FIDEL
CASTRO
AND THE
CUBAN
REVOLUTION

FIDEL
CASTRO
AND THE
CUBAN
REVOLUTION

AGE
POSITION
CHARACTER
DESTINY
PERSONALITY
AND AMBITION

CARLOS ALBERTO MONTANER

Transaction Publishers
New Brunswick (U.S.A.) and London (U.K.)

First paperback printing 2007

Copyright © 1989 by Transaction Publishers, New Brunswick, New Jersey.

This book is printed on acid-free paper that meets the American National Standard for Permanence of Paper for Printed Library Materials.

Library of Congress Catalog Number: 88-30071
ISBN: 978-1-4128-0731-9
Printed in the United States of America

Library of Congress Cataloging-in-Publication Data

Montaner, Carlos Alberto.
Fidel Castro and the Cuban Revolution: age, position, character, destiny, personality, and ambition / Carlos Alberto Montaner.
        p. cm.
    Bibliography: p.
    Includes index.
    ISBN 0-88738-235-5
        1. Cuba—History—1959- 2. Castro, Fidel, 1927- . I. Title.
F1788.M573 1989
972.91'064—dc19

88-30071
CIP

Contents

Acknowledgments

The entire documentary part of this book has been made possible thanks to the efficiency and disinterested help of Laura Ymayo. I acknowledge my first debt of gratitude to her; and, in addition, to Agustín Alles, Humberto Medrano, Juana Castro Ruz, Ramón M. Barquín, María Luisa Matos, Manolo Rodríguez Fleitas, Luis Conte Agüero, Nazario Sargén, Jorge Gutiérrez, Rosa Abella, Guillermo G. Mármol, Ana Rosa Núñez, Leví Marrero, Mario Villar Roces, Miguel Olba Benito, Angel González, Tony Fernández, Tulio Díaz Rivera, Juan Tapia Ruano, Lesbia Varona, Leonor Villa, Ariel Remos, Jesse Fernández, Tony Evora, Gastón Fernández de la Torriente, Julio Rodríguez, M.C., Aurora Calviño, L.M., and to all the others, some of them unnamable, who have contributed to the task.

Preface to the English-Language Edition

I want to dispel any erroneous notions. I am a Cuban who for strictly political reasons left Cuba in 1961. I was not adversely affected by the revolution's economic policies and could have easily benefited from the changes that have taken place in my country. I call the reader's attention to these aspects of my background to ward off suspicious conjectures, while admitting that my being a Cuban exile can call into question the objectivity of my evaluations regarding Cuba's revolutionary process. I refer the reader interested in the subject of exiles' objectivity to an illuminating essay in *Cuban Communism*, "Social Science Writing on Post-Revolutionary Cuba," by Irving Louis Horowitz, a scholar who is beyond the suspicions that perhaps I arouse. In this essay, Horowitz points out that the most valuable and dispassionate studies on contemporary Cuba are the work of exiled Cuban intellectuals. Horowitz's findings are not surprising, since the first voices that should be taken into account for an analysis of any historical event are those of the main actors. None are more qualified to relate historical events vividly than those who, like Jonah, have lived them. An a priori rejection of the player's opinions solely because he is an integral part of the drama is dangerous. The acceptance of such criteria would force us to ignore what men like Franklin, Jefferson, or Paine wrote about the American Revolution of 1776. That would be both unjust and unwise.

Prologue

A first version of this book appeared in 1976 entitled *Informe secreto sobre la revolución Cubana* (*Secret Report on the Cuban Revolution*), and the following year it was reissued with an appendix on the Cuban presence in Angola. With this title as well, it was translated and published in English in 1981.

There are three reasons why the name of the book should now be changed. The first is that this version—I believe, definitive—offers a different structure from the original in that certain essays were eliminated, others were recast, and some new ones were added about the most important events in the last few years. The second is that what in 1976 was "secret" today is public domain, and it would not be in good taste to lure the reader with a promise that would inevitably turn out to be unfulfilled. The third and perhaps most important reason is that the new name, *Fidel Castro and the Cuban Revolution,* more faithfully reflects the contents of the book. Probably the least insignificant reflections of these papers have to do with the intense and definitive relation between the personality of Fidel Castro and the frightening history of the Cubans. Chapter after chapter I insist on this theme, perhaps because it seems to me impossible to understand the revolution without understanding Castro, perhaps because I am afraid that I will not be sufficiently persuasive in the key aspect of this now quite lengthy historical process.

Further clarifications: This is not a history book, but an essay in historical interpretation. I am assuming that the reader knows the rudiments of the question at hand. If he is lost, the most sensible thing to do is read Hugh Thomas's *Cuba: The Pursuit of Freedom,* an incomparable manual of contemporary Cuban history. *Fidel Castro and the Cuban Revolution* is something different. When I decided to write it, I first faced a methodological question: How does one analyze a revolution? After attempts that floundered either in disorder or in the accumulation of facts, I chose to address a series of topics of general interest: Batista, Fidel, women, race, sex, the power structure, the opposition. I ventured to deal with them directly and—I now realize with some embarrassment—also with a certain intolerable ease. This collection of brief essays, despite its loose appearance, has hopefully a coherence that allows the reader to make a definite value judgment after he has finally put the book down. This is its aim. The reader, overburdened for years with contradictory information, will now be able to take a look behind the confusing images and formulate an unequivocal judgment about the Cuban Revolution. This book proposes to provide a general interpretation of events, and then to let one extract his own conclusions.

Publication of papers such as these has brought me in the past a good number of personal attacks and criticism. Since I know where these are coming from, I want to clarify a few things before any misinterpretations take place. To my benefit, the writers that have taken issue with me have been more repetitive than convincing. Their lack of imagination has allowed me, without great risks, to foresee the source of their main objections and articulate my answers. The procedure, certainly, is not very orthodox, but with it I am trying to keep what generally are no more than simplistic prejudices from being used as mufflers. I am not disregarding the possibility of my own mistakes in judgment in the analysis of certain facts, but this has to be proven with something more than mere growls.

First objection: The analysis of the Cuban revolution is invalid because the author is in exile and will thus always give a negative vision of that process.

If the above were true, Goytisolo, Arrabal, Madariaga, or Sender, for example, would have no authority to judge the Spanish political situation; Lenin—from London, from Switzerland—to talk about the Russia of the Czars. Or Martí, Sarmiento, and Bolívar, who wrote at such length from exile. Or Solzhenitsyn to write about the USSR which banished him by force. The opposite is probably true: Whether we like it or not, the most valuable testimonies are of those who have directly participated in events, be they winners or losers. These are slippery categories that time ends up by erasing. (Does anyone remember that Josephus, the great historian, was a loser?) But moreover, as Irving Louis Horowitz, an intellectual above suspicion, has pointed out, it happens that the best analyses of Castroism have been done by exiled academics (Mesa-Lago, Domínguez, Suárez, Clark, et al.).

Second objection: The analysis is defective from the outset because of the anti-Castro stand of its author, an acknowledged liberal in the European sense.

I suppose then, that analyses of communist dictatorships should be done by communists, those of fascism by fascists, and those of bourgeois democracies by liberals. With this criterion, *Das Kapital* would never have been written, since it is an analysis of capitalism done from communist assumptions. To pretend objectivity in this matter is laughable. No one achieves it. We all operate from profoundly subjective criteria. Is it not superstition to believe— as Marxists do—in the superior destiny (in the *mission*) of the proletarian class? Would not being a Marxist, in spite of the impossibility of verifying the theory with half a century of practice, be the most tangible proof of subjectivity? We are all subjective, among other things because it is impossible to move in the field of ethics—which is what we are talking about here—venturing judgments if one is not well endowed with a chart of values. I am indeed a liberal in the European sense, probably because my enthusiasm does not enable me to be anything else, but surely because with its imperfections I do not know other more hospitable societies. I have no other way of judging the Cuban Communist dictatorship than from my private repertoire of preferences and rejections. I accept that the Communists subscribe to a certain vision of humanity and having set themselves in it conceive relations among men accordingly, but I do not accept that someone be the sole possessor of truth and therefore have the privilege to "enforce" it.

Third objection: The work is totally ascientific. Being subjective, it contains assertions often passionate and arbitrary that are not supported by data.

We are almost in agreement. *Fidel Castro and the Cuban Revolution* is a long essay—or many short essays around the same theme—and not an academic monograph. It is highly doubtful that history might be interpreted scientifically. These scientific attempts usually end up in thick volumes of scarce use. Opposing parties, if put to the task of analyzing the Cuban Revolution—or any revolution—would end up making arbitrary assertions. What are those vague formulas of "the revolutionary people," "indoctrinated masses," "the oligarchy"? What is the scientific meaning of terms such as "petit bourgeois," "lumpenproletariat," "bourgeoisie"? The scientific analysis of history is not possible, among other things, because the language we use belongs to that lighthearted chapter of political essays. I do not believe that the explanation of any historical fact can always be supported by objective data. Neither is it necessary to do so. The beating and humiliation of a man in his cell block is a fact that does not require any process for its censure. Statistics, besides, can be deceiving even when accurate. A strict inventory of German economic growth between 1933 and 1939—kilometers of roads, price indexes, per capita production—would show a very favorable image of Hitler's Germany. Would such immaculate information be worth anything at the time of judging Nazism? Much more important, of much more historical weight is the noncomputable fact of anti-Semitism and intolerance of that frenetic tribe. And Hugh Thomas must have supposed something similar when he reviewed the monumental work by the Harvard academic Jorge Domínguez, *Cuba: Order and Revolution,* and asked himself whether "an average Cuban, submerged in the thousands of secrets and frustrations of a controlled society, would be able to recognize in those careful chapters something that appears to him to be the problems of the island." What I have tried to do, exactly, is to have this book reflect the problems of the island by trusting not only the rigor of objective "data," but also common sense, observation, and the capacity to establish ethical judgments, because when all is said and done the only use of academic information is to serve as *another* base for moral inflections. What objective measure can be used to assess my assertion that the Cuban citizen lives in a constant state of terror and shock? This assertion is not a superficial one, but has been made after having interviewed hundreds and hundreds of Cubans who have been able to escape, after having talked with officials of the regime who are living abroad and who, in virtue of old ties, have agreed to secret, pathetically mysterious meetings. I acknowledge that the reader, be he pro-Castro or simply suspicious, might doubt these undemonstrable assertions, but this would be consistent only if the same were done with those dealing with the touching story of happy children and contented workers due to the defeat of imperialism. I don't see how the revolution can prove that it has people's support but its coryphaeus playing "scientific" roles do not hesitate to affirm this backing. The punctilious reader who due to methodological problems casts doubts on my assertions, must do the same with those coming from Havana. I acknowledge that this is shaky ground, but it is obviously so for all of us.

1

The True Story of the Cuban Revolution

For that tenuous thing called "posterity," a story will remain that in a few lines will tell of the deeds that took place during the insurrectional period of the Cuban Revolution. It will go more or less like this: "After several years of intense struggle, Fidel Castro and his guerrilla followers in Sierra Maestra defeated dictator Fulgencio Batista." And perhaps then the story of "the twelve" will be mentioned—the mythical twelve men who survived the first combats and later led various guerrilla groups. This sketch will suffice for history. But it is a trifle.

A Portrait of Batista

A book about the Cuban revolution should start with Batista. What was he like? What were the predominant traits of the ex–Cuban dictator? The first thing that comes to light is the tremendous incongruence between his personal limitations and the positions in which he served. He was a vulgar and ignorant man—a malicious biographer has solemnly stated that "he had mastered the secrets of shorthand." Nevertheless, he managed to acquire the repertoire of gestures of the learned bourgeoisie. He was a military leader with no talent for fighting. Castro's war—which would have been terminated in short order by other Latin American strongmen—was all that was needed to put him on the run. As a politician he had little popular support. Yet this mediocre man was able to rule over politicians and the military, the middle class and capitalists, conservatives and Communists. Until Castro's arrival, no other Cuban had held such power in the country's republican history. This can only be understood if one realizes that Batista's weaknesses were his main assets to those forces that insured his political longevity. Batista was useful to the interests of the Cuban oligarchy, to American investors, to the Stalinist Communist party in Cuba, to the bourgeois political parties, to the Department of State in Washington, to the army he built and later destroyed, to

1

organized labor—to all the pressure groups that operated in Cuba during the tiresome quarter of a century that elapsed between 1933 and 1958. His "ability" rested in choosing the most appropriate ally at the most opportune moment. He sold and collected favors from all parties involved. To all he conveyed the certainty that his bulky deficiencies made him pliable and usable and thus made him the suitable man to carry out the designs of the group with which he happened to be allied. He manipulated and was manipulated. He served and was served. Such was the secret of his "success."

He managed to be a progressive politician (in name) in the thirties and a reactionary (also in name) in the fifties, because in the first period he was living in an atmosphere of revolution and in the second period, in the institutional order of capitalist middle-class structures where there was a certain prosperity. During the forties he was able to become an ally of the Popular Socialist party—blindly subservient to Moscow—and later in the fifties, he outlawed it, because in the first period he needed some popular support that his barracks' power base could not offer, and in the second period, he needed only the use of force to rule a country in which the relative economic boom and disgust over the corrupt use of power by traditional political parties had sown a cynical spirit of resignation. Batista sensed—he was more intuitive than logical—the rules of the Cold War, and in the fifties endorsed the mythology of that period with the same enthusiasm he had shown during the Spanish Civil War and World War II when he was pro-Popular Front and pro-Soviet. He was like a chameleon: fluid, protean, malleable to the interests with which he would temporarily strike deals (from which he would benefit). I suspect he had a realistic image of himself and his weaknesses. This would have to be considered one of his assets. He was discreet in a country of raving braggarts. He was not a hopeless egomaniac like Castro, but an astute fellow: sly, distrustful, with a cautious sense of timing, always ready to "sell" his limitations to the best buyer.

What did this man look for in government? In the first place, money. He stole, permitted stealing, and benefited from others' stealing with a neurotic frenzy. Ten percent of the budget from the Department of Public Works ended up in his pockets. Let no one be surprised, therefore, by the impressive buildings and highways with which he endowed the country. With his close relatives he shared the gambling profits (legal and illegal). He would sell sinecures, decrees, favors, customhouse directorships, government positions, and any other "merchandise" within the reach of an uncontrollable and dishonest ruler. It must be acknowledged that he did not invent such practices, and that his predecessors did the same things, but Batista carried corruption to unheard-of limits. His estimated fortune was $300 million. He was said to be one of the richest men in the world. In all likelihood, this is not an exaggeration.

Aside from wealth, the sergeant-stenographer frantically sought social prestige. I doubt that power enticed him as it does other political chieftains. He was not interested in the presidency in order to change the world—as André Breton writes in a poem—but to obtain the social ascendancy that the Cuban upper classes otherwise denied him. He merely wanted to be accepted, not to become an outstanding leader. Batista was a man of very humble origins with no prestigious ancestry to be traced back to the recent Cuban wars of independence. (There existed in Cuba a peculiar aristocracy, different from the landed one, which originated with the heroes of the wars against Spain. The descendants of these military leaders were active in politics until Castro came to power.) Batista was a half-breed, and in Cuba there were profound, though hidden, racial prejudices. When he was an ex-president, for example, he was denied entrance to an exclusive social club because he was a mulatto. In that social sphere, it was worse to be Black than to be a thief.

Batista was boorish, and to avoid appearing so, he would end up being pretentiously uncouth. Thousands of ridiculing jokes about him were told throughout the island. Behind his thirst for power there was no psychological motivation other than his deep-seated social resentment. He made pathetic efforts to be accepted by the Cuban aristocracy (an entity out of opera buffa) which were later expanded by befriending the European aristocracy. There is no more naive and awkward chapter in his biography than the one that chronicles his pilgrimage to the town of Zaldívar, Spain, in search of his mythical lineage.

He did not leave any political heritage when he died. There was no political loyalty, no coherent doctrine. Not even a trace of ideological precepts can be found in the life of the dead strongman—only a system of temporary compromises based on mutual benefits. Batista's wake does not exist as a political entity, but as a nostalgic bond among certain people of little intellect or dubious past, proclaiming themselves Batista followers. Time, in the same way it extinguished Batista in Marbella, will erase all traces of his following. In a few years, it will all be a pitiful anecdote.

The Collapse of Batista's Régime

On December 31, 1958, Havana was calm but tense as it awaited the New Year. There were few parties or celebrations. The opposition slogan "moderation, silence, no lights," devised by Emilio Guede, one of the July 26 Movements's propaganda chiefs, was being taken seriously. Everyone knew it would be unwise to provoke the police, but some way had to be found to show Batista that virtually the entire population was against his dictatorship.

The news from places where the struggle was in progress was encouraging. In Oriente, Huber Matos's guerrilla column was advancing on Santiago de

Cuba as Fidel Castro had ordered. In Las Villas province, Che Guevara and Rolando Cubelas's men had taken Santa Clara, one of the country's main cities, while guerrillas attached to the Escambray Second National Front were raiding or besieging half a dozen sizable towns. A few days earlier, this organization's leader, the twenty-four-year-old Spaniard Eloy Gutiérrez Menoyo, had pulled off a remarkable coup: he had infiltrated an army barracks in disguise and, after disarming the senior officer present, persuaded it to surrender.

There could be little doubt that from a military viewpoint things had been going badly for Batista's army. The two offensives launched by his General Staff had failed. One of these had been mounted to deal with the situation in the Sierra Maestra, at the far eastern end of the island; the other had as its target the guerrilla forces operating in the central region about 190 miles from Havana.

But despite such setbacks, for all practical purposes the armed forces were still intact. Nine-tenths of the army had not left barracks, and Batista had total control of the air. There was also his navy, which, though small and obsolete, could at least be used to bombard guerrilla strongholds on the coast. Batista's position, then, could hardly be described as desperate. In the entire country there were fewer than three thousand guerrillas; he had thirty thousand men under his command. In strictly military terms Batista should have been able to recover all the ground he had lost—it amounted to less than 2 percent of Cuba's territory—and defeat the opposition. Nonetheless, on January 1, 1959, after saying good-bye to the old year with shouts of "viva" and champagne, Batista, along with his family and his closest associates, boarded two air force planes and told the pilots to take them to the Dominican Republic. This development was so unexpected it astonished the entire country, including Fidel Castro who, in his Sierra Maestra redoubt, had been getting ready for a long guerrilla campaign whose outcome was far from certain. It had simply never occurred to him that his still immensely powerful foe would suddenly flee the country.

But the motives behind Batista's astounding decision had little to do with anything happening on the battlefield. The most important factor was his realization that the Cuban people no longer wanted him. This had been made plain in the rigged elections of November 1958, just seven weeks before his flight. Hardly anyone voted and it was obvious that the vast majority had turned their backs on him and on any electoral solution that would imply some degree of continuity. Batista had been rejected by everyone and he knew it. The psychological significance of this for him was considerable. Thirty years earlier, Batista had erupted into public life on a wave of popular approval, and he had had an aura of revolutionary prestige conferred on him by his then ally, a Cuban Communist party known as the Popular Socialist party. Unlikely as it later came to seem. Batista did not see himself as a right-wing dictator but as a populist *caudillo*, the friend and protector of the Spanish Republican government in exile and enemy of the tyrant Trujillo, the man who would give him asylum. In his own mind, he remained close to the very poorest classes from which he had been lifted up by the revolutionary movement that in 1933 transformed him from sergeant typist into Colonel and Chief of the Armed Forces.

His gloomy awareness that he had been rejected might not have been enough to make him relinquish power had his secret services not placed on his desk two very well documented reports. One informed him that some supposedly loyal army officers had been in contact with Fidel Castro in an effort to arrange a peace formula, something that would have been bound to entail his removal and also, perhaps, his arrest and trial. The other report was even more serious. It told him high-ranking United States Embassy officials had been meeting opposition representatives in Havana in an attempt to work out a political deal that might prevent the complete collapse of the country's institutions. Washington knew Batista's dictatorship was not viable in the medium term and thought it would be unable to survive even if power were handed to Dr. Andrés Rivero Agüero, the wily pro-Batista lawyer and politician who had been designated president after November's election farce.

Confronted with this situation, Batista panicked. Suddenly, he saw himself spurned by the people and "betrayed" by two of the main pillars of his régime, the Americans and the armed forces. He could not help but remember the events of 1933 when another dictator, Gerardo Machado, had been undone by the same factors: public opinion, the army, and the United States embassy. Like Machado in 1933, he knew he would not be able to keep his grip on the levers of power. He was also afraid of what might happen to him at the hands of the mob should revolutionary anarchy spawn riots like the ones that had shaken the country twenty-five years before. Haunted by these nightmares, without a thought of the glory or greatness that so frequently figured in official speeches, the general fled at dawn, leaving behind, utterly exposed to their enemies, thousands of people committed to the defense of his ignoble cause.

Fidel Makes His Move

As soon as news of this unexpected turn of events reached his headquarters, Fidel Castro, the thirty-three-year-old lawyer commanding the 26 July Movement, ordered a slow advance on Havana by highway, with a halt in Santiago de Cuba so the columns led by Che Guevara and Camilo Cienfuegos, which were already halfway to the capital, would have time to consolidate their hold on power. This was essential not just to avert a counteroffensive by the armed forces, but also to prevent guerrilla groupings attached to other opposition factions from taking over important military or political organizations. Castro never shouted "all power to the Soviets," but he did have the ability to maneuver astutely enough to make sure all power would go first to his July 26 Movement and then, a few months later, to himself.

But who was this Hollywood-style individual who did so much to create the shaggy-haired and romantic Latin American revolutionary archetype? Fidel Castro was one of the five children of the second union of a Galician immigrant named Angel Castro who had arrived in Cuba about 1898 as a Spanish soldier to fight the *mambises* rebels. After the Republic was established, Angel Castro stayed and became a farmer. He first married a woman whose surname was Argote and had several children by her. Later he set up a household with Lina Ruz, a woman who had been his servant. She bore him three boys and two girls: Fidel, Raúl, and Ramón; Emma and Juana.

A landowner, Angel Castro was comfortably off and his common-law wife, Lina Ruz, made it her business to see that her children received some education. Fidel studied with the Jesuits and distinguished himself as an athlete and member of the school debating team. Oddly enough, the final debate of his school years was over education in the Soviet Union: young Fidel harshly attacked Soviet education while José Ignacio Rasco, now an exiled Christian Democrat leader, defended it. Fidel proved fiery and eloquent. Even then it was clear he was leadership material.

As an adolescent, Castro was viscerally anti-Communist, so much so that he was the only border in Belén school who supported the Axis. Using a map that he kept in his dormitory, young Fidel followed the feats of the German army with fascination. But the object of his enthusiasm seems to have changed even before the war ended.

Castro's political ideas really began to take shape in the mid-1940s, soon after he started studying law, thanks to his relationship with Alfredo Guevara, a young communist studying philosophy and literature. Unlike Guevara, Castro did not join the Party, but he did accept its radical diagnosis of the ills of Cuban society: ever since then he has taken it for granted that his country's relative poverty is due to corrupt politicians, American imperialist greed, and the bad distribution of land; he also assumed that the eradication of these evils would lead to an immediate expansion of the economy and the strengthening of the country's institutions.

But although his political baggage on entering university was limited to these few simple ideas, Castro never for a moment doubted that destiny had chosen him to play the role of a leader. This conviction soon brought him into violent confrontation with the young people who dominated the University Student Foundation. Even though at the time the country was ruled by a law-abiding and freely elected government, Havana University was a political cockpit. Gunfights and murders were common. Castro soon got involved in the violence, trying to kill a rival leader, Leonel Gómez, by shooting him in the stomach. During that period he was accused of two murders: one victim was Federation president Manolo Castro—no relation to Fidel—and the other a university guard sergeant, Fernández Caral. However, nothing could be proven in court.

In 1947 Fidel played a part—a humble one as a simple soldier—in a plan to invade the Dominican Republic and unseat Trujillo. Nothing came of it because international pressure obliged the Cuban government to disarm the would-be expeditionary forces and dismantle their organizations. The following year, Castro, along with other student leaders, was invited to an anti-imperialist get-together in Bogotá. His visit there coincided with the murder of Gaitán and the riots that led up to the savage confrontation between liberals and conservatives known as the *bogotazo*. While the bloodletting was going on Castro was arrested for trying to stir up a mutiny in a police barracks, but he was released from jail thanks to the good offices of the Cuban ambassador, Guillermo Belt, who managed to get him home aboard a cargo plane.

In 1948 Castro took his law degree and joined the Orthodox party, a populist organization whose ideology was vaguely social-democrat but that had a distinct penchant for striking radical postures. It was then that he married Mirtha Díaz Balart, the daughter of a prominent pro-Batista politician. The couple had a son, Fidelito, and went to the United States for a year. Castro toyed with the idea of studying political science at Columbia University in New York and forgetting Cuba for a while: he had too many enemies there and might easily lose his life in one of the vendettas among rival political gangs.

But Castro's political vocation finally proved strong enough to overcome these promptings. He went back to the island with the aim of becoming a legislator. In 1951 he stood as a candidate for the House of Representatives for a Havana ward. His friends at the time thought him an indefatigable idealist; his enemies saw him as a dangerous gangster; both agreed he was a remarkable personality who would be sure to win fame if suitable circumstances arose but who also might easily come to an abrupt end with a bullet halting his turbulent progress.

On March 10, 1952, the kind of situation Castro could thrive in was created by General Fulgencio Batista who, together with a group of old military cronies, staged a coup d'état toppling the democratic government of Carlos Prío Socarrás. Batista wanted to prevent the holding of the upcoming elections, which would probably have been won by the Orthodox party, one of whose listed candidates was Fidel.

Castro's immediate response was to set about organizing an anti-Batista uprising. He was far from the only person to do so. University students began to plot within days of Batista takeover. The Authentic party, which had just been removed from power, assigned some of its best men to the job of preparing an insurrection. Once again, Cuba found itself transformed into a hotbed of conspiracy. Nobody had a clearer idea of what his own future course would be than Fidel Castro.

Castro never forgot that twenty years previously, an earlier revolutionary leader, Antonio Guiteras, the man behind the Young Cuba Movement, had attacked a barracks and then managed to foment an uprising in the hill country. Castro took over both the program and the strategy of Guiteras, whose creed was an anti-imperialist, anti-capitalist, and anti-Communist hodge-podge. On July 26, 1953, with less than 100 men, all recruited from the Orthodox party's youth wing, he staged an attack on the Moncada barracks, the most powerful army installation in Santiago de Cuba (east of Cuba).

The Moncada attack, which was harshly criticized by the Cuban communists, did not unseat Batista, but it did give Fidel a nationwide reputation and turn him into the key opposition leader, a position he consolidated from his prison cell by skillful correspondence with journalists and the country's most important politicians. Just twenty-one months after being sentenced to jail, Fidel and his comrades were amnestied. Sticking to the trail blazed by Guiteras, he decided to foment an uprising in the Sierra Maestra (mountains he had roamed as an adolescent), as a prelude to a much bigger guerrilla war. He committed himself to embarking from Mexico on this enterprise before the end of 1956. In December, with eighty-two others, he returned to Cuban soil.

The actual landing proved almost as disastrous as the attack on the Moncada barracks. Most of Fidel's force either died or were taken prisoner. Only a score, with Fidel at their head, managed to reach the rugged outcrops of the Sierra Maestra range, and they did this thanks to the fortuitous help they received from an old peasant called Crecencio Pérez, who had been living as an outlaw in the area for decades.

Militarily, neither the landing nor the Sierra Maestra uprising posed any kind of danger to Batista. Psychologically, however, they had a strong impact on the general population and on some international organizations. The very existence of a small guerrilla group that the army was unable to destroy became a spur driving on other revolutionary groupings.

For a while, Batista did not seem unduly perturbed by this guerrilla activity. In many ways it was useful to him, making it much easier to order special defense expenditure that could then be looted. That is why he did not move to finish off the guerrillas early on when it would have been fairly easy for him to do so. It suited him to have an enemy in the hills. But this approach eventually led to the demoralization of his army and his own downfall.

In March 1957, students headed by Carlos Gutiérrez Menoyo, a Spanish exile who had fought alongside the French Resistance, attacked the Presidential Palace with the aim of killing Batista and thereby decapitating his régime. This attack failed for reasons that have never been fully explained. In it, Gutiérrez died, as did twenty-seven other rebels and five guards. Then, night after night, bombs planted by clandestine groups went off in Havana and Santiago de Cuba. Prominent individuals became targets of assassination attempts, and the army and police retaliated by torturing and murdering suspects.

With few exceptions, public opinion started to turn against Batista, demanding a political solution that would put an end to the unrest affecting the country. The bourgeoisie openly financed revolutionary groupings. The Church circulated pastoral letters hostile to the dictatorship. Thanks to the shrewd maneuverings of an engineer, Manuel Ray, professional associations formed the Civic Resistance Organization, set up to back the rebellion. With a mixture of enthusiasm and fear, the entire country flung itself into the revolutionary adventure. At that time nobody even thought about communism, let alone Moscow. The talk was all about democracy, freedom, and respect for human rights; the only objective was to restore the rule of law that had been swept aside by Batista's coup. There was just one small corner of the revolutionary map where a different kind of political discourse prevailed: rumor had it that up in the Sierra Maestra an Argentinian doctor went around talking about Marxism. The doctor was said to hate Yankees because he had been in Guatemala in 1954 when the military under Castillo Arias, with the backing of the CIA, had mounted a coup against Jacobo Arbenz. But all that seemed of minor significance. In the 1950s, communism was of no concern to Cubans. It was assumed that such disasters could only happen in Europe or Asia in the sphere of influence of the Soviet Union. In Cuba, ninety miles from the United States, people were fighting for freedom.

The Road to Moscow

Despite this consensus, within weeks of the revolution's success, Castro's new government began to change course and soon came into open conflict with the United States. But there had been nothing in the original program to suggest this would be the case. What had happened? Today, half the Left attributes the change to Castro's need to defend himself against American reprisals and the other half, led by Castro himself, insists that a communist society was a logical objective for Marxist revolutionaries. But it does not seem very likely that a secret plot to transform Cuba into a communist state was hatched in the Sierra Maestra. Among the guerrilas, there was, it is true, a radical faction headed by Che Guevarra and Raúl Castro that was openly Marxist, and Fidel flirted with it even though he never committed himself decisively. But Castro was then fully aware that the adoption of a Marxist program would finish him as leader of the Cuban uprising because most of the Cuban opposition, including the urban cadres of his own 26 July Movement, detested communism.

Be that as it may, Castro did have plans for himself that, as he pursued them, would inevitably involve him in a confrontation with Washington and an alliance with Moscow. In a letter addressed to Celia Sánchez from the Sierra Maestra on July 6, 1958 and published twenty years later by Carlos Franqui, Castro revealed that his principal aim was to fight relentlessly against the United States and that he would do so after the revolution had succeeded: "Once this war is over I will start what for me is a much longer and bigger war, the war I am going to wage against them [the Americans]. I realize this will be my true destiny."

Castro then may or may not have been a communist. But there can be no doubt that even then he was rabidly anti-America. Indeed, his inborn sense of public relations told him that anti-Americanism was just what he needed to make himself the most important Latin American leader of the century. This was his secret objective. The young man who had tried to invade the Dominican Republic in 1947 and who a year later added to the chaos in Bogotá found himself with a chance to turn Cuba into a launching pad for the projection on a continental scale of his own leadership.

It is of course feasible that Castro would never have found himself a place in the Soviet orbit had the United States silently resigned itself to the confiscation of U.S. property and maintained economic relations favorable to the island, paying more than the market price for sugar and granting soft loans, while at the same time, turning a blind eye to the worldwide subversive activities Cuba has been engaged in ever since 1959. But it is unrealistic to assume that the United States could have helped finance a revolution obviously hostile to its own interests, contenting itself with standing by passively while a government that treats it as an enemy made its appearance.

In other words, the Cuban revolution ended by selling out to Moscow and adopting the kind of state communists recommend because Fidel's anti-Americanism and taste for international adventures led inevitably to a confrontation with the United States and Latin American countries, and once this took place, his only possible hope of salvation lay in the protection afforded by Moscow.

Once safely under the Kremlin's wing, Castro, with almost complete impunity, could indulge his revolutionary dreams and embark on that "long war" he had promised Celia Sánchez and that has left a trail of Cuban dead in Venezuela, Bolivia, Angola, Ethiopia, Syria, and—most recently—Grenada. The Yankee did not push him into Moscow's arms. He was pushed by his own interests and his neurotic need for a great role in history.

Appendix

Jacobo Arbenz (1913–1971). An army officer and politician of Swiss origin who led the triumvirate that ruled Guatemala after 1944. He became president of his country after general elections in 1950 and tried to change its archaic structures with land reform and overtures to Communist countries. He was overthrown in 1954 by troops under the command of Colonel Carlos Castillo Armas and died in exile in Mexico.

The attack on the Presidential Palace. The armed attack carried out by the Revolutionary Directorate on the afternoon of March 13, 1957. No other forces joined in. The objective was physically to eliminate Batista in his own offices. Its failure was followed by a wave of revenge murders by the police.

Authentic Party. A political movement formed after the demise of the Machado dictatorship. It was dominated by Ramón Grau San Martín, who governed in accordance with the constitution from 1944 to 1948. Its name comes from its members' belief that it loyally followed the "authentic" line of the Cuban Revolutionary party founded toward the end of the nineteenth century by José Martí. It was considered moderately right wing.

The "bogotazo." This was the name given to the explosion of mob violence in Colombia's capital, Bogotá, in 1948, when liberals and conservatives fought one another with firearms following the fortuitous death of the liberal leader Jorge Eliecer Gaitán. Castro is said to have participated in the fighting and was taken prisoner, but Cuba's diplomatic representative saved him from jail.

Civil Resistance. A widely supported anti-Batista movement founded by Manuel Ray (see below) and other revolutionaries during the 1950s. It succeeded in establishing itself in every important city and town in the country.

Commandante Rolando Cubelas. A physician. When the revolution took place he was president of the University Student Federation (FEU). Prior to that he had fought with the guerrillas operating in the central part of the island and reached the rank of commandante. He was accused of plotting to kill Castro and was sentenced for this. He lives as an exile in Madrid.

Emilio Cuede. A Cuban journalist who was chief of the 26 July Movement propaganda section in Havana. He was the revolutionary representative who on the morning of January 1 announced officially that Batista had fled. He is currently an exile in Puerto Rico.

Carlos Franqui. Cuban essayist and journalist. When young he was active in the Socialist Youth (communist) and joined in the Key Confites expedition against Trujillo in 1947. He worked for the magazine *Carteles* and the daily *Hoy.* After Castro took power, he edited the magazine *Revolución* until it was closed down. Among its contributors were the best liberal and progressive Cuban writers. In 1968 he went into exile, making his home in Montecatini, Italy. His works include *El libro de los doce, Diario de la Revolución Cubana,* and *Retrato de Familia con Fidel.* He has experienced the revolution from the inside and described it from the standpoint of a member of the ruling élite.

Commandante Camilo Cienfuegos Gorriarán. One of the most popular revolutionary guerrilla chiefs. He fought under Fidel Castro in the Sierra Maestra and with "Che" Guevara led the column that in late 1958 cleared Las Villas to prepare the siege of the provincial capital of Santa Clara, thus precipitating Batista's flight. In 1959 he held important military positions and in October that year Castro gave him the job of taking commandante Huber Matos prisoner in Camagüey. When returning to Havana, the light airplane in which he was traveling with two other people disappeared over the sea.

Alfredo Guevara. A Cuban revolutionary and, for many years, director of ICAIC (the Cuban Cinema Art and Industry Institute). His activism in the communist Popular Socialist party since the 1950s did not stop him being Fidel Castro's friend when both were at university. He is now Cuba's representative to Unesco, having left ICAIC where he was accused of committing too many mistakes. He is one of the most long-standing and influential pillars of the Castro régime.

Antonio Guiteras Holmes (1908–1935). A Cuban politician with nationalist, anti-imperialist ideas. He became a revolutionary while struggling against Machado. After the fall of the dictator, he rose to become interior minister in the Grau administration and he nationalized the electricity industry. But when he lost his backing, he fell victim to the country's new strongman, former sergeant Batista, whose soldiers killed him in El Morrillo in 1935. He founded Young Cuba, a secret political society, and was the author of important social reforms. His political heirs came together in ARG (the Guiteras Revolutionary Group), an organization that in the 1940s was prone to indulge in political gangsterism.

26 July Movement. A political and military organization founded by Fidel Castro and a group of intimates during the 1950s with the aim of overthrowing Batista and carrying out a reform program in Cuba.

The landing. The eventual landing of the yacht *Granma* took place on the swampy beaches of Birán, to the southwest of Oriente province, on December 2, 1956. Fidel Castro and his men had made the crossing from Yucatán, Mexico.

Celia Sánchez Manduley. A Cuban revolutionary leader who was with Castro during the attack on the Moncada barracks and later accompanied him on his Sierra Maestra adventure. After the revolution she had some influence over Castro and acted as his secretary. She died in the 1980s.

Commandante Huber Matos. Doctor in pedagogy, the leader in Manzanillo of the teachers' union and the freemasonry connected to the Orthodox party. After Batista's coup in 1952 he became an active opponent of the dictatorship. He was a member of the 26 July Movement and after some actions in Oriente went into exile in Venezuela and Costa Rica. At the start of 1958, he flew to the Sierra Maestra with a substantial consignment of arms. He was named commander of the "Antonio Guiteras" Eighth Column and was given the task of besieging Santiago. When the revolution succeeded, Castro made him the Camagüey military chief, but in mid-1959 he wrote Castro a private letter the dictator used to accuse him of high treason. He was in prison for twenty years and left Cuba in 1979. He lives in Miami and is president of the Independent and Democratic Cuba (CID) organization.

Commandante Eloy Gutiérrez Menoyo. A revolutionary born in Spain who made his home in Cuba. His family had been members of the UGT Spanish labor union organizations and he fought on the Republican side during the Spanish Civil War and then in the French maquis against the Nazis in the Second World War. He was one of the leaders of the Escambray Second National Front in Las Villas province. After the revolution, he was pushed aside because of his anticommunism. He went into exile but returned to the Escambray hills to fight against Castro. In 1966 he was taken prisoner and condemned to life imprisonment. He refused to be "reeducated" and was harshly treated in consequence. He was freed, thanks to international pressure, in December 1986.

General Gerardo Machado Morales (1971–1939). Cuban army officer and politician who became president of the country in 1925. During his second mandate, his rule became dictatorial. In 1933 he was overthrown by a revolutionary movement in which Fulgencio Batista played a notable part. He died in exile.

Orthodox party. A Cuban political organization formed by Eduardo R. Chibás. It was given its name because it was supposed to follow the "orthodox" line of the Revolutionary Cuban party founded by José Martí at the end of the nineteenth century in order to advance the struggle for independence. It embraced a considerable proportion of the liberal middle class and workers with middle-of-the-road positions, and called for clean administration and, a balanced budget. It was viscerally anticommunist. Had democratic elections been held in 1952 it would probably have won them, but they were cancelled following Batista's coup d'état. After the revolution, the Orthodox party vanished from the Cuban scene. Fidel Castro was an active member of its youth wing.

The plan to invade the Dominican Republic. An expeditionary force composed of Dominicans and Cubans proposed to overthrow the dictator Trujillo. This political and military enterprise was organized in 1947 and baptized the "Key Confites campaign" after the key or islet where the forces were based.

Popular Socialist Party (PSP). This was the name used by the Cuban Communist party in the 1940s and 1950s. For opportunistic motives it backed the unpopular Batista during his first (constitutional) term between 1940 and 1944. In return it got control of the Confederation of Workers of Cuba (CTC). After Batista's coup d'état, the party was outlawed and was persecuted until 1958. When the Castroite revolution succeeded, the PSP militants jumped on the Integrated Revolutionary Organizations (ORI) bandwagon and merged with the new Cuban Communist party formed in 1965.

José Ignacio Rasco. Ph.D. in law and philosophy. Founder of the Cuban Christian Democrat party and later an official of the Inter-American Development Bank (IDB). He is now a professor at Miami University. Among his works are: *Cuba 1959, Trasfondo histórico de la Revolución,* and *Integración y desintegración 1966.*

Manuel Ray Rivero. A Cuban engineer and revolutionary who was a member of Fidel Castro's first government and later the leader of the opposition to Castro's plans to communize the island. He managed to escape into exile.

Carlos Prío Socarrás (1903–1977). A Cuban politician belonging to the Authentic party and Cuba's last democratically elected president. His term started in 1948 but he was overthrown by Batista's coup in 1952. His presidency was noted for its sensible economic policy, which brought about financial stability and encouraged development (by such institutions as BANFAIC, the Cuban Farm and Industry Development Bank) but also for widespread corruption. He committed suicide in Miami.

General Rafael Leónidas Trujillo (1891–1961). A Dominican Republic army officer and politician who in 1930 forced President Vázquez to quit and then established an all-powerful dictatorship answering to him and to his chosen representatives alone. He enjoyed the open support of the Dominican National Guard and the tacit backing of the United States. He built many public works, put the economy on a sound footing, and when it suited him turned a blind eye to corruption. He was assassinated by his own underlings.

Young Cuba. A radical, anti-imperialist organization formed by Antonio Guiteras (see above) on the basis of Martí's ideas and the libertarianism of Mazzini (hence the name). It was active during the 1920s and 1930s.

Zaldívar or Zaldíbar. A Basque Country municipality with 3,200 inhabitants from which the ex-dictator Fulgencio Batista said in his memoirs he derived his second surname.

2

Anatomy of Power in Castro's Cuba

Who Rules Cuba?

Fidel rules. He delegates responsibility to a few intimate followers but it is obvious that he holds the reins. The only indispensable requisite needed to reach power's inner sanctum is total loyalty to Castro. All the key political and military positions—the only ones which guarantee the regime's continuity—are under the control of Fidel's men. How has it been possible for this elite to come to power? How was part of Castro's team formed? Essentially as a result of the Sierra Maestra adventure. Participation in the Moncada attack does not mean anything. There are some Moncada-attack veterans who have been in exile or in prison for years. Fidel recruited his definitive group in the Sierra Maestra. He confides only in those who came to know him *after* the myth. Those who have been his companions in the university struggles or in the Orthodox party—before the myth—he maintains at a certain cautious distance or in high administrative posts, but never in key positions. This is natural: The most genuine and spontaneous submission is the one given him by those who always saw him as a hero and a genius. The ones that are most inclined toward this naive admiration are the *guajiros* (Cuban peasants) and those with little education. There is also a predictable gratitude. After all, Castro freed them from the purgatory of anonymity and made them celebrities. This is the case of Tomassevich, Calixto García, Guillermo García, Almeida, Joel Iglesias, and so many others. These are the men who guarantee Castro's overwhelming military support in the event that his will is not obeyed or his power is challenged. They are not conventional Communists; they are Castroites. They play the political roles that Castro reserves for them. They lack the most elemental autonomy. For the Maximum Leader, this is an invaluable state of affairs.

But is there any element in power that is not entirely pro–Fidel? Of course. The government apparatus was born of a compromise between the July 26

Movement and the Communist (Popular Socialist) party. Cuban government propaganda tries to convey the impression that it is a monolithic structure, but the crevices and divisions are easily detected from afar. The July 26 Movement has itself been fragmented into two great divisions since the struggle against Batista. On one side, what has been called the Plains, formed by clandestine urban guerrillas; on the other, the Sierra, the rural guerrillas. The Plains did the bulk of the fighting against Batista, but the show was stolen by the rural guerrillas. The human element of both sectors is also different. The Plains was made up of students, professionals, and the middle class, almost all of them White; while the Sierra incorporated hundreds of peasants with little education, frequently mulattoes or Blacks. Tensions between the two groups developed as a consequence of the control exercised from the Sierra, where the leadership was, over the cities, where the danger was. When urban guerrillas were intensively hunted by the police, it was said that they were "burned," and they would be sent to the relative safety of the Sierra. This situation provoked a certain rivalry between the two sectors in the struggle, in which underhanded class differences played no small part. The clandestine urban guerrillas became, since that time, the "right wing" of the July 26 Movement. The first opposition to Castro, once he was in power, was organized by these moderate sectors. Faustino Pérez, Marcelo Fernández, David Salvador, Manuel Ray, Víctor Paneque, Aldo Vera, Emilio Guede, Enrique Oltuski, Carlos Varona, Manolo Fernández, and other key elements of the National Directorate of the July 26 Movement held semiconspiratorial meetings when faced with the evidence of the communist direction that Castro and Guevara were imprinting on the revolution. Of these men some definitely chose the path of armed opposition, and others —Faustino Pérez, Marcelo Fernández, Enrique Oltuski—ended up by accepting communism as an unmodifiable calamity before which there was no better alternative. Castro accepted the reintegration to power of these critical and skeptical revolutionaries, but he was very careful not to place them in key positions. The Plains— the clandestine urban guerrillas—who have remained loyal, have been used by the revolution, but far from where the bunker's inner circle decides the country's fate. Castro never completely trusted these men. *His people* are the Sierra's peasants, ready to kill or be killed defending the Maximum Leader without questioning the ethical justification of his deeds.

The old Communist (Popular Socialist) party is the other force present in the power structure, but it is mainly visible in second-level positions and has little access to the military apparatus. Castro does not trust the Communists, and reasons abound. The PSP, which betrayed the forces that were fighting against the Machado dictatorship, was pro-Batista during this dictator's first rise to power, and rabidly sectarian during the insurrection against Batista's second dictatorship, an event in which it hardly participated. It was only at the end, during the tyranny's last months, when the collapse was foreseeable, that the PSP sent several men to Sierra Maestra and organized a guerrilla group in Las Villas province with the purpose of placing it at Castro's disposal and thus neutralizing the influence of other anti-Communist guerrilla groups in that area. The PSP was very vulnerable. Only if Fidel gave it a hand would it share in the revolution's spoils. Some incredibly vile episodes were discussed sotto voce among the different revolutionary groups. Marcos Rodríguez, a well-known PSP member, had turned over to Bastista's police force (with the object of having them eliminated, as they were avowed anticommunists) four of the better-known leaders of the university students' Revolutionary Directorate. The Communist party leaders had encouraged this treacherous act and later protected the traitors. In reality, the PSP was composed of two very different groups: the hierarchy, corrupt and cynical, more or less intellectually well endowed, and the militant base, patient and honest, almost always composed of men with little education.

When Fidel decided to undertake the revolution's "communization," the old PSP nurtured the fantastic illusion that they would "use" Fidel and his people, ignorant amateurs unfamiliar with party doctrine. Escalante, Ordoqui, and other elements of the PSP's central committee began the task of infiltrating their cadres in decision-making positions and in the military command. But Castro never lost track of them, and it did not take him long to find out what they were planning. He put an end to their game with an unexpected shove that sent Escalante to jail and placed Ordoqui and his wife in a public trial over the somber Marcos Rodríguez affair.

Fidel did not need the PSP to serve as Moscow's interpreter. He had established his own communication channels, and Moscow limited itself to asking for leniency for the old party satellite now in disgrace with the Cuban Jupiter. The tacit accord consisted of keeping the PSP busy running the cultural spectacle. Well-known Communist personalities such as Guillén, Rodríguez, Mariano Portuondo, Marinello, and Alicia Alonso could tend to literature, painting, music, ballet, and cinematography—activities that were profoundly mysterious rituals to the pro-Fidel people. Being kept occupied in those pleasant pastimes, the old comrades enjoyed the feeling of power without remotely embodying a serious political risk for Castro.

During more than twenty-nine years Castro has personally monopolized all political power. This has allowed him to launch the revolution in different and even contradictory paths without having to answer to anyone for his unpredictable whims. From adopting Marxism-Leninism as a theoretical safeguard, to "decreeing" the need to industrialize the country, then later backing off and forgetting the whole idea; trying to do away with the single-crop sugar industry, then changing his mind and coming up with the wild project of harvesting 10 million tons of sugar. These erratic changes in such a short time would not have been possible with the existence of a party and an independent legislative branch of government with the capacity to criticize and mold government policy. Institutionalization—Fidel feels it intuitively— would signal the revolution's finale. Or at least the end of *his* revolution. That is why the regime's institutionalization process is nothing but a clumsy alibi to seek political legitimacy insofar as time gradually erases the memory of the military victories of the Sierra Maestra. To Castro, a man born to give orders the likes of whom has never existed in the country's history, it would be very difficult to accept the fact that some institution could limit his frenetic capacity for action. That is why he postpones institutionalization. It is simpler to govern by decree, by simple memoranda, by speeches that the people interpret as if they were laws and commands of obligatory compliance.

This circumstance strengthens the power structure, but it raises some doubts about the regime's survival if Castro were to die or disappear in an assassination attempt. In a clear panorama, in which Castro himself has impeded the emergence of national leaders and in which there are no institutions capable of offering an undisputed substitute, it is probable that clashes between different sectors in power will take place. Of course, Raúl Castro, Fidel's vicar in the armed forces, would momentarily be the dominant figure, but Raúl is hated within that institution by many officers, especially those who graduated from the Czechoslovakian military academies.

What real power do the Russians have in Cuba? Not as much as the anti-Castro propaganda claims nor as little as Castro would like to pretend. The Russians' weight in Cuba cannot be felt as in its European satellites, among other reasons, because Cuba is very far from the Soviet military arm, and because the old Communist party—the Soviet agent—has no influence whatsoever. Soviet influence and power are measured in terms of the amount of financial support and military supplies which Moscow is willing to give Havana. Due to the fact that the revolution meant supplying a costly and uninterrupted lifeline, Moscow has demanded in return almost absolute control of the Cuban economy. Thousands of technicians work at trying to organize the Caribbean chaos and keeping the Soviet Union informed, but they do not directly operate in the sphere where political decisions are made. There are no "older brothers" giving Castro orders, but rather officials that look after Soviet investments so that they will not be completely wasted in the Cuban morass. As the magnitude of Cuba's failure increases, these Soviet officials have increased in importance. Beside each Cuban minister and vice-minister there is a watchful Russian "technician" who directs the depart-ment's work. Theoretically, his role is similar to that of "advisors" in the Alliance for Progress, the Inter-American Development Bank, or AID, and like his counterpart's relationship with the CIA, he keeps the Soviet intelligence apparatus well informed.

Soviet power is more potential than effective. Because of the aid that Russia gives Cuba, there is a potential for blackmail—Cuba only has oil reserves for thirty days. If the Soviet flux of oil were to stop, the country would be paralyzed or forced to acquire it in Western currency, of which Cuba does not have large amounts. It would also be left at the mercy of the United States, for the only thing that has detained the liquidation of Castro's regime by or under the instigation of the United States has been the United States-Soviet pact of 1962.

The Soviet Union has used this blackmail capacity with some discretion, but it has become shamefully evident on three occasions: during the October crisis, when Khrushchev made a pact with the United States that sealed Cuba's fate without even consulting with Havana; in the aborted springtime of Prague when Soviet tanks crushed socialism with a human semblance; and in the Middle East conflicts. Fidel, in the really vital issues, has been forced to stridently support the Soviet position. In other matters, the Soviet Union appears resigned to being unable to control its remote appendix with the same unrestrained impunity it has customarily enjoyed in Eastern Europe.

The makeup of the higher echelons of the onerous Cuban government bureaucracy is a clear indicator of the regime's objectives. For example, the top officials of the Ministry of Agriculture number 9 bureaucrats, while the Ministry of Foreign Affairs has 187. The Ministry of Education has 21 top officials, but the Ministry of the Interior—which handles the affairs of the police state within a state—has 121. The Public Health Ministry has 28 ranking bureaucrats, while the armed forces have 199 high ranking officers. The Cuban government's bureaucratic design is not typical of a country struggling with underdevelopment, but of an imperialistic power that wants to influence—and does influence—world events. It would be ludicrous to consider the Cuban government as the state machinery of a poor Third World country desperately trying to develop in spite of the obstacles the superpowers place in its way. If Cuba were really a conventional underdeveloped country seeking a more human standard of living for its citizens, surely its bureaucratic configuration would be radically different.

How Does He Rule?

Régis Debray published in Paris his version of Che Guevara's Bolivian adventure. Debray was a young French intellectual, author of a mediocre little book, *Revolution in the Revolution*, and later a guerrilla apprentice in the Che Guevara's group. According to Guevara, Debray lacked the physical resources which the tough life of a guerrilla required, and soon the latter came up with a weak excuse to join the urban guerrillas. Finally, the Bolivian army found him, and after several years in prison—during which he learned Spanish and acquired his habit of making superficial analyses—he found himself free again and willing to curtail forever his deviations from the strict (and safe) field of theoretical thinking. Personal involvement undoubtedly leads to prison, death, or to painful and ridiculous contradictions.

Debray interned himself in the Cuban madhouse in the mid-sixties. During those years, Fidel was going through a violently contagious paranoid period from which the young philosophy professor could not escape. The Cuban leader had resolved "to make the Andes into another Sierra Maestra," "to start a long American march" (à la Mao), to ignite the continent with a total revolutionary war, to raise the consciousness of the Third World; and in order to accomplish this, he sent guerrillas to Africa and "volunteers" to Vietnam (almost all died). This costly public relations effort was directed toward gaining recognition as the undisputed crown prince of the Third World. At that time Fidel held secret ambitions of independence from both Moscow and Washington, claiming for Havana the title of capital of the Spanish-American world, after Che, of course, had completed his wars of conquest. It had been agreed that Fidel would move his headquarters to the continent as soon as a safe "liberated" territory had been conquered. All these demented lucubrations, exhaled between cigar puffs and sips of coffee, in the midst of the surrealist spectacle of a meeting of bearded men, sounded strangely believable. Fidel would convoke the Apocalypse with the same seriousness with which Duvalier or Trujillo used to practice voodoo. Debray was overcome by the magic. The charisma and vehemence of the Cuban overwhelmed him. After four hours in Havana, he had forgotten Descartes' *The Discourse on Method*. Fidel, brilliant, eloquent, and the captive slave of a simple but twisted and convincing logic—features typical of a genial paranoid— bewitched the young French Marxist. Perhaps Debray would have suspected that he was falling into a trap had he known that the Maximum Leader, in addition to being known as "The Horse," was also called "The Madman," the name with which Kuchilán, with his customary sagacity, had baptized Castro (behind his back) at a social gathering being held one day at the Carmelo Restaurant. "The Madman" took Debray's imagination by assault.

Recent Cuban history is absolutely unexplainable if one forgets the psychological makeup of its principal and almost sole protagonist. None of this will be recorded by future history books. They will speculate about "economic conditions," "power structures," "international opportunities," and other high-sounding words of historiography. But they will forget Fidel's childish temper tantrums, his paranoia, his abnormal fits of anger, his insane jealousy directed toward any person who might stand out or might begin to win the people's love or admiration. It might be just hearsay, but it is said that Castro personally had two television leading men fired because their fans were becoming too numerous. It is a terse statement about Castro's maladjusted relationship with his people. Fidel sees himself vaguely as a supermacho who exercises a lover-tyrant authority over the country he has conquered. The bedroom where everything is aired is the rostrum. From the speaker's platform Fidel punishes, loves, or scolds his lover, and all is done according to how "obedient" and "loyal"—traditional female virtues—the Cuban people have been. Angry or happy, in a posture of intimate promiscuity that no other political caudillo has attained, Fidel manipulates the Cuban people. He reserves for himself, as his special macho duty, the announcement of bad news. He informs the country of scarcities, hurricanes, the failure of the sugar crop, or the reestablishment of the death penalty. He thunders, threatens, and lashes out at the Great Female for her fickle behavior. His immediate subordinates have suffered, seized by fear, the man's screams and abuse. José Llanusa—who managed to become secretary of education with the outstanding academic background that being a basketball coach conferred—was physically shoved and pushed by Castro in the presence of other leaders. The reaction of these subordinates, humiliated and offended by the lover-tyrant, is of a pathetic congruence; they become resentful and dejected. Once, while leaving a television station, Major Faustino Pérez, a resistance hero punished by Fidel, became hysterical, took hold of Fidel by the lapels, and half in repentance and half in anger asked him for another opportunity to be loyal. Castro placed his hands on Pérez's shoulders, looked at him intently, and gave him a second chance. Since then Faustino cannot help but maintain toward Castro an ambiguous attitude of sadness and spite. The disillusionment and bewilderment that follow are not results of the failure of an ideological adventure which ended up as a dictatorship, but a consequence of the supermacho's initial seduction and subsequent betrayal. Differences are settled within the sphere of personal relationships. They love and are loved by the caudillo in a passive-active relationship.

How did this literary character manage to become the owner of a country? The answer is simple: riding on the crest of a revolution. In a territory without institutions or rules against which to measure the competency of men, revolutions are the only fitting scenery for epic heroes. Fidel is the epic hero par excellence: daring, energetic, dogmatic. Within the republican framework of a bourgeois democracy, the majority of those characteristics would become defects; in the middle of a revolution they become virtues. How was he able to win followers? Guevara, for example, was much more intelligent than Fidel, and certainly better educated, more refined. Yet the Argentine, subdued by Castro's charisma, was able to leave aside his exemplary sobriety and dedicated a pitiful poem to Fidel in which he offered himself to his worshipped hero. Fidel seduced him, and the young physician, in spite of knowing himself intellectually and morally superior, subordinated himself. This strange erotic-political relationship so frequent in the Cuban madhouse, always ruled the relationship between the two men. When Guevara wanted to break off the affiliation, when he wanted to end Castro's "influence," Fidel considered it a sign of faithlessness. The relationship between the two was left in this strange state when Guevara went to Africa in 1965. That is why from all of Che's documents, Fidel has chosen as a "political statement" a letter in which Guevara rectified previous postures of independence and again totally endorsed his lord and master's vision. From the speaker's platform—the bedroom—Fidel revalidated his position as an indisputable lover–conqueror.

Debray—and I am returning to the orgin of these reflections—does not deal with these considerations in his book. Of the writers that have written about Cuba, only Karol, Dumont, and Enzensberger have sensed the monstrous significance of Fidel's relationship with the Cuban people. Debray, stubbornly superficial, contents himself with immediate reasons. One, a weighty one, appears to obsess him with respect to his adventure's failure: the colossal stupidity of deriving universal conclusions from the particular and unrepeatable Cuban experience. Debray, and with him the protagonists of the Cuban Revolution, ended up believing the revolutionary mythology: the fantastic tale of the twelve men who defeated an army of thirty thousand backed by the United States, and other ridiculous conclusions drawn a posteriori from the folkloric anecdotes of the struggle against the incredibly maladroit Batista. Today, years after Che's death and the bearded men's first days in power, the small actors in the historical process—Debray among them—are beginning to shake loose from Castro's madness. In Paris, safe from Castro's contagious paranoia, far from his manly seduction, Debray, little by little, is recovering his lucidity and is writing some sadly revealing books.

Whom Does He Rule?

Since democracy remains a magic word in those countries in which it does not exist, a label is sought in order to proclaim that, yes, it does exist in Cuba but in a different way from that in other countries. In Cuba, according to the legend, there is "direct democracy." Fidel controls the country with the same mentality with which Trujillo ruled the Dominican Republic. He is a Trujillo who has read (portions of) Lenin and who has social sensitivity. Cuba is his hacienda. He knows the *guajiros* (Cuban peasants) and he tells and listens to some very boring stories about cows and hens. He visits the orphans and plays basketball with them. He goes into mines, out in the fishing boats, or visits the charcoal workers. He welcomes anyone—Sartre, Gina Lollobrigida, and Sukarno—they are all the same to him. Since Mussolini's death, the world has not seen a more photogenic dictator. He is blessed with an insatiable curiosity. He sticks his Hellenic nose into everything, and enjoys it. Power is fun, and if it is absolute, it is absolute fun. Castro enjoys walking around wearing a construction helmet or interrogating a CIA agent or inaugurating a hospital for the lame. He observes and lives through every event in his little (114.424 km^2) hacienda. Everything that goes on is his personal concern. With the aid of his elephantine memory, he accumulates facts, ideas, and anecdotes. "You, señora"—he said once to a cigar vendor while walking in Prado Street in 1959 following the triumph of the revolution and in the presence of hundreds of journalists—"you refused to give me a cheap box of cigars on credit right before the Moncada attack." The woman almost fainted, and Fidel smiled, proud of his amazing memory, which he manipulates the same way Trujillo did. "How are Fefa and the kids?" Perhaps once, fourteen years ago, he had met the person now standing before him, and had learned on that occasion about Fefa's existence.

There is a certain pathological incapacity in all this mnemonic nonsense. Fidel Castro does not know how to establish priorities. He gives equal time to petty matters and to serious business. To some foreigners and some natives this characteristic is one of his more charming traits. It is so amusing to have as your president someone who pitches nine innings, shoots baskets, and traps sharks! Drinking coffee with one of history's protagonists is so delightful that people forget that the job of a country's head of state is not to train himself to win the decathlon or to entertain customers at a barber shop. Englishmen would never tolerate Fidel's clowning in their heads of state; but in exotic, rumba-dancing Cuba anything goes. Something similar happens with Amin. Amin is a darker Fidel. Fidel is superior to Amin in his coherence and in his search for political objectives. Amin is superior to Fidel in that he knows how to play the maracas. In any case, one has to credit both dictators with a good sense for public relations. Pinochet has probably been less cruel than Amin, but he is by far the more unpopular of the two. Pinochet kills seriously, and Amin kills jokingly. Fidel—in scale—does what Stalin did, but Stalin was censured and Fidel receives winks. Stalin did not play basketball and did not send regards to Fefa. That personal style of the Nation's Little Father is usually effective in provincial societies like Cuba's. The nation's leader is not the remote person who teledirects life, but a man made of flesh and blood with whom you may one day talk about the weather, the sugar harvest, or the immortality of lobsters. Fidel knows this, and he exploits it successfully. This quality is part of what some preposterous people call "direct democracy."

"Direct democracy" is also exercised from the public podium. In the island's squares, from a height, Fidel asks the people: "Does our Revolution deserve voluntary work?" And the people roar "Yes!" happy to devote their Sundays to the delightful task of cutting sugarcane. At other times the questions are tougher. "Do you want elections?" "No, no!" the people shout with disgust. Foreign correspondents, full of enthusiasm, fervently jot down notes which explain the miracle of "direct democracy." It does not matter that throughout the square *listeros* ("list makers") also go around taking note of the attendance, name by name, or that the terrifying little eyes of the partisans direct and measure the controlled enthusiasm. Foreign correspondents will go on writing about "direct democracy." Fidel has a good press. He is a likable fellow. He is quite funny, especially if you do not live in Cuba.

But is it good or bad to know cows by their names? This is a slippery subject. Castro is the most popular ruler in Cuban history. It is a matter of style, not of whether the people approve or disapprove of the measures he dictates. Castro's style is totally popular. There are various signs. He is the first head of state that Cubans have called by a first name. The others were "Batista" or "Prío" or Menocal" or "Grau." Castro is "Fidel" or "Fifo" or "El Caballo" (the horse). He is much more than the man installed in the government. He is a familiar figure, an inevitable presence that floods homes through radio, television, newspapers, conversation, and children's games. His sayings, his accent, his gestures are imitated by 9 million Cubans, victims of history's most promiscuous politician. While previous Cuban politicians, facing a microphone, would enunciate their *s's*, *d's*, and even *z's* in a desperate effort to appear educated, Fidel speaks "Cuban" with spontaneous candor and not a trace of inhibition. He is not exactly the most eloquent of public speakers. He is a man who grabs the microphone by its neck and laughs, struggles, admonishes, praises, converses, throws a tantrum, insults, and says whatever he damn pleases, unashamedly. Spontaneity saves him from ridicule.

This "direct democracy" has its established power which is Fidel, and its opposition which is also Fidel. Fidel is his government's only serious critic. He commits blunders and later censors them. He proclaims the 10-million-ton harvest and later fires the person in charge when the goal is not met. On several occasions, from the speaker's platform, he has placed his absolute power at the people's disposal. The people shouted "No!" that they wanted him, that he should go on sacrificing himself. And then Castro, humbly, accepts the dictates of the loud majority. Faced with such spectacles, there is always at hand some gentleman who sings the praises of Athenian democracy and the Socratic square, while spewing Latin citations taken from the pink pages of *Le Petit Larousse*. In the midst of such buffoonery one can only remain bewildered.

Why Does He Rule?

Months after attaining power, the Cuban Revolution's leadership directed the rapid radicalization process. The new leaders changed from being a petty bourgeois reformist group and came to embody the role of Marxist-Leninist revolutionaries. Many factors played a part in this radical change: Castro's authoritarian character, the services the Communist party provided just before and after the revolutionary triumph, fear of the reaction of the United States, and a certain social sensibility. All of that, compounded, tipped the scales in Moscow's direction. But there is more. There is a factor of tremendous importance in Cuba's communization: It was the only choice that guaranteed Castro a role of worldwide preponderance as chieftain of the first communist revolution in Latin America. If one loses sight of Castro, any analysis of Cuban contemporary history becomes obscure. Fidel is a Messianic man with a sickly vocation for power and glory. All his life, from adolescence, he has untiringly sought newspaper headlines. In 1959, after the failure of the Bolivian revolution, the extinction of the revolutionary Mexican mystique, the erosion of Perón's prestige, and the cautious moderation of the democratic Left exemplified by Rómulo Betancourt, José Figueres, or Luis Muñoz Marín, what shining road did he have left to attract world attention? The installment of communism in Cuba was the type of ideal enterprise for the indefatigable Castro—the proper task for the warrior who does not wish to rest. When the possibility of communizing the country was discussed by Fidel, Raúl, Guevara, and other intimate members of the revolutionary conclave, a morale-building esprit de corps was reborn among them. Again there was a crusade, a struggle, and the possibility of glory. Moscow did not exactly understand what was happening in the Cuba of 1959. For the first time its conspiratorial agents were less effective than those of the Cuban leadership. Neither was Moscow able to foresee that it was bringing to its side a fiery competitor. Once inside the system, Fidel Castro convoked his intimates and communicated to them the new objectives of the revolution: in the domestic realm, the establishment of the first communist nation in the world. The Soviet Union had fifty years of socialism and of dictatorship of the proletariat; of traveling on the eternal road to communism. Cuba would skip stages, it would modify the behavior and habits of the people, it would eradicate money and the profit-making zeal in a few years. Cuba (Castro) would show the world, et cetera, et cetera.

In the area of foreign policy, the challenge to the Soviets was no less disquieting. Fidel's reasoning was of a naive simplicity: Asia for the Chinese, Europe for the Russians, and Latin America for the Cubans. He claimed for Cuba (for himself to be more exact) the leadership of a third Communist bloc that would sprout as a consequence of the subversive efforts organized by Havana. Fortunately for his plans, political leaders all over the world began to recite a Third World rhetoric. The Third World was claiming a protagonist role in the face of the policies of the big powers. Fidel conceived of himself as the axis and spokesman of that Third World. He organized in Havana the

Tricontinental Conference; he supported, trained, and sent guerrillas everywhere. With one hand he would fight imperialism, and with the other, symbolically, he would challenge (gesticulating) Moscow's Communist supremacy in certain parts of the world.

Moscow, an old giant who has already tried these utopias, resignedly admitted the vehement gesticulations of the curious satellite. It needed only to patiently wait for the impulsive Caribbean leader's failure. In the end, Castro would tire of sending guerrillas who would repeatedly suffer defeats, of supporting Marxist dilettantes, and of ignoring the aging local Communist parties. In the long run, he would discover that the best way to destroy an economic system is to take those mythical short cuts toward prosperity. Far from building the first communist nation in the world, Castro ended up by creating socialism's first military dictatorship, in the midst of a shameful chain of economic failures, scarcities, foreign dependency, and penury.

As failure became evident, those vibrant initial objectives began to slowly dull. The guerrillas did not prosper, the intellectuals ended up by rebelling, the students did not respond or finally accused the Cuban government of being reactionary. The melancholy certitude that there is always someone to the Left (or to the Right) finally took hold of Castro. Havana, for many maverick Communists, for the divine Left, is a Stalinist regime of little attraction. All the great objectives of Castroism began to crumble in the face of a reality much more complex than Castro had suspected. Euphoria and optimism are usually ominous in politics. What is left of the imperial dream? Resigned to the failure of the Cuban model, they have opted for exporting the army to foreign adventures such as the colonial wars in Africa. Now they are not trying to convince anyone they are especially interested in a domestic triumph, they plan simply to win, faithfully devoted to the Soviet model.

Is Fidel Castro Crazy?

In short: Is Fidel Castro crazy? Mr. Castro, who believes himself to be Napoleon (and who is probably right), in 1981 stated that the United States sent him a dengue epidemic with the grim aim of still further undermining the health of his bewildered subjects. Years ago he bitterly complained that the CIA had destroyed the tobacco harvest by spreading the terrible "blue mold," while it damaged the sugar harvest at the same time by unleashing the wrath of the "blight," a tiny insect trained—obviously—by the treacherous "strangeloves" of the Pentagon. But these fantastic accusations are not new. Twenty years ago he alerted the world about another singularly vile trick: The CIA had diverted cyclones and directed them in sinister gusts against the coasts of the island of Cuba. All this leads to the inevitable question: Is this imaginative gentleman crazy? Jeane Kirkpatrick, the brilliant U.S. delegate to the United Nations, thinks so, and that is how Madrid's daily, *ABC*, reported it. Nasser and Tito joked about the mental health of the character, and even Che himself, in the midst of his evident admiration, showed serious reservations: "You have to forgive him those things, Pardo; you know that Fidel is a little loony."

A little? How little? What kind of madness does he suffer from? Evidently he has paranoic characteristics: pathological distrust, persecution manias, perfectly articulate rationalizations of an insane origin. But he also reveals neurotic symptoms: manic-depressive crises, fits of euphoria, oral and motor hyperactivity, episodes of transitory rage. Perhaps one is not dealing with an insane-asylum or straightjacket lunatic, but, yes, undoubtedly with a psychotic personality. The "psychologist/psychiatrist clan"—as Szasz calls it— puts to bed, sedates, and treats millions of patients even when this luckless fauna may only be given to disturbing the little world of the neighborhood family, while Fidel Castro has at his disposal a cornered clientele of 10 million petrified Cubans subject to the consequences of his outbursts.

This is very serious, because we shall never know whether Castro is crazy, and probably we shall not even manage to figure out this question of "being crazy," but there is no doubt that when a subject of such strange behavior reaches power, the roles are turned upside-down. Under normal circumstances, when the neighbor on the fifth floor insists that the CIA is sending cyclones or that his cousin is being injected with dengue, he is locked up, calmed down, given an aspirin, two slaps, three electroshocks and/or a little print of Saint Judas Tadeus, or—in any case—he is advised to get married to see if he can get rid of his nervousness by means of the bed, which is a very effective remedy. But when the author of the nonsense is not the fifth-floor neighbor but the one in the house of the chief of state, may God catch us with our confessions made, for it is the "normal" people who end up in the insane asylums, as happened to my friend, historian Juan Peñate.

What is to be done, then, with Mr. Castro? I think here we have made a mistake in international forums. The problem of Cuba has nothing to do with the Security Council of the United Nations but with the World Health Organization, the Viennese School, and sedatives.

Here what needs to be shouted is "Long live *librium* Cuba!" (play on words for the Cuban expression "¡Viva Cuba libre!"—"Long live free Cuba!"). On the one hand this is a pharmaceutical problem and, on the other, a secret service one. In other words, the same CIA commando who introduced dengue on the island should stealthily enter Castro's rooms in Havana while he is sleeping and inject in his veins thirty-eight gallons of a tranquilizing serum of any calming substance. Let's see if once and for all history may absolve the rest of the Cubans who in the end are the ones who have been condemned to foot the bill for the disturbed personality of this alarming gentleman.

A Case of Crisis

But his adversaries are not the only ones who suffer. At times the regime itself becomes a victim of Castro's personality. The most notorious case is that of the Peruvian Embassy. In April 1980, Fidel Castro, indignant because a handful of Cubans had managed to force their way into the Embassy, removed the guard from the door, thus, in a few hours, causing 10,800 people—all that could fit into every square centimeter—to enter the diplomatic precincts in order to escape the country.

Why did Fidel Castro provoke this flagrant discredit to his regime? Why did he make evident in a pair of Peruvian nights what he had, with extraordinary ability, been hiding for two decades? The answer must be sought in a trait of his temperament: pride. Fidel does not admit contradictors, nor critics, nor threatening situations. That is the way he has been since data has existed on his personal behavior. Fidel subscribes, even to the point of suicide, to the old Castilian stupidity of "maintain it but don't change it."

He always attacks, always retreats by moving forward, never retracts. To have a place in his personal retinue it is necessary to lack one's own criteria and—if possible—be able to show a flat encephalogram. This is the origin of the spiritual poverty of his acolytes. Ramiro Valdés, Armando Hart, Sergio del Valle, the very brotherly Raúl, Juan Almeida, Pepín Naranjo, Guillermo García—his private henchmen—are always only people with soft necks and dull neurons.

They have no other function than to execute orders (or people), laugh, and roll the ball around on the tip of the dialectical snout. There are few intelligent people close to Fidel, and those that are cannot excel. Carlos Rafael Rodríguez, Humberto Pérez, and one well-endowed comrade or another are experts in the difficult art of making themselves anonymous. The most brilliant, the most imaginative, the most creative man has to be Fidel. Mirror, mirror, on the wall, who's the most beautiful tyrant of them all? Nobody matches him. Nobody can challenge him.

The fight between Castro—in this corner of the ring, with ten tons of egocentrism—and Peru and Venezuela in the other—with reason and right—occurred because, for once, this nearly sexagenarian boy, stubborn and proud, could not have his way and preferred to break the game. But his little temper tantrum landed right in the bull's eye of his prestige.

This incident clearly ought to make the palace clique do some thinking. The profile of the revolution, its ideological direction and international importance, are due to Castro. But, at the same time, it is Fidel who is digging the grave of its process. He is the father and the enemy, the wing and the anchor, the only Cuban who could put Cuba on the international map, but the one who will end up wiping it out. His impulse toward pride is much stronger than his instinct for prudence, and there is the incident of the Peruvian Embassy as proof.

The simple recognition of this fact is a source of subversion within the power structure of the regime. Every Communist, every civil servant convinced of the incurability of the Maximum Leader, of his chronic condition as a disorganizer of the state, as a chaoticizer of public life, ought to arrive at the relentless conviction that to substitute him is much more feasible than to educate him.

Neither are the Russians unfamiliar with this scheme of reasoning. The invasion of Afghanistan was due to a similar analysis: Amin, the Communist leader of Kabul, was the source of the instability and the capsizing. Moscow, an expert in realpolitik, decided to eliminate him and substitute him for another milder and better organized supporter. The Russians have poured into the bottomless Cuban sack more than $30 billion and a thoroughly impressive amount of equipment. If popular disturbances occur, rash attempts at coups d'état, and the danger of the Cuban regime's collapse occurs, it is likely that the consequences will reach a Kremlin in which there will be no lack of candidates to inherit Chernienko's easy chair—people always ready to fatten up on the errors and lack of foresight of others. A similar event cost Nikita Khrushchev his job.

The Russian hierarchy has good reasons to be worried about the doubtful fate of the Cuban revolution and the irrational conduct of its favored viceroy. It is practically impossible that the events of Afghanistan would be repeated in Cuba, but not out of the question that the Russians, very nervous facing an impending crisis, would try to put a straightjacket on a madman.

Appendix

Alicia Alonso (1920–   ). Cuba's leading classical ballerina and founder of the Cuban National Ballet. She has danced throughout the world, chiefly for the American Ballet Theater company and the Bolshoi Ballet of Moscow. Thanks to her ideological links with the communist PSP, after the revolution she was entrusted with the foundation of the national ballet company. She is now in semiretirement.

Rómulo Betancourt (1908–1981). Venezuelan politician who was president between 1959 and 1964, replacing the dictator Marcos Pérez Jiménez. In his youth he was a Communist, but he broke away from this allegiance and later founded the Democratic Action party. During his mandate he consolidated Venezuelan democracy, fought against left-wing guerrilla movements in the mountains, and confronted the dictatorships of Castro in Cuba and Trujillo in the Dominican Republic.

The CIA versus Cuba. Castro has accused the CIA of the reappearance on the island in the seventies of swine fever which decimated herds. He has also suggested that contagious diseases affecting humans have been introduced into Cuba by the CIA. But the frequent outbreaks of hepatitis, malaria, AIDS, and the like are due primarily to the lack of health controls for the many visitors from Africa south of the Sahara, Central America, and other regions where these diseases are endemic.

Régis Debray (1943–   ). A French writer and politician famous in Cuba for his short work *Revolution in the Revolution?* He was with "Che" Guevara on his Bolivian adventure in 1967 but was taken prisoner that year. He was freed in 1970 and wrote about his experiences. He has been an official advisor to President François Mitterrand and has moved away from radical Marxist militancy to a very different moderate outlook.

Dengue. A relatively benign infectious disease caused by a virus. It can be transmitted by the bite of the aedes aegypti mosquito. In the last few decades Cuba has suffered several *dengue* epidemics and the Cuban government has repeatedly accused the CIA of being responsible.

Waldo Díaz-Balart. A constructivist Cuban painter who lives in Spain. He is Castro's brother-in-law.

René Dumont (1904–   ). French agronomist famous for his struggle against hunger first in the rice-growing area of the Tonkin Gulf and later in China. After being invited to Cuba as a farming expert he wrote an essay *(Is Cuba Socialist?)* in which he questions the virtues of the Cuban experience and of the Maximum Leader. For this he has been ostracized by the Cuban leadership.

Effects That Reached the Kremlin. Chernienko's successor, Gorbachev, is even further from the Castroite position. His *glasnost* and *perestroika* policies have been strongly opposed by Castro who tirelessly reiterates his long-standing revisionist viewpoints.

Hans Magnus Enzensberger (1929–   ). German writer, critic, poet, and political expert who has translated Neruda into German. He is very critical of present-day Germany, but although some of his writings have praised the Castro regime, he has kept a certain distance from it.

Aníbal Escalante. A leader of the (communist) Popular Socialist party and well known in it for his authoritarian personality and his policy of infiltrating key posts in the revolutionary leadership. Fidel Castro denounced him in his speech on 13 March 1962. In 1968 he accused him of being the leader of the so-called microfaction that favored a total sellout to the Soviet Union. Escalante and many of his supporters, some from the old PSP, were removed from their positions and spent some time in jail. He has not been given another job and spent several years as an exile in the Soviet Union. Castro has sidelined him completely as he invariably does with anyone who threatens to overshadow him.

Juan Peñate Fernández. A Cuban historian who has lived in Madrid since 1980. He was persecuted for his ideas and interned in a lunatic asylum for being "antisocial." He went into exile after managing to get into the Peruvian Embassy in 1980.

Manolo Fernández. A member of the July 26 Movement and the first labor minister in the first revolutionary government. He went into exile in the United States in 1961 helped by the good offices of the Venezuelan embassy.

Marcelo Fernández. A leading figure of the July 26 Movement when it operated underground in Havana. For a time he was regarded as something of a right winger, but despite this he has held important jobs such as minister of trade as well as other posts of a technical nature.

José Figueres Ferrer (1906–   ). Three-time president of Costa Rica (1948–1949, 1953–1958, 1970–1974). He did much to increase the prestige of his country's democracy. He visited revolutionary Cuba and his public appeal to the regime for moderation led to his being ostracized by Castro ever since.

José Llanusa Gobel. An active member of the July 26 Movement in Havana and head of INDER (National Sports Institute) in 1961. In 1965 he became minister of education. But he was accused of making too many mistakes and removed from the revolution's decision-making circles.

Nicolás Guillén (1902–   ). A poet, born in Camagüey, and the principal exponent of Cuba's black poetry. He has been linked to the Cuban Communist movement since the 1930s. He worked as a typesetter and typist in the Interior Ministry under the dictatorship of Machado. In 1930 the publication of *Motivos del son* made him famous. Later volumes include *Poemas mulatos, West Indies Ltd.,* and *Songoro Cosongo.* In 1937 he joined the Communist Revolutionary Union which later became the PSP. He then traveled throughout the hemisphere giving lectures. The governments of Prío and Batista, especially the latter, forced him to go into exile. In 1954 he received the Lenin Peace Prize. From 1955 to 1958 he lived in Paris before taking up residence in Argentina thanks to the good offices of Rafael Alberti. After the revolution he returned to Cuba to work on the newspaper *Hoy* and in 1961 was named president of UNEAC (the Cuban National Writers and Artists' Union). His most recent work is *Cuatro canciones para el Che.*

Incidents at the Peruvian Embassy. The events of April 1980 when the grounds of the Peruvian Embassy in Havana were invaded by almost 11,000 "inner exiles" after police protection was withdrawn. This led to the Mariel exodus.

Joel Iglesias. As a young man he fought against Batista in the Sierra. On account of his peasant origin he became president of the Union of Young Communists in the 1960s.

Kewes S. Karol (1924–   ). A writer and political expert of Polish origin who fought with the Red Army against the Germans but after the war moved to Paris where he wrote for the *Nouvel Observateur.* He was in Cuba four times between 1961 and 1968. In 1970 he published *Guerrillas in Power,* a book critical of the Cuban revolution which earned him the permanent hostility of the Cuban leadership.

Mario Kuchilán A Cuban journalist of Asian origin whose writings are notable for their caustic quality. Even before the Batista dictatorship he was known in the Cuban media. Since the revolution he has supported Castro.

(List Makers). In the Plaza de la Revolución, trusted trade union members, work-center officials, and police have the job of making sure that their fellow workers all turn up for the big demonstrations organized by the regime.

José Pardo Llada. A journalist who was popular before the revolution for his political commentaries on Cuban radio. He was linked to the Orthodox party. At first he supported Castro's revolution and was the target of an assassination attempt by anti-Castro forces but escaped unharmed because he was wearing a bullet-proof jacket. He was with Castro in the Sierra during the final months of the guerrilla campaign but in 1961 requested political asylum in Mexico.

The Long March. The famous trek that lasted from 1934 to 1936 in which the Chinese Communist army led by Mao Zedong traveled 12,000 kilometers, crossing 12 provinces, to escape the pursuing nationalist troops by taking refuge in Shanxi province. A large proportion of Mao's effectives fell by the wayside.

Luis Muñoz Marín (1898–1980). Puerto Rican politician who in 1938 formed the Popular Democratic party and in 1948 became governor, being reelected in 1964. He drew up the statute for a free state associated with the United States which was approved in 1952.

Líder Máximo (Maximum Leader). The Cuban propaganda media's customary epithet for Fidel Castro.

Joaquín Ordoqui. A PSP leader married to Edith García Buchaca, another leading member of the PSP. He was jailed by the Batista police in 1953 following Castro's attack on the Moncada and when released went into exile first in Eastern Europe and then in Mexico. After the revolution he served as the army's chief of supplies until, at the trial of Marcos Rodríguez, he was accused of giving economic and military information to the CIA. After being tried he and his wife were kept confined to a farm near Havana until his death.

Enrique Oltuski Osaki. A member of the July 26 Movement and, for a time, communications minister. He came from the well-off middle class and brought to the movement a solid technical background.

Víctor Paneque. Also known as Commander "Diego." He was the member of the July 26 Movement who, in Pinar del Río, tried to set up an anti-Batista front. For a time after the revolution he held a high post in the Revolutionary Armed Forces. After a few months he fled to exile in the United States.

Faustino Pérez. A revolutionary commander and one of the twelve rebels who survived the Granma landing of 1956. Later, he led the sabotage squads of the July 26 Movement in Havana and shared responsibility for the failure of the strike staged on April 9. His anti-Communist attitute soon led to his being sidelined from decision-making circles. Nonetheless he has remained loyal to Castro.

José Antonio Portuondo (1911–   ). A Cuban intellectual and writer who has been a militant Communist since the 1930s. Before the revolution he benefited from scholarships and grants in Mexico and the United States and has been a professor in several U.S. universities. After the revolution he was ambassador to Mexico from 1960 to 1962. Since 1965 he has been professor of aesthetics and literary theory at Havana University's school of literature. He has also served as Cuban ambassador to the Holy See. He edited the anthology *Cuentos cubanos contemporáneos* (Contemporary Cuban Short Stories) and *Bosquejo histórico de las letras cubanas.*

Revolutionary Directorate. A Cuban revolutionary movement that fought against Batista. It was formed mainly by FEU members and other revolutionary university students. Its baptism by fire came with the attack on the Presidential Palace and the CMQ radio station that was carried out with the aim of killing Batista and broadcasting a statement saying the country has been liberated. In the fighting, FEU president José Antonio Echevarría was killed by a police bullet. The directorate survived the ensuing crackdown and joined the revolutionary struggle proceeding in the Sierra del Escambray in Santa Clara. After the revolution its formal leader was commander Faure Chomón.

Mariano Rodríguez (1912–   ). Cuban painter linked to the Communist movement since the 1930s. He has held important positions in UNEAC and served the revolutionary government as cultural attaché in India. His artistic motifs derive mainly from multicolored roosters.

Marcos Rodríguez. A member of the (communist) Popular Socialist party who played a role in the revolution. He was tried and shot (in 1964) for allegedly betraying to the Batista authorities revolutionaries hiding at 7 Calle Humbolt after the 13 March 1957 attack on the presidential palace. He appears to have done this for reasons of personal vengeance against one of the participants. In 1960, with the revolution under way, he was arrested by the Czech police in Prague, sent back to Cuba, and, several years later, tried. His trial turned into a confrontation between the leaders of the Revolutionary Directorate and members of the PSP whom it accused of sectarianism. When Rodríguez fell he dragged down with him PSP members Joaquín Ordoqui and his wife, Edith García Buchaca, who lost all their political influence.

Juanita Castro Ruz. Fidel Castro's sister. She went into exile and has repeatedly attacked the Communist dictatorship led by her two brothers.

David Salvador. A leader of the revolutionary CTC (Central de Trabajadores de Cuba, the trade union umbrella organization). At first he supported Castro but later plotted against him and spent several years in jail before going into exile in the United States.

Thomas S. Szasz. An American psychiatrist. His books on antipsychiatry enjoyed a vogue in the 1970s.

When the Target Is Not Met. After the failure of the "10-million-ton harvest" in 1970, Castro called on his followers to "transform the setback into a victory." The minister of sugar, Lieutenant Orlando Borrego, was sacked and has not held a position of responsibility since. He was the scapegoat.

Tobacco Mildew. A mold of bluish color that plagues tobacco leaves and stems. It thrives in damp conditions. It has periodically destroyed large tracts of the best plantations in Vuelta Abajo, Pinar del Río. The Cuban government has attributed it to enemy agents.

Tricontinental Conference. Large-scale congress with left-wing delegates from Asia, Africa, and Latin America which was held in Havana from 3–15 January 1966, and which gave birth to the Organization for the Solidarity of the Peoples of Asia, Africa, and Latin America. This short-lived body was less than effective.

Carlos Varona. A Cuban lawyer, deputy labor minister in the first revolutionary government. He is a university professor and lives in exile in Puerto Rico where he received a doctorate in psychology.

Aldo Vera. Castroite revolutionary commander, chief of the action and sabotage department of the July 26 Movement in Havana. After the revolution he headed one of the regime's police organizations but later went into exile and took part in several attacks against the Cuban government officials when they were abroad. In the mid-seventies he was murdered by persons unknown in San Juan, Puerto Rico.

Juan Marinello Vidaurreta (1898–1977). A veteran leader of the Cuban Communist movement of which he was named president in 1937. He has worked for many publications. In 1940 he was elected member of the Constituent Assembly and in 1948 was a candidate for the country's presidency. He left Cuba soon after the Batista coup and returned with Castro's revolution. In 1962 he became rector of Havana University where he set in motion its "reforms." The following year he was appointed Cuban delegate to Unesco. As a student of Martí, his most important work was *Martí, escritor americano,* published by Editorial Grijalbo of Mexico.

The visit by "Che" to Africa. In 1965 "Che" Guevara traveled to several African countries (Ghana, Guinea, etc.). He took advantage of his stay in Algeria to criticize the lack of economic support of the socialist countries for the Third World, with special reference to the difference in prices between farm and industrial products.

3

A Revolution in Search of an Ideology

Idiosyncrasy and the System

The term *idiosyncrasy* has lost its credibility. It is very difficult to take inventory of the characteristics of the people who make up a nation. One runs the risk of stating a trivial cliché. One generalizes senselessly and ends up talking about the "phlegmatic English." It is a dangerous topic. It audaciously borders on nonsense. But I must try it. And I must try it because it does not seem absurd to me to assume that the economic organization of a country would function better (or worse) if it fits with the idiosyncrasy of its people. I am not talking about the political system. A democracy and a parliament can function in any culture and economic latitude (Sweden, India, Japan, Guyana). It suffices to have a minimum desire to collaborate, and that the will of the majority be accepted within certain rules of the game. These elemental principles are within the reach of any idiosyncrasy that does not deny mathematics. Economic organization is another story. The Paraguayan communes of the nineteenth century and the Jewish Kibbutzim of the twentieth have been glorious communist experiences, because these economic modes of production harmoniously fitted in with the idiosyncrasies of the Guaraní Indians and of the Israelis. More or less for the same reasons—among others—capitalism has failed in the Andean plateau and succeeded (relatively) in the urban centers. If this premise is correct, before choosing a new development model for a country, a new economic organization, the prudent thing would be to examine the profile of those who are to implement the system, to know what the persons who are going to do the work are like.

What is the Cuban like? I fear—to the Communists' chagrin—that we are dealing with a creature who is an individualist. Undisciplined, imaginative, irreverent, anarchist—a Spaniard who has been metabolized by the tropics, divested of any solemnity, and inoculated with the ludicrous spirit of the Africans. The Communists have their hearts set on engineering a New Man, but while they try to achieve it—Frankenstein is the only truly new man up to now—they are going to have to deal with the existing breed. That is why they are not accomplishing much. The Cubans just do not take to communism, more or less as the Indians did not take to catechism. They went to mass, yes, but they also paid homage to their Indian deities. No one ever knew when they were praying or making believe they were. Those in Cuba who while voluntarily cutting sugarcane have seen a spontaneous dancing party develop in a canefield, know what I am talking about. The Caribbean is not suitable for Marx's ideas. His son-in-law, who was Cuban, should have warned him.

The incongruence between the Cuban and his present economic organization have given birth to a new invention: the Committees for the Defense of the Revolution. According to the regime itself—very conceited about its police force—there are more than 200,000 of those small domestic forts. They are a group of followers in charge of prying into everything, making an inventory of everything, knowing every detail about everyone in the country. They are the ones who put into practice the guidelines which come from the leadership. Nothing human is foreign to them: with whom does the lady in apartment 5 go to bed, when does the bald man in apartment 1 take a shower, why didn't so-and-so go cut sugarcane? Repression and vigilance are in direct proportion to potential disobedience. The police force has to correct the idiosyncratic flaws. They have to forcefully manufacture Germans. Mussolini would pull his hair out trying to organize Fascist youth groups in the midst of his Napoleonic uproar. Fidel tears out his beard trying to organize a laborious and efficient beehive with rumba-dancing bees. Since he cannot, he tightens control of everything. He represses in the political sense as well as that of psychiatric jargon. He molds with prohibitions, sanctions, and fears. It is obvious that the Committees for the Defense of the Revolution are not defending themselves against American marines, but against Cubans themselves; it is a telling statement. If there are 200,000 miniforts it is because there are millions of potential transgressors. Of course, the revolution is not to blame for having to feed the economic boiler with repression. The Cubans are at fault who have the nerve not to be Germans.

Marxism-Leninism cannot accept the existence of idiosyncrasies. Part of the dogma is to assume that a country's traits and those of the classes that compose it are the result of certain peculiar economic relations, and that when you alter them, these traits will change. How long is it going to take the revolution to alter Cuban genes until they fit into the system? The Cuban is not very different from the Southern European. What can be said of him can also be said of the Spaniard, Greek, Italian, Portuguese, or French. The Cuban, a mestizo variant of the Latin, has a social mentality developed through millennia of history, which obviously did not begin with Columbus's recent visit. How long will it take the revolution to mold a Cuban to be orderly, obedient, responsible, respectful, etc. When will he become a Teuton so that Cuba will at least function with East Germany's efficiency? Do Castro and his team seriously think that they are going to change in several generations the results of thousands of years of history? Does our Caribbean Midas think that he only needs to touch Cubans with his telescopic rifle in order to transform what is Latin into a Germanic creation? Does a government have the right to play with utopias? Many Cuban traits, within a congruent economic organization, could, as in the case of the French, be turned into assets. But communism is the new scholasticism: a capricious interpretation of reality, which, when it does not coincide with life, opts to ignore it, or to create Committees for the Defense of the Revolution, which is worse.

The "Cuban Model"

Deciphering the scheme of values that governs the Cuban Communist hierarchy—especially among the neo-Communists spawned by Fidel—is not simple. The old guard—which knows more because of age than because of wisdom—is more classical. It covers up its contradictions more skillfully, more modestly. The Fidelists are more erratic. In 1960, for example, they were sure that abortion was evil; in 1970 they did not doubt that it was good; and in 1980 they were almost on the verge of making it obligatory. At the beginning of the revolution, an abortion quack could end up behind bars for performing his job; nowadays, he might receive an award if he works additional hours. Castroism's axiological scale departed from a liberal premise (1959), and took off at full speed toward Stalinism, with an unsuccessful stop at the neo-Rousseauean mythology of the New Man elaborated by Che. This New Man was the most original contribution that Cuba could have offered to the universal socialist experience, but the heart of the generous and patriotic worker simply was not there. The unselfish design failed, and they had to return to the usual: a reward if you work, punishment if you do not, which worked so well for grandpa Stalin.

What is the "Cuban model" then? I am afraid that what is special in the Cuban experience is not exactly Marxist. Neither the group which took over power nor the manner in which it went about it had anything to do with Marxist catechism. To Cuba's credit—for whatever it might be worth—it should be said that Communism has never attained power according to Marx's predictions. Cuba is ruled by an army which came to prominence during the revolution, and not a Communist party with a workers' base. The "Cuban Marxist model" is a contradiction in terms. Whatever is Cuban in it is not Marxist. And vice-versa. Let us see what is Marxist. The Cuban economy is based on the most rigid Soviet model. Castro has been transparent in these extremes: He has rejected the human socialism of Czechoslovakia, the mixed socialism of Yugoslavia, and even the Maoist's beehive. In every Cuban ministry there are Soviet advisors to set the standards. Castro's only differences with Moscow have arisen when Moscow has taken a step toward the West. Fidel is more of a Papist than the Pope. It is he who has discreetly pulled the Russians' ears when the Soviets have deviated from Marxist-Leninist orthodoxy. Cuba condemns peaceful coexistence and the nuclear arms nonproliferation treaty, because both those treaties appear to be against the interests of a worldwide proletarian revolution. Cuba condemns Latin American Communist parties because they have deviated from Leninism. Fidel is the one who is conservative—he is the preserver of the traditional mythology of the Sect's sacred books—which, since he is a newcomer, is rather ironic, but this intransigent conduct is typical of new adherents to any dogma. With time and increasing dependence on Moscow, these attacks have been muffled. Fidel, more docile, more aware, older, today understands that in Moscow as well as in London or Washington, the state rules according to its interests, and that great powers do not owe their existence to certain rights, but to certain material interests. This accommodation to political realities—which made Washington support a bloody tyranny such as Trujillo's, and Moscow sign a pact with Hitler partitioning Poland—will lead Castro to an agreement with his neighbors to the north, to a renewal of commerce, discarding those "nevers" that he has so insistently repeated over the years.

What, then, is the Cuban model? When the Portuguese armed forces chose the socialist route, there was a certain naive talk of the "Cuban model." Immediately they thought of establishing "local councils of the revolution," a Lusitanian variant of the Cuban Committees for the Defense of the Revolution. Strictly speaking, the only contribution that Cuba could offer the Portuguese would have been its very efficient police state. Cuba's innovation was not Marxist; the revolution's novelty is in its system of repression. Havana was not able to transmit one single valuable production formula, nor suggest a type of administrative organization, accounting system, or any other positive and transferable innovation. It limited itself to this advice: "Organize your supporters street by street, give them arms, and have them watch over the rest of the population. There is no better way of maintaining power." That is the only exportable aspect of the so-called Cuban model: an asphyxiating repressive structure.

If there is no Cuban model, why do people talk about it? Very simple: the ones who talk about it are not Marxists. They are not insiders. Cuba is a contradiction of Western liberals, who persist in blocking out the sun with their index finger. At a cultural performance at New York University, I have seen the audience stomp the floor and shout against the Soviet Union, then immediately afterward madly applaud the first mention of the Cuban Revolution. It is neither elegant nor "liberal" to declare oneself a critic of the Cuban

Revolution. Fortunately that has changed. Today there are very few people who dare defend publicly the sad Cuban slaughterhouse, but before the scandal of the Peruvian Embassy and the exodus later from Mariel, the acts in Russia that a liberal called "crimes" were ignored when they occurred in Cuba. It was not exactly a hypocritical attitude, but a renewed willingness to make concessions to Castroism, a willingness that could operate on a subconscious level. Solzhenitsyn's *Gulag Archipelago* might be believed without questioning one comma, but a similar book compiled by a Cuban exile would have been automatically rejected. Progressive elements in America and Europe placed too many hopes in the revolution to accept later the brutal fact that Fidel and a group of his followers had selected for the country a Leninist dictatorship with all its Cuban consequences. The curious thing is that Havana—Fidel—has not tried to mask these facts, nor pull the wool over anyone's eyes.

Whenever necessary, Castro talks about the liberals with infinite contempt. He states that he endorses Communism and the implications of prison and repression for its adversaries. The world's Communists, who know the intimate details, either like him or dislike him—the "liberal" Communists detest him—because of their affinity or their differences, but they do not believe they are facing a romantic national leader. Progressive non-Marxist elements persist in admiring an imaginary revolution which does not exist outside of the confines of their best wishes. What future but prison, the firing squad, or exile would a leader like Mitterrand, Palme, De la Madrid, or Felipe González have in Cuba? There is a last and repulsive way of nullifying the contradiction: recognize the revolution's excesses, its somber and depressive tone, but assume that it is all appropriate for the Cubans. For the Swedes, Mexicans, or French, it would not be correct, but it is perfectly acceptable for those imbeciles in the Antilles. Castro's warm embraces with Palme or Mitterrand can only be explained this way: Mitterrand and Palme supposed that those Caribbean creatures were either inferior to or different from the Swedes and French.

On a personal level one often finds progressive elements, well-intentioned liberals who reason with the same unjust and racist scheme: "I could not adapt to that country, but for the Cubans it is fitting." (Apparently the Cubans must be animals from another world.) A racist and cynical variant of the above is also frequent among certain intellectuals: "The revolution is magnificent, but my bourgeois habits would not permit me to live in the country." Alejo Carpentier was fond of saying that bad writers were those who were not on good terms with the Left. Few people are willing to risk their image denouncing Cuba. Certainly every public man—politician, artist, writer, singer—is so insofar as he has an image (that is what being a public man consists of, in being, besides oneself, an image) and that image includes the political ideology of the public man. The same non-Communist intellectual who forcefully asks for freedom for Chilean prisoners will refuse to risk his image as a progressive, painstakingly built on the basis of certain virile stances and as many more shameful concessions. This dishonest atmosphere of half truths helps keep alive a Cuban revolution that existed only for the first few months of 1959, and supplies oxygen to such ridiculous inventions as the "Cuban model," the "Cuban way to socialism," and other monsters of an imaginary bestiary. The truth is painful, and it finally ended up imposing its authority: The only Cuban contribution to socialism has been a new and efficient internal vigilance system; a greater efficacy in repression. This explains the almost total loss of the Cuban revolution's seductive power. Now it is only loved by authoritarian temperaments.

Che and the New Man

The Cuban Revolution has given birth to only two important men: Fidel Castro and Ernesto Guevara. Without Fidel there would not have been a revolution; without Che, it would probably have been different. When Fidel and Guevara met in Mexico, the "July 26" was only the insurrectional branch of the Orthodox party. The "26" was essentially an action group—a few young men who constantly talked about guns and bullets. Che, on the other hand, had mastered another language. In Guatemala, he had absorbed the ideas of the committed revolutionary. He brought with him a different type of schooling. He had known Peronism, and was familiar with the most radical thought of the time. He did not belong, as legend has it, to the Communist party (PSP), but had subscribed to some of its myths. Guevara was not a profound theoretician. He was a 26-year-old revolutionary dilettante who had recently left medical school, irrepressibly lyrical, who saw himself as a kind of transcendental ascetic, halfway between Mahatma Gandhi and Leon Trotsky. Before meeting Fidel he had traveled over half the South American continent on a motorcycle, had planned to dedicate himself to taking care of lepers in Bolivia—à la Schweitzer—and had attained little success in Jacobo Arbenz's Guatemala. Che wanted to become involved in a useful adventure. When this psychological type takes to religion, he becomes an apostolic missionary. When Che met Fidel, he took to revolution, which in the final analysis is an apostolic mission. He enrolled in the Granma expedition after talking with Castro a couple of times and falling into a trance from the dose of enthusiasm with which the Cuban injected him. Guevara was better read than Castro and could conceptualize better than his mentor, but there never was any doubt about the hierarchical order. Fidel commanded and Che obeyed; Fidel was the leader and Che voluntarily complied. In a deplorable rapture-filled poem of some forty verses written by Guevara, he calls Fidel "dawn's captain." This poem and his letter-testament—a document in which he frees the Cuban Revolution of all responsibility in his death and accuses himself of the error of not having always understood Fidel—are the alpha and omega of twelve years of irrational submission by a man who was spiritually superior to his leader, not only in intelligence and education, but also in ethical makeup and its application to everyday living. Guevara was the first, last, and only New Man to come out of the revolutionary process. That future Cuban—unselfish, hard-working, honest, critical—was himself. That creature that would come, to whom work was a privilege, to whom the best remuneration would be a job well done, was himself. Che wanted to make other Ches. He tried—perhaps unconsciously—to impregnate nine million Cubans with his seed. As all apostles, he projected in others his own heroic self-concept. He turned his type into an archetype, repeating a phenomenon as old as man. Nevertheless, his search for the New Man invested dignity in the revolutionary enterprise. Almost no one noticed in those times the trampling of the old men, of all those bipeds who could not or did not want to look like Guevara, of all the people who believe that working is a painful boredom and to whom the future of humanity is a much more fragile abstraction than the future of the family. Guevara was a hero and he wanted to set up a factory of heroes. The engineering of this new revolutionary animal appeared to him a simple enterprise because of that rare mechanism that operates in the brain of apostles. If he, with an asthmatic condition which would prostrate him, and two thin legs which hardly supported him, had carried out the revolution, why not the rest? To Savonarola, to Loyola, to Robespierre, these things were easy.

To the plump little man who goes and returns from work, to the city bureaucrat, to the man who sings in the shower, Guevara was asking for the moon. Very soon he had proof that his enthusiasm was not contagious. The New Man did not meet production quotas. Che has been one of the worst public administrators of Cuba's history. If a secretary of industry or the director of the national bank of any civilized country were to make the blunders that Che made, he would have had to commit suicide—more or less what Guevara did. As soon as he verified that the New Man was not viable and that he himself had failed in the task of governing Cuba, he mounted Rocinante (Don Quixote's horse) and went away to attack windmills. All very touching, very literary, and hardly Leninist. An analysis—Marxist or whatever—of the objective and subjective conditions which destroyed Batista's dictatorship should have sufficed to convince him that the Cuban experience was absolutely unrepeatable. But what useful task could he tackle now? The Granma and the Sierra Maestra epic brought about the liberation of a country, which is not bad. Later he projected the liberation of humanity through the ideological manipulation of his genetic seed: the much heralded New Man. It is evident that Guevara, under his shy mannerisms, under the layers of artificial curtness which covered his lyricism, had a messianic personality.

The saddest thing is that when the Guevaran utopia vanished and the Soviet pragmatism of state capitalism—which does not care about the age or style of its workers—was imposed, the only original contribution of the Cuban Revolution to the history of Communism disappeared. Fidel, who is an inexhaustible source of energy, is incapable of theorizing. He is more Stalin than Lenin. All that virginal, amiable, and Rousseauistic search for a man that would not know avarice or exhaustion, a man that would feel in his own flesh the injustice committed against others (against others not in opposition to the revolution, of course), began to be forgotten until no one remembered him. The laboratory which was assembled at the Isle of Pines, with young Communists uncontaminated by the "old regime," true "noble civilized savages," ended up a resounding failure. It is not honest to criticize the Cuban Revolution because it turned away from utopian roads on which other dreamers had already lost their way, but it is less honest to ignore the fact that for many years nothing original or dignifying has taken place in the country. A long time ago, Fidel decided that Guevara was mistaken and that he had to stop all that foolishness and start dealing with real people. Thus he resurrected the old and infallible trick of reward and punishment. If one works, reward; if one sits down, punishment. It does not fail. Old or new, it never fails.

Sovereignty as a Historical Alibi

Someone could say, "Sovereignty, how many revolutions were committed in your name!" Cuba's revolution was not carried out in sovereignty's name, but the notion ended up justifying it in the eyes of half the world. Fidel-David flung his sling at USA-Goliath and stoned him in the middle of his sphere of influence, which, as is well known, is the place where it hurts the most. Cuba, the backyard where the gringos used to land marines, gamblers, and whore-loving Americans, suddenly became forbidden territory. Fidel closed the red-light district. He kicked out the gangsters, bade farewell to American businessmen, redeemed the prostitutes, made the pimps aware of their evil ways, and warned the whole world that Cuba was the first free territory of the Americas. Since the gringos had a bad press, and Cuba was overly dependent upon the United States, the fact that Cuba was exercising its sovereignty was accepted as a good thing. A substantial part of the sympathies that this revolutionary process enjoys is due to this interpretation of Cuban events. Is there any truth to it? In the first place, if sovereignty is the right of a people to determine its own destiny without foreign intervention, one would need to have a strange imagination to affirm that Cuba is a sovereign state. In any case, Fidel, who has decided the path that Cuba is to take, is the territory's only sovereign. But not even that is true. The Soviet Union is the new colonial power. Not everything, of course, is the same.

The Russians do not offend the Cubans' genital nationalism. Either because there are almost no prostitutes, or because the Russian comrades do not do those nasty things, the sacred honor of Cuban women has not been tarnished by the foreigner's breath. This is touching. Henry Miller would become automatically unemployed in such a chaste country. Once some girls got themselves into the ship cabins of certain foreign sailors, and Castro himself intervened in the affair with a pathetic speech about public morality. In such matters Castro does not budge. He is 100 percent nationalist. He is like those primitive people who resent *foreigners* going to bed with *their* women. The Cuban cultural hierarchy's rejection of Camilo José Cela began when he was asked (while visiting Cuba) if he wanted a dinner in his honor, and he replied that he would infinitely prefer a mulatto girl. Cela's hormonal preferences placed him on the list of imperialism's agents.

Nor do the Russians land their marines in order to force the Cubans to keep the peace. Their military men are more discreet. They control the bases to which (for security reasons) the Cubans have no access, like the submarine base in Cienfuegos, but this is not a matter aired in public. These technicians and military advisors, of course, enjoy impunity before the law. As might be expected, due to the number of years elapsed, dozens of accidents and incidents resulting in death or injury to Cubans have taken place without a single foreigner being prosecuted. The whore-loving Americans of before—those boisterous gringos—would end up in jail every once in a while. The Socialist comrades have better luck. Everybody is equal in Cuba. It must be that there are some who are more equal than others, as Orwell used to say.

In Cuba's capitalist society the Yankee businessman, with his inevitable portfolio, was an important fixture who had influence and to whom people would constantly say "Yes, sir." That specimen has its doppelganger in the official Russian commissary. There are many of them in Cuba. They move around with black briefcases, giving orders through interpreters. The Cubans have made up a classification scheme teeming with prejudices: the Russians are despotic and stink (they are pejoratively called "bolos"—"ninepins"); the Germans also stink but are only ill-mannered; Czechoslovakians and Rumanians are usually kind and do not stink; Bulgarians are definitely stupid. The most cordial and least haughty foreign advisors were the Chinese, but they left when the "rice quarrel" took place. The rice quarrel was a Sino-Cuban confrontation related to the price and conditions which China established to sell Cuba its rice. Fidel ended up calling the venerable Mao "a decrepit old man." Silently, smiling, the Chinese left and never again has anybody in Cuba been able to catch even a glimpse of them.

But let us get back to the important part: What real degree of independence does Cuba have with respect to the Soviet Union? After all, the fact that the gringos in previous times and now the Russians have privileges is not decisive. The vital question is whether Cuba is a satellite, and if so, how near is its orbit to the planetary mass that governs her movements. Cuba is fundamentally a satellite. She does not digress even one inch on the key issues from the (adopted) Mother Country. Havana hates and attacks Mao and Tito, Chinese and Yugoslavians, supports the Czechoslovakian intervention and the invasion of Afghanistan, persecutes Trotskyites, accuses Israel, and submits to all the orthodox rites. The Soviet Union, in exchange, lets Cuba be more Papist than the Pope (no offense intended). Such is the gist of its independence. Cuba, for example, may support certain Communist groups to the Left of local Communist parties. Moscow does not demand that it approve of or help the old guard, and even allows Fidel to test out his native rumba International style. With complete freedom, Castro makes his the cause of 5 percent of Puerto Ricans who want independence. Or he will stubbornly persist in as profound an anti-Americanism as any we have seen since the worst days of the Cold War. The Soviet Union patiently accepts Cuba's orthodox role. There is no risk in it. There cannot be a schism similar to the Sino-Soviet rupture because Cuba is insignificant. Besides, Castro's only guarantee that the Cuban Revolution will remain a Communist space station is for the Soviet Union to protect it. If there were to be a rupture, the island would be helpless and the Yankees would strike. This might appear to be an argument in favor of Cuba's subservience to the Soviet Union, but were we not talking about the exercise of sovereignty? What sense is there in changing proconsuls? Paradoxically the countries in this hemisphere are more independent of the United States than Cuba is with respect to the Soviet Union. Carlos Andrés Pérez and even Balaguer permit themselves whimsical autonomous plans that Castro could not even dream of. This is in the political realm; when we talk about economic affairs, the picture is different. Cuba has nowadays as many commercial ties with the Soviet Union as she once maintained with the United States. Yet this fact by itself does not mean anything. Cuba had, 150 km from its shores, the largest buyer, seller, and producer of goods that history has known. Was there any logical and feasible way of avoiding its influence? The famous "Yankee blockade" had not hurt Cuba so much for what the United States does not buy, as for what it does not sell. Cuba, no longer exploited at home, now has to let herself be exploited abroad. And on top of that, it is more expensive.

Thus a political and economic problem is viewed from a sentimental angle, which is, like the Cuban peasants say, "grabbing the banana bunch by the leaves." Fidel, no doubt, has played the role of David with inspired talent. Much more has been said: that the Cubans have recovered, thanks to him, a certain national dignity they lacked; that nowadays they feel like their own masters; that they are proud of their place in the world. It is true that Castro has placed Cuba on the political map, but one must question the usefulness of being on the front page of newspapers. Amin has made Uganda popular, and Qaddafi has done the same with Libya, without the Ugandan or Libyan people getting anything out of the spectacle except headaches. It has been years since Switzerland and Austria have received front-page coverage, and I do not think they are losing any sleep over it. Besides, it is not very sane to transmit one's own megalomania to the population. Countries do not have individual fragmentary delusions of grandeur. That is a virus spread by a certain class of people. The naive satisfaction that a man from an insignificant country might feel before his country's sudden fame is a symptom of primitive enthusiasm, a close heroic relative of the sports fan or the art lover. Fidel could not resign himself to accepting his territory as an anonymous and delightful bathing resort, a factory, or pleasant cultivated land—which is exactly what it is—and he fabricated a destiny that has nothing to do with the country's reality. On a disproportionate scale, it is like the tragedy of the midget who wants to be big and ends up by happily accepting fame. For some fools this notoriety is equal to "national dignity" and other empty platitudes. This is not serious. Sovereignty, which is always relative, is the expression of the consensus of the majority, and not the whimsical decision of one man with a vocation for ending up in the history chronicles. It is also a coherent position of independence before all powers. Otherwise, it is a farce.

Appendix

Abortions. This was just one case among hundreds. In 1966 Dr. Ventura Ventura, the cousin of the then public health minister, Dr. Machado Ventura, was sent to one of the concentration camps euphemistically known as Military Production Support Units (UMAP) for carrying out abortions. Recent economic difficulties and the spectacular increase in unmarried mothers have forced the authorities to adopt a very different approach to the problem.

Joaquín Balaguer (1960–). President of the Dominican Republic. A man of considerable intellectual achievement, he actively served the Trujillo dictatorship, being vice-president from 1957 to 1960. The year after the 1965 U.S. intervention he won the presidential elections but was defeated by the opposition in 1978. In 1986, even though he had become blind, he won the presidential elections once again.

Alejo Carpentier (1904–1980). Cuban writer. His father was a French architect and his mother a Russian dancer. He wrote novels, short stories, essays, and academic work on music. During the 1930s he lived in Paris and then in Haiti and Venezuela where he taught at the Central University. After the revolution he returned to Cuba to direct the Editora Nacional de Cuba (national publishing house) before being sent to Paris as a cultural diplomat. He was deputy president of UNEAC and professor of history at Havana University's History School. Among his best-known books are *Ecué-Yamba-o*, *El reino de este mundo*, *Guerra del tiempo*, and his most mature work, *El siglo de las luces*.

Camilo José Cela (1916–). A Spanish writer who became known with the publication in 1942 of *La familia de Pascual Duarte* and consolidated his reputation with *La Colmena* in 1951. His recent publications include *Mazurca para dos muertos* and *Cristo versus Arizona*. He is a member of the Royal Spanish Academy and was designated senator by the crown during the early stages of Spain's democratic restoration.

"Che" as a Public Administrator. As an official, "Che" Guevara divided his working hours into time spent on voluntary labor such as cutting sugarcane, bricklaying, and working as a stevedore, and time devoted to making political speeches, playing chess, and producing articles on military affairs. The administrative work entrusted him was carried out with spectacular incompetence. He had no interest in business efficiency as he knew that any losses would be made good in the national budget.

Doppelgänger. A German word meaning a double or alter ego.

Isla de Pinos. An island to the south of Cuba. It is administratively a special municipality depending directly on the central government. It was baptized "Evangelista" by Columbus and is now known as the "Island of Youth." For some years it has been home to several thousand African, Asian, and Latin American students who must combine their studies with work.

Paul Lafargue (1842–1911). A doctor by profession who, although born in Santiago de Cuba, was a French citizen. He married Karl Marx's daughter. During the 1880s, together with Pablo Iglesias, he helped found the Spanish Socialist movement. He and his wife committed suicide together in Paris.

Carlos Andrés Pérez (1922–%). A Venezuelan politician and a leading founder of the Democratic Action (AD) party. He has held many different posts during AD's periods in power. He lived in exile before the fall of Marcos Pérez Jiménez's dictatorship in 1958. He was president of Venezuela between 1973 and 1979. During his term he nationalized the iron and petroleum industries.

The Rice War. An economic and political confrontation between Communist China and Castro's Cuba caused by Peking's decision to reduce, in order to palliate its own shortages, the rice quota it sent to Cuba. Castro bitterly criticized the Chinese leadership for this decision.

4

Cuban Military Imperialism

What are thousands of Cubans doing fighting in Angola and Ethiopia? Why does the Cuban government—directly or with the help of the Palestinians— train African guerrillas? Why does it aid the Polisario insurgents? Why does it give military aid to bloody dictators like Macías and Amin? Why does it intervene in the Yemen war and offer its troops to the Argentines during the Falklands' war? When it hears the bugle call, Cuba is always willing to participate in military adventures and mount the Soviet Mig-Tank cavalry to save or finish off all Sitting Bulls. This option (redeemer or conqueror), of course, depends on Havana-Moscow's ideological interests.

Where the Orders Come From

The first, simplest, most inevitable answer points to Fidel Castro. Through-out the years I have been making statements similar to those in which I attribute to the Cuban president the course and destiny of the revolution, the choice of its allies, many of its economic errors, and the country's global fate. When one is intimately familiar with Castro's relationship with *his* Politburo, collective decision making must be discarded, and it should not surprise us that it is Castro alone who leads the small island in the direction he euphemistically calls proletarian internationalism, a phenomenon more com-monly known as military adventurism, Third World Napoleonism, or, very simply, imperialism. To be sure, it is hungry, barefoot, poor man's imperi-alism, but unmistakably imperialism, even though it does not pursue economic benefits but rather political hegemony. What member of the Politburo is capable of bridling Castro? Perhaps his brother Raúl? Raúl, above all, is Fidel's military bodyguard. His presence in the armed forces looks after the bayonet's loyalty to his brother. Since earliest childhood, Raúl has pathologically admired Fidel. Fidel is tall, strong, bold, virile, and charis-matic. Raúl is small, beardless, taciturn, and almost insignificant. Their relationship has always been rigidly hierarchical. Fidel gives orders, at times curtly, and Raúl quietly, obsequiously obeys. Raúl does not dare contradict Fidel. He never has. Whenever he has said or done something behind the Maximum Leader's back, it has always been fearful and discreet. For example, when he helped his sisters leave Cuba; or when helping people who had fallen out of grace; when he sent his daughter on a summer vacation to the French Riviera; or when he got his half-crazy, half-poet, half-brother, Angel Castro Argote, out of jail. Raúl is powerful (he is second in the nation) only to the extent that he enjoys Fidel's confidence, and this can only be attained by submitting to and agreeing with the commander-in-chief's illuminated point of view.

President Castro's favorite pastime is the construction, using elementary but logical reasoning, of political, economic, military, theological, agricultural, judicial, esthetic (not too often), scientific, cinematographic, pig-breeding, axiological, and whatnot theories, to show the retinue at hand his infinite memory, intelligence, and sagacity. He will do this while visiting a shoe factory of a potato-growing commune, with a Communist leader he is seeing in private or with the charming capitalists who come looking for business possibilities. Castro rationalizes and takes apart anything, explaining it to the dazzled person sitting at his right. When some unhappy person dares contradict him, at first Castro will patiently present "solid" arguments until he crushes his conversation partner. If his interlocutor insists, Castro—this time with less patience—will offer more facts, arguments, and eloquence. If by now the interlocutor continues to insist (he is insane), Castro will insult him, threaten him, or if circumstances compel him to hold his tongue, he will place the unruly person on a blacklist of undesirables or opponents. In 1959, while sitting in a small café in Havana's Vedado district, I witnessed a "debate" between the Maximum Leader—who had recently descended victoriously from the Sierra Maestra—and an old friend of his. They discussed the efficacy of agrarian reform. Castro's interlocutor, who was much better informed on the subject, managed to corner Fidel. Coldly, Castro looked at him severely and said: "Antonio, I understand you were a candidate in the 1958 elections. That is a very serious matter and I'm not surprised that someone who participated in that counterrevolutionary farce would have such absurd ideas on agrarian reform." Obviously, Antonio said nothing. He emitted a nervous cough, left the café, and a week later left the country.

Who then, among the members of the Politburo, is going to face the thunderbolts of this awesome Zeus? Carlos Rafael Rodríguez? The vice-minister is a cordial, temporizing man deeply aware of Cuba's present tragedy and willing to dialogue with the opposition. He is also deeply aware of Castro's nature, but Rodríguez does not have an army to support him, not even the remains of a party—the discredited PSP—to back him up, because the old comrades see in him a neo-Fidelist rather than a member of the old team.

Rodríquez dares not raise his voice. He simply waits patiently for something to happen. ("He is our Mikoyan," as Nicolás Guillén is fond of saying.) What about the other members of the Politburo? What about Arnaldo Milián, the old party's aging bureaucrat? He is only the efficient organizer of repressive activities. What about Carlos Aldanra? What about Jorge Risquet? And Pedro Miret, Juan Almeida, Sergio del Valle, Machado Ventura, good old Armando Hart? These last seven men are mere Fidelists, high-ranking *apparatchiks* used to taking orders—Pavlovian style. Since 1953 these last seven men have done little more than follow Fidel's more delirious adventures. Fidel rings the bell of revolutionary action, the Fidelist-harnessed dogs secrete Jacobin saliva, and later the heroes receive the affectionate backslap, public acclaim, promotions (they become generals), and all the other privileges of power. Positive reinforcement, in the crudest behaviorist version known to contemporary politics, follows. They are accomplices and henchmen, not leaders, and in the time-worn obedience derived from rewards and punishments, have lost all autonomy. Their outstanding characteristic, as that of almost all unconditional followers, consists of renouncing their place as intelligent persons and giving the adored leader a vote of confidence so that he can think and determine for them. No, not even the Politburo has decided the imperialist slant of the revolution. This is nothing more than the sound box for the imperious voice of Fidel.

Why?

As in the book of Genesis, in the beginning there was Fidel. In the beginning of everything. The country's communization and alignment with the Soviets, the model of society chosen, the economic course taken, and at present, the military adventures continuously organized in Havana. But I must still provide the reason for the military undertakings. Such a complex question cannot have a simple answer. The most obvious and indisputable reply is that Fidel Castro personally makes the decisions. He finds bellicose activities, firearms, and the games of men of action attractive. Let us review the landmarks of an exceptional book, *Fidel Castro: From the Jesuits to Moncada,* written by José Pardo Llada. When he was seventeen, Castro carried a revolver. When he was nineteen, he participated in a typical ambush, characteristic of the university gangster's feuds, and he wounded a fellow student named Leonel González. In 1947, when he was twenty-one, he proposed to his companions in the Federation of Cuban University Students the assassination of President Grau San Martín, a democratic politician who reached power with popular support, for the purpose of establishing a republic led by students. Shortly afterwards, he embarked on an abortive invasion against Trujillo. In 1948, surprised by the popular uprising known as "El bogotazo" while on a trip to Bogotá, he tried to lead a revolt in a police barracks and was deported. In 1951 he tried to convince the leaders of the Orthodox opposition party to detour the massive funeral caravan for Eduardo Chibás—which filled the streets of Havana—toward the Presidential Palace and there "seize power with the corpse," as he put it. In 1953, one year after Batista's takeover, it is no longer Fidel with his pistol and his delusions but Fidel with a just revolutionary cause and an armed group willing to obey his orders. The conditions for Napoleon's development are present. His immediately attacks a military barracks. Later, in the Sierra, he organized an army— *his* army. How can one ask this adventurous spirit to calm down after victory? How can one expect serenity to take over so that the construction of a better world for the Cuban people can begin? This is an absurd pretention. In 1959, Batista had been overthrown, but Castro's insurrectionary impetus had increased after the victory. He already had a country and armed forces at his disposal. Beginning in 1959, the relationship between the growth of the revolutionary armed forces and Cuba's interventions in other countries can be easily verified. In 1959, with Castro's consent and secret handling, small guerrilla groups were sent to liberate Panama and the Dominican Republic. Diverse groups established contacts with the Spanish, Haitian, and Nicaraguan opposition. Yet the most glaring intervention took place, not against these countries, but against Rómulo Betancourt's Venezuelan democracy, only because the Venezuelan leader had expressed his dislike of Castro during a tense meeting held in the spring of 1959. Their interview sealed the Cuban decision to contribute arms, men, and money to the "struggle" against the Venezuelan people's freely elected government.

Since 1959, from the moment Castro came to power, he immediately transformed Cuba into a base for exporting revolutions. And those "exports" have always been directly related to the size and training of the Cuban armed forces. When Cuba, in 1959, was a country governed by revolvers and hunting rifles, it already sent guerrillas abroad armed with revolvers and hunting rifles. In the mid-sixties, with a well-organized espionage apparatus and a firmer, more reliable international underground network, Castro undertook operations similar to the one which cost Ernesto Guevara his life. Fifteen years later, possessing an imposing, well-trained, superbly equipped army, Cuba exports divisions, Migs and tanks, without abandoning the old, veiled ties with some of the world's clandestine organizations.

The existence of a terrorist "International" with main offices in Havana and Algiers is not a well-kept secret. Both were promoted by old guerrilla fighters (Castro and the late Houari Boumediènne). This International supplies arms to the IRA, trains the ETA (Basque separatists), and nourishes numerous subversive groups; and its intricate mazes hide terrorists like the notorious

Venezuelan Carlos or efficient gunmen from the PLO. Some members of the Nicaraguan Sandinist front began their training in Cuba, and later continued learning under the watchful eyes of the PLO, a revolutionary group without a country which can evade all international responsibilities. Cuba, Algeria, or Libya may be asked to comply with international laws, but not the PLO. All clues wind up in thin air in the Palestinians' imprecise marketplace. Because of the irresponsibility they enjoy, they are Cuba's, Algeria's, or Libya's best allies. Moscow can use them to carry out its "dirty work" with absolute impunity.

In the direction of clandestine operations, made up on the basis of secret complicities and openly military ones (Angola and Ethiopia), Castro moves the pawns of *his* war. The first war—the secret one—is handled by his ministry of interior; the second one, by means of the armed forces. These activities monopolize most of the indefatigable Cuban warrior's interests and efforts. The Angolan and Ethiopian wars, the Zimbabwe war, the Yemenite war, the Nicaraguan war, the Caribbean and Chilean wars, the wars of the oppressed Blacks, of the Sahauris humiliated by Morocco, of a Vietnam bombed by the United States or China. All these wars. There is no foreign war in Castro's eyes. There is no country which can attack its neighbor without fearing that the "victim" will call the Antilles' Seventh Cavalry. No country—especially in the Third World—can be completely sure that the Cuban government is not secretly plotting against it with an opposition group. Cuba's long arm can be seen—and has been seen—in such murky affairs as Italian terrorism (the Feltrinelli affair) and the links between Cuba and ETA. Castro is the embodiment of an endless war.

The Ethical Reasoning

We have seen the who and the how of Cuban interventionism. Now we should examine the reasons Cuba wields in justifying its wars of conquest. Neither Castro nor anyone else has ever admitted that behind the bellicose events the protagonizing urges of the "chiefs" are hidden. No one is willing to accept that history is also a product of the gall bladder, hemorrhoids, heredity, or birth trauma. It is always necessary to seize a moral justification by the neck. All political action, however drastic or monstrous, can only be carried out within an ethical framework. The Germans came up with the notion of *Lebensraum* in order to justify war and the racist anthropology of Arian superiority in order to carry out the "final solution to the Jewish problem." With his iron-fisted, quasi-fascist dictatorship Franco was "saving Europe from communism." Castro also possesses a schematic rationalization which justifies his imperialistic behavior. First, the people's struggle against dictatorship is an inalienable right. Second, it is Castro's prerogative to decide what is really a country struggling for liberation and what constitutes a dictatorship. Nicaragua was a dictatorship and its people were fighting for liberty. Neither Czechoslovakia nor Hungary are dictatorships, nor are their peoples at war. Italy, which is a capitalist country, is a type of dictatorship, and its people, the Red Brigades, are struggling. Thus Cuba, using the Palestinians as intermediaries, helps the Italian terrorist group. Third, Cuban aid to the struggles against capitalist dictatorships bears a direct relationship to geopolitical possibilities.

Whole armies are sent to Angola or Ethiopia, very simply, because no one can do anything about it. Nicaragua, on the other hand, received money and arms through the Costa Rican Communist party and Cuba trained anti-Somoza guerrillas in the Middle East. Troops were not sent to Somoza's fiefdom because startling the Caribbean neighborhood with direct intervention could be very dangerous. Fourth, these revolutionary activities, as Cuba's minister of foreign affairs has pointed out, constitute the country's primary objective, while the island's other political and economic goals are subordinated to it because—this is the key to the theoretical justification—the Third World will never develop until an international economic order dictated by the Communist countries comes into being. In the fifth place, that global political and economic vision that demands a universal revolutionary triumph can be complemented with partial euphemisms. For example, when Angola is invaded to combat the White racists, Cuba regains its lost African roots. On the other hand, Cuban armies rush to Ethiopia in order to help a sovereign state in danger of disappearing before the onslaught of Somali and Eritrean secessionists (hiding the sad irony that before the coup d'état that overthrew Emperor Selassie, Cuba trained Eritreans and helped Somalia's army). Israel is combated because it is a capitalist stronghold plunged like a scimitar in the heart of the Third World. And bloody dictator Macías, or the horrid Congo-Brazzaville dictatorship, are helped and counseled because, after all, they are circumstantial allies in the long march toward the creation of a Communist planet.

Castro's urgent imperialistic needs hide from him the fact that not even on a planet made ideologically uniform by Communism—as the imperial wars between China and Vietnam or Vietnam and Cambodia attest—should we wait for fraternal relationships to develop among men. But the acceptance of this poor, flimsy evidence would bankrupt the reasons for Cuba's interventionism, and we already know that the simple, brutal act of killing or dying for abstractions requires some scheme of ethical values as justification.

The Severity of These Acts

According to the most reliable analysis, Cuba has the world's ninth largest army and the second in size in America. That army has not grown—as the Cuban government has tried to explain—in response to United States threats.

In the first half of the sixties, when the threat was real, Cuba's defense spending was $213 million. Twenty years later, when the United States is no longer a real threat and Cuba is protected by the Soviet-American pact of 1963, the island spends 1,000 million pesos (approximately $1.4 billion) to maintain a war machine of more than 100,000 soldiers, hundreds of tanks and planes, and a powerful reserve army of more than half a million men.

It is not a question, furthermore, of a passive army, dedicated to executing harmless maneuvers, but of a formidable military force molded through several wars into an unmistakable morale of invincibility. In 1961, after the Bay of Pigs invasion, they boasted of having defeated the Americans. In 1975 they vanquished the South Africans. In 1976 "the Somalians." It is an army that has never lost a war, and is thus overcome by the natural temptation of intervening with all its considerable weight wherever possible. Practically everything has been a failure in Cuba with the exception of the military-police state undertakings. Cuba has not been able, after twenty years, to achieve something as simple as ending the scarcity of coffee, but it has "defeated imperialism" (it does not matter whether it is Somali or Kikuyu imperialism) each time it has put its mind to it. The belligerent role Cuba has assumed is sad, but it is the only part which it has been able to play with any efficacy. Logically, now the growing tendency is to export not a useless revolutionary model but an expeditionary force that confirms the Revolution's importance and the specific weight of its Maximum Leader, with blood and fire.

The Soviets

For the Soviets this phenomenon is genuinely new. Moscow has never been able to count on satellites willing to serve as cannon fodder. Poland does not avidly ask the Soviet Union to give its generals permission to cut Finland's throat, and Bulgaria is not interested in invading Greece. Yet Cuba offers itself in sacrifice for the greater glory of Moscow—in all territories where the circumstances are favorable. Moscow has discovered a comfortable way of extending its hegemony throughout the Third World with impunity. It simply hands its warrior proletarians—the Cubans—the instruments of war and they do all the work with admirable efficacy. The combination is very profitable for the Soviets. For fighting in the Third World—a region of poor, dark people— what could be better than an army of poor, dark people? The interventionist power is no longer arrogant, blonde, and White, but underdeveloped, harried Antilleans, sacrificed in the honorable cause of internationalism. But the Cubans, who are brave, expert fighters, tend to be maladroit in administering the affairs of state. For that purpose the East German army is more useful, because, as everyone knows, German efficiency in everything is clearly superior, including in the organization of the death of others. In Africa, along with the Cubans, there is a growing number of East Germans. The Cubans provide the troops and the long knives; the Germans provide the officers. That concubinage could turn into a very dangerous affair. In 1978 France sent troops to the Congo to abort an invasion of Katanguese exiles. If European intervention in Africa should increase—the intervention of Eastern and Western Europe—so would the chances of an African conflict involving European nations, and the consequences of that clash could be enormously risky. The most viable way to avoid that real and imminent danger is to make the Cuban troops return to their Caribbean bases. This objective is probably more easily accomplished by pressuring the Soviet Union rather than Cuba. The Cuban presence would be impossible almost everywhere without the Soviet aegis. For Cuba (for Castro) these wars and interventions are the Revolution's own raison d'être, and he will never abandon those territories or clandestine activities of his own free will. When the United States naively offers to lift the blockade or establish full diplomatic relations in exchange for an end to interventions, it does not realize that its offer is not enough for Castroism. For Castro, a tireless, unrepenting fighter, military adventure is more important than the possibility of selling sugar or having access to the United States capital markets. There is no other way to limit Cuban interventionism than to make it pay a high price for its colonial wars. That is the logic behind China's decision to intervene in Vietnam. The United States, France and the responsible nations will only muzzle the Cuban *gurkas* with a mixture of serious threats, of serious losses in the intervened areas, and by means of direct negotiation with the Soviets.

Cuban Consequences

One final aspect of the Cuban question has been revealed by these manifest examples of military interventionism: Honorable persons can no longer continue to say that Cuba is a poor country trying to develop in spite of United States hostility. Cuba is a fanatical, aggressive military power whose primary objective is the implantation of Communism at any price. But besides the international consequences which we have been examining, there are truly dramatic internal Cuban consequences.

The most tragic aspect of Castroite militarism is the creation in that small island of a military caste and of an institution which will outlive Castroism and Communism. When Cuban Communism becomes an anecdote of the past—in ten, twenty, thirty years—those monstrous armed forces will continue being the most onerous factor in the country's institutional life. The vast system of privileges that the military class enjoys, the high rank and recognition it is accorded within the power structure, will make it practically impossible to dismantle the military apparatus. Perhaps then several Latin American countries will have converted their armed forces into simple police departments, but Cuba will have begun once again its cavalary of military coups and countercoups, only because in 1959, Genghis Khan, Alexander the Great, Napoleon and Patton—all of them—reincarnated in a man by the name of Fidel Castro.

Appendix

The Cuban Politburo. This is Communist Cuba's main governing body and is headed by Fidel Castro. Its role is merely consultative and decorative as it invariably carries out the wishes of its leader.

Ramón Grau San Martín (1882–1969). A Cuban politician and physician who was provisional president in 1933 and 1934 after the fall of Machado and then was himself overthrown. He lived in exile between 1935 and 1938. In 1944 he won the presidential elections against Batista's candidate. His four years in the presidency were extremely corrupt and gang warfare erupted between rival police factions. His term is considered one of the most corrupt in Cuban history.

Murder of Gian Giacomo Feltrinelli (1926–1972). A Milano publisher connected with left-wing groups and a friend of Castro's Cuba. He was the first to publish Lampedusa's *The Leopard* and Boris Pasternak's *Doctor Zhivago*. His death was apparently caused by a bomb that went off while he was trying to blow up an electricity pylon.

The National People's Power Assembly. This was formed in 1976. To head it Fidel Castro designated Blas Roca, secretary general of the Popular Socialist party until this became defunct. When Blas Roca died he was replaced by Flavio Bravo.

Osvaldo Dorticós Torrado (1919–1983). A Cuban politician and member of Castro's regime. In the first revolutionary government he held the post of minister of revolutionary records and in the summer of 1959 he was named president of Cuba following the overthrow of Urrutia. In 1976 he stepped down in favor of Castro and became justice minister. In 1983 he committed suicide for what were described officially as health reasons.

Revolver. Ever since his involvement in the Key Confites adventure (1947) against the Trujillo regime, Fidel Castro was known always to carry a revolver. This reputation was consolidated later when he was active in gangster-like political organizations such as the UIR.

An Unbeaten Army. In 1983, the Cuban soldiers who surrendered in Grenada to U.S. forces were described as "civilian collaborators" and "heroic fighters who laid down their arms because of their lack of equipment." On their return to Havana, the defeated Cuban military leaders were noisily welcomed as heroes. Later, however, they were quietly degraded and sent to the front in Angola as privates. One officer who received this treatment was Colonel Tortoló. He had been ordered to Grenada to organize resistance "to the very last man." His flight from the battlefield inspired a large number of sarcastic jokes in Cuba.

5

Beneficiaries of the Revolution

Then the ones below move up
And the ones on top go to hell.
—Refrain from a popular Cuban song of the forties

What happened after the revolutionary upheaval? How was the structure of Cuban society left after the Communist explosion? I shall not waste time describing how prerevolutionary Cuba was. For this purpose I refer the reader to one of the appendices of this book. There he will find a highly reliable summary. In prerevolutionary Cuba only 30 percent of the population was rural, and there existed in the country a wide stratum of what modern economists call "middle social levels." (The class concept is going through a crisis, as is the abstraction "proletariat"; there are, however, social levels that in Cuba used to be characterized by their fluidity.) The transition of the agricultural worker toward industrial production was not rare, and from both of these toward the tertiary sector of services or commerce, and from all of these toward the urban center to work in all types of activities. During the forties and fifties, the country has seen a notable improvement in income distribution, which forced Noyola, a Marxist economist, to state at the beginning of the revolution that Cuba was one of the Latin American countries where income was less poorly distributed. It was an accurate statement. There were great differences in the Cubans' purchasing power, but the situation was much better than in Peru, Ecuador, Colombia, Venezuela, and even in the Spain of the fifties. The middle social levels covered a large stratum, mainly White and urban. The latter was also the case for the upper social levels. The middle and upper social levels, this vast and multicolored world of merchants, traveling salesmen, specialized workers, technicians, small, middle, and large owners of industries, physicians, lawyers, teachers, journalists, advertisers, public relations men, engineers, in other words, professionals of all kinds, plus employees in the beer and tobacco industries, power and petrochemical plants, laboratories, telephone companies; all these hundreds of thousands of Cubans have been roughly called "the bourgeoisie." They are the cyclone's victims.

57

The middle and upper social levels have had to pay for the revolution. These hundreds of thousands have seen their diet, clothes, entertainment, autonomy, freedom of movement, and their political weight substantially curtailed. But as revolutions apparently are subject to the laws of "action and reaction" which take effect in physics, there is a group of Cubans that benefited economically: the poorest sector of the lower social levels—that army of chronically unemployed, many of black origin, who before had survived with difficulty in the outskirts of urban centers or in impoverished agricultural ones. To these Cubans the revolution has meant an improvement, even though it offers them in exchange for their work (obligatory, as with everybody else) only the same quantity of clothes and food as the rest of the population.

Cubans who have benefited are those without a trade or other income, what Marx called the "lumpenproletariat," the uneducated citizens who would crowd into slum tenements, the legion of car parkers and washers, the thousands of servants, especially those who worked for the middle levels, the ambulatory salesmen of trinkets and lottery tickets, shoeshiners, sugarcane laborers, the charcoal makers on the coast, fishermen, and the peasants in the mountains. The lowest levels of the poor have improved their living conditions. But the same cannot be said of the other low social levels. The badly remunerated worker of before, the poorly paid employee of a business, the seamstress and the barber have increased neither their income nor the quality of their lives. But fair information would add that the lower and middle social levels were infinitely wider than the upper ones.

The inevitable question is whether more persons benefited materially than have been damaged or vice versa. I believe more have been damaged, but I am not discarding the possibility that I am mistaken. To offer an honest answer, one would have to start by defining "damage" and "benefit." In a consumer society the quality of life is measured with a different yardstick than in Communist societies. Cuba has renounced being a consumer society, but it has not clarified the new objectives, except for the very vague ones of creating a new society and a new man.

It is logical to suppose that Castro recruits his faithful from the lower social levels and his enemies from the middle and upper social levels. The first exception to this generalization is the Cuban revolutionary hierarchy, which comes from the middle and even upper social levels. But in general terms this statement holds true. Two thorny problems then come to light. First, the racial ingredient involved in the tensions. For embarrassing historical reasons, Cuban Blacks and mulattoes occupied the lower social levels; these groups have now been favored and their adherence to the government is logical, especially because the revolution has opened doors to them which before were closed due to racism. The impressive fact that among the thousands of female political prisoners there are no more than half a dozen Blacks illustrates this point. There are Black men in prison, but in a much smaller proportion than in the census. Opposition—as well as power, but that is another question—basically has been a white man's activity. The other wave of political clients comes to Castroism from certain peasant sectors, especially from sugarcane laborers and from the forgotten and destitute peasants in the mountains, but this statement should not be interpreted in a general sense. The peasantry of Escambray, for example, began to be anti-Castroist in the sixties and fed guerrilla groups for more than five years.

As the revolution not only protects but also turns its partisans into militants, all the previous power structures and decision-making centers have changed ownership. The revolution has massively substituted some men for others, one power structure for another. It has taken control away from the middle and upper social levels and has given it to the lower level. Since other ethnic and geographic factors concurred, Blacks and peasants have begun to play an unprecedented role in Cuban society. In a sense any revolution is but a precipitate process of transmission of privileges. The Cuban Revolution has not been an exception. But has this been harmful to Cuba?

The harm done by improverishing the middle and upper social sectors has probably been much greater than the benefits derived from protecting the lower ones. One of Cuba's biggest accomplishments was its large and open middle levels. Their sudden impoverishment was a stupid and brutal act. It was not indispensable to depress the middle sectors to benefit the lower ones. This was the result of the sudden change of economic direction and of a series of incredible errors in the administration of the country. The goal was to raise the lower social sectors to the middle levels, not to impoverish the whole country in the name of progress. What was being promised was the socialization of development, not misery.

Characterizing the middle levels as "the exploitive bourgeoisie" to justify the head rolling is a sweeping injustice. This enormous middle class was the product of hard and honest work in the imperfect society and hard times in which they had to live. Many were workers of privileged syndicates, as in the case of the tobacco, alcoholic spirits, and petrochemical workers, exceptionally well paid, and other professionals who finished college through work and hardship. It is true that they did not live in a just society, but they were perhaps the only just thing of which that society could be proud. To dramatically cut off the buying power they had won with so much difficulty, to unfeelingly and rudely lower their standard of living, has been as great an injustice of this new order as was the previous order's lack of protection for the destitute. The revolution's work, in its social aspect, does not hold. The people who have been injured are too numerous, and they did not deserve this mistreatment nor was it necessary. For each capitalist exploiter who has lost his privileges, for each dishonest politician who has lost the spoils of his corruption, for each gambler, pimp, or thief fortunately evicted, thousands of hard-working Cubans who had been able to overcome poverty through hard work have now been impoverished. There is no justification for what has been done to them.

The Successes

It has been stated that the revolution has generally benefited the poorest fringe of the lower social levels. That, of course, is not the only positive thing which can be said about the revolutionary process. There is more. Cuba's new leaders are not guided, as was frequently the case before, by economic ambition. They are not interested in money, but in power; though it is undeniable that the current important names in Cuba enjoy obvious privileges such as confiscated houses, cars, imported foodstuffs, trips abroad and exclusive clubs, and private hospitals like those serving officers in the armed forces and state security. Cuba needed to dust off centuries of government corruption. Theft and speculation—old practices which date from colonial times—have disappeared. There are, certainly, small murky business deals, buyers for the Ministry of International Commerce who discreetly demand commissions, minor civil servants who take advantage of their positions, but nothing comparable to the traditional scandals of the pre-Castro era.

There is a will for progress and development on the part of the government, and an acute social sensitivity. The government feels responsible for Cuban destiny—for their education, diet, health, and dress. When all or some of these responsibilities cannot be fully met, the government cadres acknowledge the failure. Then one of the most irritating aspects of the revolutions takes place: the concealment of data. In Cuba no one dies of gastrointestinal disorders, no one lacks a roof over his head, no one fails to attend school. The image's ghost—Communism's worst neurosis—provokes a coarse concealment of reality.

In some aspects progress has been notable. In the social order, the end of racial discrimination in the labor, student, and recreational sectors is worthy of much praise. Another type of discrimination has developed, but there is no doubt that Blacks and mulattoes have seen their opportunities for economic and social integration in the country multiply. Athletic events have expanded and improved. Certain sports—tennis, swimming, basketball, rowing, water polo—which were played only by the middle- and upper-middle-class youth—today are within the reach of much larger sectors of the population. Other sports—baseball, boxing, chess, track-and-field—are played by a larger number of fans, and generally with better trainers and facilities. The government enthusiastically sponsors participation in sports activities, probably because it has subscribed to the old and debatable superstition of "a sound mind in a sound body" and is able to use sporting results as propaganda instruments, but in any case enthusiasm for baseball and devotion to certain athletic idols have served as shady breaks in the tense revolutionary trajectory. Cuba is the Latin American nation where sports are practiced the most and the best.

Medicine

Medical attention has been another of the revolution's priorities. It has been taken to the most secluded rural places, and a successful effort has been made to replace the 3,000 Cuban physicians who opted for exile. The present number of physicians has been established at 9,000, which averages one physician per 1,000 inhabitants, a notable figure for an underdeveloped country. The numerical increase of medical services, however, conflicts with their quality. The lack of organization at Havana University's School of Medicine, due to the almost total emigration of faculty and the political criteria which prevailed in the selection of substitutes, resulted in a noticeable drop in academic standards, partly mitigated by the intense practice to which recent students have to submit in the new study plans put into effect by the revolution. Lack of medical supplies also ties physicians' hands; although able to make the correct diagnosis, they cannot prescribe the proper medicaton. It is not strange, then, for Cubans who enjoy a certain hierarchy—Alicia Alonso, for example—to discreetly go abroad to undergo an operation or treatment for a serious illness. They generally go to Western countries, as medicine in the socialist world, sotto voce, has fallen into disrepute among Cubans.

There is an embarrassing chapter in Cuba's medical practice: the treatment given to sick political prisoners. The prisons—we are talking about several thousand Cubans—have become deposits of human "scum." Prisoners with tuberculosis, syphilis, and other contagious diseases, have been cruelly thrown in with the rest. With the same needle, without even being able to boil it, prisoners have injected themselves dozens of times to try to escape the different epidemics that have broken out in prison. Dozens of maimed prisoners, maimed by the guards' cruelty—Armando Valladares, Rigoberto Pereda—have been denied treatment. Ricardo Cruz Font had to close an open wound in his head with his own hands—a rifle butt blow—until the lacerated tissue began to heal. Neither is there any dental care, only extractions, at times. It is said that a prisoner writhing in pain with a toothache once pulled a tooth with a spoon. I do not see how it is possible to separate the dismal story of the medicine practiced in prisons from the neat statistics offered by the government. Unless—and this is exactly what happens—political adversaries are considered a species of animal who can die of pain or infection without the voice of those physicians responsible ever trembling, without the prisoners meriting the effort it takes to fill out a medical report.

Education

Education is another conquest of which the Cuban government is proud, and in some aspects is certainly entitled to be so, especially in the case of rural education and in the attention given to illiterate adults. Of course, it is a rigid schooling, conceived to create orthodox Communists, but even that is better than no education at all.

Children's education is at the service of Communist indoctrination. The primers where one reads, under *F* "Fidel's rifle" (*fusil*), under *CH* "Che," and under *R* "Raúl," are a shameful chapter in the history of personality cults. All educational systems educate within the general system to which they subscribe, but there is no doubt that *liberal* education—that word which horrifies Castro—is responsible for the most portentous adventures in thought, including, of course, Marxism, and above all, the revision of Marxist thought.

Among the fallacious practices of Cuban pedagogy is the one of combining studies with agricultural work. Students must move to the country several months every year to sow and reap crops. Supposedly, this activity helps in the production task and destroys the tendency of class grouping—removing the adolescent from pernicious family influences. In reality, it is only a variant of Virgilean mythology, so profoundly rooted in the West. The perception of the countryside as purifying territory is one of the most pertinacious naivetés maintained through the centuries. The revolution falls into it, but it rationalizes in the usual Communist dialect.

Politicization, agriculture, and ideological orthodoxy have produced a notable decrease in the quality of studies, in spite of the fact that students formed within this revolutionary tension live obsessed with a critical word: responsibility. The same simple rule indicates that a bad worker is a bad revolutionary operates on a student scale. A bad student is a bad revolutionary, because the revolution demands excellence in any human activity. The ruling hierarchy does not realize the inhuman aspects of this permanent state of tension. Apparently for these gentlemen, the *ultima ratio* of life is the fulfillment of certain duties such as those defined by certain books, a policy which undoubtedly ends up by turning into a stunted horizon.

The government makes every effort to offer all Cubans the opportunity of elementary school studies, and to most, secondary education. But the same cannot be said for university studies. Universities are for those who have been "integrated." They belong exclusively to the partisans, or the "cadres." We are not dealing with a secret prerequisite, but with something publicly acknowledged. The high ideological class is the only one which has access to a university education. No matter how brilliant he might be, a "nonintegrated" young person—who does not belong to some revolutionary organization or who is a Protestant or a Catholic—will not have the opportunity to cultivate his talents. In the decade of the sixties and later during the revolutionary offensive of 1968—a kind of cultural minirevolution—Havana University was "purified." Students and professors who were morally or politically suspicious—as seen by Fidel's Calvinistic eye—were expelled from the university. In 1980, after the events of the Peruvian Embassy and Mariel exodus, the witch hunt was repeated.

Castro, who during his student days was rather active as an agitator—he shot and wounded two fellow students—feared the source of rebellion which Havana University has always been. When he assumed power, he dedicated a good part of his efforts and those of the police force to liquidate the old tradition. Today, "the Hill"—as it used to be called—is a campus of tamed students, very zealous for orthodox thought and totally unprepared for nonconformity. As to the quality of studies, little can be said for them. Following the country's ups and downs, during the sixties the university insensibly deteriorated, but as the seventies began, a slow recuperation took place. Today, after the latest convulsions, it has sunk once more into mediocrity.

A Country Without Unemployment

One of the evils of capitalism is chronic unemployment. In Cuba it no longer exists. There was plenty before. What has happened? Very simply, the economic organization of Communism conceives of work in a different light. It would be more accurate to say that in Cuba there are no unoccupied persons. Even more, to be "unoccupied" is a very grave crime. This distinction between employment and occupation is not an empty one. Employment is a result of the relationship between demand, consumption, and cost, while occupation is an arbitrarily assigned task, for which some emoluments are received which are not tied to productivity, demand, and consumption. The difference is obvious: the case of an unoccupied slave never existed. In the Middle Ages, among the guilds, unoccupied persons did not exist. A few gentlemen—overseers, lords, masters—would assign a task, and the employees would carry it out. The Communist system operates on similar principles: officials assign a work center and a salary.

Employment or occupation—has it been advantageous or detrimental to Cubans? It depends. To the chronically unemployed—20 percent of the population—it has been advantageous. It is better to have an arbitrarily imposed occupation than to have none. To the previously employed—80 percent of the population—it has been detrimental, as opportunity for promotion no longer depends on objective factors, such as productivity or diligence, but on subjective factors such as "revolutionary consciousness" and "integration to the system." Neither is it possible to change occupations freely or look for other jobs with ease. Everything is zealously regimented. Moreover, thousands of university and polytechnic graduates do not find a place in the Cuban labor organization and they are exported abroad by the State which takes charge, of course, of collecting the currency assigned to these "internationalists." There are Cuban workers and technicians in Libya, Algeria, Czechoslovakia, and East Germany, and if there are none in Siberia it is because Moscow did not take into account Castro's offer to supply it with ten thousand woodcutters. There is a peculiar form of alienation in the Communist world of labor: the worker cannot perceive the relationship between his effort and the material reward involved. The Communists, masters of materialism, presume to pay effort with spiritual money—I am referring to voluntary work. How long can the revolutionary enthusiasm of a worker last who has been arbitrarily assigned to a task for which he received a subjective remuneration? That is where the system breaks down and the repressive outcome results, because the officials of a Communist system treasure power much more than capitalist employers do. The rapacity of capitalism is inevitably restrained by the workers' union actions and the result of competition. In the Communist working world there are no shock absorbers. You work because you are a partisan or because you may end up in jail. It is true that in Cuba there are no unemployed, but the consequences have been fatal. Nor are there employees. There is no free selection of place, manner, or time of rendering services. There is no reward according to effort.

The Cost of Benefits

The reader probably expected a broader and less positive record of the revolution. I could mention the spectacular growth of the fishing industry, drastically diminished when the fleet was used for imperial adventures such as occurred during the Angolan expedition; the increase of hydraulic energy production; and the development of the citrus fruits industry. All of that, however, is substantial. Let us assume that in the economic order the Cuban experience had not been a failure. Even if it had been successful, would that justify the establishment of a Communist dictatorship? Can one judge Hitler, Stalin, Mussolini, Trujillo by the length of their countries' highways or the cubic meters of water in dams? There has to be some relationship between means and ends.

The greatness of the pyramids will always be less than the brutal fact that they were built using slave labor and at a cost of thousands of lives. Will the dictatorship be justifiable? In order to take more children to mediocre schools, and more sick people to some badly equipped hospitals, was it indispensable to establish a totalitarian regime with thousands of political prisoners, one million political exiles, a vigilance committee in every street, and a politically terrorized population? In order to fish more, to harvest more oranges, was there no other road than the brutal imposition of a dictatorship? Were there no other means to end or mitigate the economic differences of the various social strata? The price paid for the "benefits" of the revolution is much higher than the real value of what has been obtained. After all, Uruguayans, Argentines, Costa Ricans, and Puerto Ricans do not have illiteracy either, and provide, without so much ado, medical assistance to the sick. Peruvians, on the other hand, have started a profound revolution without executing thousands of adversaries or imprisoning tens of thousands of people.

The moral dilemma for anyone who has not become insensitive to fascism or Communism is very clear: What are the limits of repression which rightfully belong to a state engaged in the task of development? To fascists and Communists the answer is obvious: There are no limits, everything is permitted to the government. For those who do not subscribe to a totalitarian concept of society, it is indispensable to find a balance between development and the means to achieve it. In Cuba that balance has been brutally broken.

Blacks

Pre-Castro Cuba was racist. Post-Castro Cuba is also racist, but in a subtle manner and with a different emphasis. Before the revolution, Blacks and mulattoes were denied admission to exclusive social clubs, to some private schools, and to certain trades controlled by racist unions (banking, gastronomic enterprises, electric plants, telephone companies, etc.). Blacks were accepted in politics, and had access to armed forces and public administration positions. Racism was the nation's perversion, not the state's; more than an official problem it was a social phenomenon. It was not an aggressive and open racism, as is South Africa's, but that did not make it less repugnant. There was, however, the curious habit of denying the existence of this injustice. Blacks and Whites swore that they lived in total harmony in spite of evidence to the contrary.

The revolution, in one of its most reasonable acts, eliminated racism from the beaches, labor unions, and schools, proclaiming the triumph of a new, egalitarian, and fraternal society. After that just act, it began to send the bill to Black Cubans. Due to the revolution's "generosity," Blacks and mulattoes had/have to sympathize with official Marxism-Leninism. The Black or mulatto who has not "joined" the revolution is a traitor twice over. A White might not be a revolutionary; and if he is prudent, quiet, and obedient, perhaps he can crouch behind an unassuming attitude and watch events unfold. Blacks and mulattoes *have* to incorporate themselves. They *have* to repay the revolution, with the most strident militancy, the services which have been "loaned" them.

The Blacks and mulattoes who landed in Cuba during the Bay of Pigs invasion were doubly ill-treated: for being traitors to their country and to their race. Racism, in this sense, is now official: Blacks are forced to subscribe to a political color; Blacks who want to emigrate are mistreated. There were times when they would not be given a passport, or it would be unduly delayed. In addition they were forced to go through a spiteful series of insults and threats because of their "double treason."

There are other aspects of the revolution's racism that make Black American revolutionaries tremble. Cuban Blacks had faithfully kept their original traditions, sects, and African rites. The *ñáñigos*, the *yorubas*, the congos, would form civic-religious communities that not only served to preserve traditions, but also reinforce the identity of these minorities. This Black cult, tolerated and even imitated by Whites in prerevolutionary racist Cuba, is nowadays the object of more or less veiled persecutions. It is very simple: A good revolutionary cannot be a *ñáñigo*, use a "protection," or belong to a *potencia*. A Black, in order to be a "good" revolutionary—to which, because of his Black condition, he is doubly forced—must renounce his African heritage. He must deny his own Blackness, because "Black pride" is a luxury of the decadent and tolerant Western civilization, not of monolithic Cuba to which the revolution gave birth. If that revolution had taken into account Blacks' religious and cultural values at the time of defining—in absolute terms—the nation's values in this new stage, then it would have acted justly; but it chose to ignore 61 percent of the Cuban population, preferring a White Cuba, refusing to recognize the weight of the African tradition. From this point of view, the exporting of the well-known Cuban "Black ballet" seems innocent and eloquent. European mesh and slippers as a straight-jacket for dark Afro-Antillean skin.

Modern Communism—Fanon bitterly suspected—is a White European invention. Cuba, the moment it Communized itself, became European, even though its source of inspiration could only be Eastern Europe. Havana, which vaguely perceives this, suffers from certain painful complexes. There are hardly any Black diplomats. Sports delegations—the people—are full of Blacks, but their leaders—the state—are almost always White. In the Central Committee of the Communist party, Blacks have the ridiculously unfavorable proportion of being only 10 percent out of more than 100 members. The same is true of members of the cabinet and of the main power structure. There is no discriminating will on the part of the revolution. But neither is there a desire to rectify the situation. It is easier to ignore injustice and call "counterrevolutionary" or "divisionist" the person who denounces it than recognize that in its own way—a dogmatic and rigid way—the revolution is fundamentally racist, perhaps due to the intrinsic nature of Communism. Marx had foreseen class struggle in a homogeneous society such as Great Britain's and Germany's, but never in his wildest dreams did he imagine the multicolored Caribbean world. Why has there not been a single interracial marriage involving members of the ruling class's upper echelons in twenty years of revolution?

Racism is not eradicated by decree. In the undercurrent of Cuban life—White and Black—there are deeply rooted racist values (Blacks have accepted the White man's world). The revolution, which has been beneficial by permitting Blacks access to areas of work, recreation, and education previously reserved to Whites, has been notoriously harmful in the reinforcement of Black ethnic identity. "Black is not beautiful" in Cuba, and the ones who are right are the Black American revolutionaries who proudly display their Afro hairdos, their jazz, and their African cultural profile. We are dealing with the necessity of granting Blacks the dignity that they are per se entitled to. It was only when White American society began to perceive Black as "beautiful" because of how *he* looked, and not the degree to which he resembled a White, that Whites began to respect Blacks, paradoxically ignoring, then, the accident of his color; it was when Blacks and Whites openly went to bed—in the United States—to demonstrate in sexual intercourse that racism had begun to give way. For racism—and I do not intend in this book to theorize beyond certain limits—is always the fear of sexual assault by a strange race, and the only way to conquer it is by facilitating the speeding up in the rates of cross-breeding. In Cuba racism will have disappeared when Blacks and Whites have "integrated" into a mulatto tone, and this praiseworthy objective is little served by the revolution openly ignoring the existence of the colored half of the census. José Martí, full of good intentions, but completely mistaken, declared that the "Cuban is more than white or black," or that to speak of the races contributed to division. The fact that in Cuba half the country is White or Black cannot be ignored, especially if there are indications of racial tensions between the two. Cuban nationality was defined by White creoles who made the nation possible through wars in which they supplied the leadership and the Blacks a substantial part of the troops; a society in which the Whites' contribution was the hierarchy and the Blacks', the workers. From these origins there have developed a scale of values in which being White was noble, elegant, refined, and being Black the reverse of the coin. The correction of this aberration—common, by the way, to the whole Carribean—will be achieved only by reinforcing black identity through the revaluation of that ethnic profile. Probably post-revolutionary Cuban society would have suffered racial tension to a greater degree. But in the long run it would have served the Black cause, which is what is at issue, since the final solution to racial conflicts is not that Whites and Blacks go to schools and cabarets together, but that they go into the bedroom together; and for this, mutual admiration and esteem is necessary.

In Europe, where the absence of Black slaves avoided *that* racial prejudice, the color of Blacks is not ignored, nor are they olympically "tolerated," they are esteemed as Blacks. In Cuba, the path chosen by the revolution does not lead to the creation of a racially and culturally mixed fatherland, but to the disappearance of any vestige of the Blacks' contribution to Cuban culture. In a letter from the island, a Black writer friend of mine summarized the conflict in a concise phrase: "We are now Black Whites." The racial phenomenon taking place in Cuba has not been understood. Only Cleaver, the Black Panthers' leader, and Walterio Carbonell, a Black Communist founder of Cuba's Black Communist party (an invention which got him into prison for a while), have dealt with this matter in some depth. Both have censured Cuba's present racism, but it is not even remotely possible that the government will change its course.

Castroism is firmly devoted to the myth of "unity," even though it might only be an appearance. The world must be shown a monolithic image. No one knows for sure what the purpose of such an image is, but it is probably politically advantageous to pursue it. On an internal plane, in the small world of interracial relations, there are frequent collisions. The typical conflict—a monotonous, everyday happening—has to do with Blacks' failures and frustrations in the conquest of White women. To turn down a Black's advances is, by definition, a counterrevolutionary act for a White woman, but the revolution, which has told her that Whites and Blacks are equal, has not taught her to admire and respect Blacks. Instead, it claims to suddenly erase five centuries of prejudice. The consequences of this tension are ridiculous exchanges, in which comrade X—a Black—accuses comrade Z—a White— of racial prejudice because she has not accepted his advances; comrade Z defends herself by stating that she turned him down for other reasons—while the "revolution" watches nervously.

Women

One of the revolution's worthier efforts aims at changing the Cuban woman's traditional role, getting her out of the house, and moving her to the factory. It is time that the "warrior's comfort" start waging her own battles and begin doing something useful. The revolution wants to be feminist and also to increase production. That is very good. At the beginning of the revolution the Cuban Federation of Women was set up. Its head was Vilma Espín, a woman of singular personal talents and great capacity for work. Since then, an incessant fight to "liberate" women has taken place. People have even talked of the "battle of the sexes," but no doubt due to Marxism's poor imagination; the latter is little more than a window through which only dialectical ideas are perceived. The effort does not coincide with the achievements. Women comprise only 25 percent of the labor force, 13 percent of the members of the party, and 6 percent of the leadership. Among the 150 members of the Political Bureau, Secretariat, and Central Committee of the Communist party, there are only a few women. What has happened? In the first place, to legislate in matters of this kind is practically useless. Second, there is a serious contradiction between the revolution and feminism. I will try to explain.

In Cuba sexual roles were very rigidly established. Cuban psychologists know what I am talking about, as their most common patients were anguished males who began to have doubts about their masculinity as they noticed that they were not fulfilling some of the requirements demanded from "men." To fulfill this role, the male had to be brave, gesticulate rudely, have his vocal chords well coordinated with his hormones, be a womanizer and brag about it, come to blows at the slightest provocation, be careful about not permitting anybody to touch his behind, protect his mate from lascivious looks—at the risk of a fight—and of course, to protect his mother's sacred honor. Cubans were pure machos—the type that would have made Freud tremble. Pistol-carrying, cigar-smoking, hard-drinking, spitting machos. And these machos made the revolution. Even worse: The men who did it were called "guajiros machos" by other Cubans.

The contradiction is this: The Cuban Revolution is the business of machos, with a macho style and macho psychology. If, as in England during Heath's time, the prime minister would start directing a children's choir, people would talk about it. Juan Almeida, Castro's deputy, composed a few songs, and his boss felt uncomfortable. Machos do not do such things. Machos drive jeeps, have big pistols, and make revolutions. How on earth are women going to be able to comfortably integrate themselves into such a markedly men's world? Its own revolutionary mechanics unconsciously rejects them. The revolution, like certain brandies, is only for men. All that rhetoric of "assault brigades against the tomato," "the guerrilla fighters of the potatoes," and other beligerent formulas to get people to work, reflect the epic-machismo background of the revolution. The process has not been able to overcome its guerrilla origins. It pays for its original sin. It must be—for those who have messianic urges—very pleasant to live surrounded by heroism, but that does not contribute to the creation of a healthy society in which men and women can work side by side with ease. In order to make room for women, besides establishing day-care centers—which are fine—the nation needs to get rid of its machismo; to relax the sexual roles, primarily to decrease the index of neurotics, and secondly to make sex cease to be a determining aspect of the position of people in society. Women are not integrated because in order to be so they almost have to stop being women.

I prefer to repeat myself rather than to leave things unclear: Cuban women, also prisoners of secular values in conflict with the revolution, cannot decidedly join a process which is in contradiction with what they vaguely understand as their femininity. The revolution continues to be the work of certain heroic machos who perceive reality with the eye of the guerrilla fighter ready for the skirmish. Fidel, the supermacho, "The Horse," as his supporters call him, associating him with the impressively virile animal, is perhaps the immediate and unconscious culprit of this phenomenon. There is no doubt as to his good faith or the magnificent *intentions* of the revolution, but in order to take the correct path, they would have to concoct a different mythology, adopt other manners, and castrate the revolution. They would have to build the foundation of a totally neutral society, asexual. If to be a revolutionary is to topple structures and substitute them with more just ones, the revolutionary thing would be to eradicate the masculine accent, the machismo style which rules over Cuba's public life. But that would be like asking for a different revolution, and besides, it would be to ask of a leadership rich in testosterone, satisfied and proud of its work (each leader, each time he zips up his olive green fly and checks the lock in his pistol, reinforces his male ego and congratulates himself for being such a macho), to give up one of the aspects of the glory of power in that small Caribbean world—like expecting pears from an elm tree.

Appendix

Walterio Carbonell. A Cuban revolutionary who held important official positions. For a time he was a member of Castro's inner circle. This did not save him from imprisonment.

Chronic Unemployment. According to the findings in 1957 of the National Economic Council, 16.4 percent of the population over age 14 had no job and about 7 percent worked for family firms without receiving wages.

Corruption in Government. There have been many cases of corruption and illicit enrichment. The most publicized recent case was that of Luis Orlando Domínguez, civil aviation chief and former secretary general of the Union of Young Communists. In 1987 he was sentenced to a long jail term for helping himself to public funds.

Cuban Lumberjacks in Siberia. In 1980 Castro publicly complained that the Soviet Union was not meeting its obligations regarding the supply of sawn wood on the grounds that there were not enough woodcutters in Siberia. He offered to send Cuban volunteers to do the job. At the time, the Soviet Union rejected the offer but Major Azpillaga, an intelligence officer who deserted, stated in 1987 that young Cubans were cutting wood in Siberia under appalling working conditions and suffered from bad housing and inadequate food.

Double Betrayal of Blacks. During a televised exchange in 1961 between Fidel Castro and members of the 2506 Brigade of the invasion force captured at Playa Girón (the Bay of Pigs), Castro made use in almost all cases of the respectful pronoun *usted* (the equivalent of the French *vous*). But when he spoke with a Black prisoner he used *tú*, a pronoun then used either among friends or relatives or to social inferiors: "Hey, you, what are you [tú] doing here? Aren't you ashamed of yourself? Don't you know you've got your social role wrong? Don't you know that they've used you in a shameful way and that as well as being a traitor to the revolution you are a traitor to your race?" In the context, it was as though an American politician treated White prisoners as "sir" and Blacks as "boy."

The Escambray Peasants. A large number of men who worked during the day but were guerrillas by night. The only way the Castroite authorities could prevent the peasantry from helping the "insurgents" in the Escambray area was by forcibly relocating the population. Many young peasant women received grants so they could learn dressmaking in Havana, and thousands of their relatives were sent to inhospitable parts of Pinar del Río province where the first thing they had to do was put up their new homes. Examples of these settlements are Ciudad Sandino and Communidad López Peña.

Vilma Espín (1930–). A Cuban revolutionary, wife of Raúl Castro and president of the Cuban Women's Federation. At present she is a deputy in the Natonal Assembly and a member of the Politburo.

Franz Fanon (1925–1961). An Algerian psychologist and political theorist originally from Martinique. He was an active supporter of the FLN and was well known for his anticolonialist books, among which are *Peau Blanche, Masques negres* and *Les Damnés de la terre.*

Ricardo Cruz Font. A poet and political prisoner who spent ten years in jail. He was in bad psychological shape when he went into exile in Spain, and committed suicide in Paris in 1987.

The Great Revolutionary Offensive of 1968. An extremist movement formed by Cuban revolutionaries who wanted to make their rule even more radical by demanding greater sacrifices from the people, putting an end to all resistance and eliminating the few remaining private businesses in order to create the "New Man." The offensive was announced by Fidel Castro on 13 March 1968.

"Guajiro Macho". A pejorative epithet used in Cuba to describe a person with the appearance and manner of an uncouth and uneducated peasant with primitive and "macho" habits.

Ñañigo. A Cuban, usually Black, who belonged to a secret society with religious and corporativist overtones that was sometimes feared by the White population for its alleged violence. *Abakuá* has the same meaning.

Rigoberto Pereda. Cuban political prisoner.

Potencia. An intensely religious Black Cuban fraternity.

Proportion of Blacks in Power. Of the 148 members of the Central Committee of the Communist party only 9 were Blacks or of mixed race, even though over 60 percent of the Cuban population is either Black or of mixed race. Furthermore, only 16 committee members were women. On the other hand, 40 were high-ranking military officers.

Comments on this situation made by this author led to the reorganization of the Central Committee so that, in the words of Castro, "it would reflect better the ethnic, sexual, and age-group composition of Cuban society."

Armando Valladares (1939–   ). Cuban writer who was a political prisoner for 22 years for expressing anti-Marxist ideas and being opposed to the Castro regime. He has written several works of which the most notable are *El corazón con que vivo* and the autobiographical *Contra toda esperanza*.

Yoruba. The West African people inhabiting what are now Nigeria, Benin, and Togo who speak a language of the Kwa group. Most Black slaves brought to Cuba in the eighteenth and nineteenth centuries belong to this ethnic group.

6

Economic Failure

The Battle for Production

Production is socialism's neurotic fixation. It is a mysterious frenzy that consists of pursuing goals, meeting them—or not—and then setting other goals. Of course, what is produced is distributed, and one's share is more (or less if you are not lucky, or if it rains, etc.). But deep down what is produced is not as important as the athletic spirit instilled in the production process. In the midst of the clamor no one notices the absurdity in the behavior of some men pursuing goals that are floating just over the horizon. That is as alienating as the worst aspects of capitalism and consumer society.

In Cuba, the fatherland's honor is located in the smokestacks. It is as if Othello were the minister of industry. Each failure, a national period of mourning; each success, a fiesta is organized and another goal is set. Life, more than a stage, is voluntary work. The 10-million-ton sugar harvest, since it reached only 8 million and since it comprised national glory, left Cubans without honor. Fidel, like Ahab the Samarian king, tore up his clothes, fired a minister providentially surnamed Borrego (lamb—fool, simpleton), and the whole country wallowed in sadness. It is true that this raving atmosphere of goals, emulation, production tables, and ghostly fights against imperialism exists in all latitudes of socialism, but in Cuba the fever reaches its highest mark. The secret lies in Fidel's personality. Fidel is a born competitor, a man in permanent struggle with other men, without paying too much attention to the struggle's objective. Fidel has made the battle of production his own. He personally looks after the efficiency of milking cows, of the egg-laying hens, and of the sugar industry workers. He is very enthusiastic about all of this. He would tenderly pamper an obese bull (named Rosafé) which had been especially brought from Canada. The animal died of a hemorrhage on its one millionth ejaculation, and Fidel was left in a state of depression. The production of good semen had suffered a serious blow. Fidel showed it. There is no exaggeration here. René Dumont, the French Socialist, narrates in his book impressive things about Fidel's promiscuity with the country's economy. Castro, who plays baseball and basketball, and fishes under water, transmits to the nation his fiery competitive character. When he was a teenager at Belén Jesuit Academy, he became famous among his schoolmates because in order to win a bet he tried to open an iron door by riding at it full speed with his bicycle. He cut his head, but the tears were shed because of the failure, not the pain. Transposing the Olympic motto, for Castro the question is to compete and win.

This gossip would have no importance if Cuba's destiny were not so tied to Fidel's personality. Fidel, as Che with his New Man, wants to create the country in his image and likeness. He wishes, and becomes desperate because he is not able to achieve it, for legions of enthusiastic Cubans to meet goals as high-hurdle runners. The problem is that, with the exception of unusually tenacious persons, enthusiasm has some rather precise limits. Twenty-five years of enthusiasm are more than enough. To wake up day after day, week after week, year after year, with a radiant spirit because "we are doing our duty and meeting some goals," is a task for chosen people or cretins. Athletic enthusiasm (whether revolutionary, religious, or on the ball field—the fanatic and his pathological enthusiasms are one and the same in any activity) requires successes and pauses in order to be continued. It is not possible to maintain a permanent competitive tension as the revolution demanded. People simply get tired of all that sugarcane cutting, of piling up so many bricks, or of tightening so many nuts per minute. The first time one wins a speed and efficiency contest at work, one has the sensation of being a hero; the second time one has the suspicion of playing the fool. George Orwell vividly describes this phenomenon in his delectable classic *Animal Farm*.

Cuba has turned its back on the consumer society. That—I agree—is an aberration of capitalist societies. But in consumer societies, the worker, though being alienated, is able to see a relation between his effort and the compensation he receives, although admittedly this compensation might be an artifically created necessity. In Cuba, after the euphoria and the public rituals, it is not very clear why each person must produce more cement or dedicate Saturday and Sunday to voluntary work. The Communists hate abstractions, and end up by succumbing before the most harmful idols. Production is one of them. I am not arguing against the necessity of producing more hens and eggs to take care of the needs of the population, but against the monstrous fact that this objective should become the nation's leitmotiv. Putting Cuba's inexorable mass media to the task of making the whole country gyrate around the production arithmetic is alienating, absurd, boring, and fruitless. The poultry and porcine battles are soporific. An old and candid friend once expressed his amazement to me: "I don't understand. When they are children they do not have the maturity to take an interest in those things, and when they are mature, they do not show any interest." And then the government tries to blame the workers and repeat the history of the revolutionary consciousness to try to justify the unjustifiable: the total failure of the system as a method for the creation of wealth.

Scarcity and the Consumer Society

The ration book seems one of the fairest things in the world. It is quite appropriate: Whatever is available should be shared by all. In times of crisis (war-torn Europe, the postwar period, shipwrecked persons) a rational accumulation and distribution of material wealth is essential. But this type of crisis cannot last indefinitely without questioning the capacity of those responsible for it. In 1959, Cuba had not been through a civil war. Batista fled after the first few skirmishes. The country was intact and could brag about having the third per capita ingestion of protein on the continent. Higher, by the way, than the minimum limit recommended by the Food and Agriculture Organization. Three years after the Communists had taken power, the rationing of food, clothes, shoes, and the scarcity of the rest began. It is said that Cuba lost a great deal with the economic blockade imposed by the United States, but it is supposed that it gained more in return from the Soviet Union, Eastern Europe, China, Korea, and the family of satellites. It tightened economic ties with Western Europe and Canada. Cuba has never enjoyed a more open-door policy. The image of little David struggling to maintain his growth and development against the CIA, hurricanes, and international conspiracy, is only good to mask an overwhelming truth: The country is in the hands of a legion of incompetent people. A few years ago, a curious economist compared the ration book with the obligatory diet given by Spain to the slaves. The astonishing results were that the slaves were better fed than the Cubans of these perilous times (see table 6.1).

TABLE 6.1
Rationing in Cuba

Item	1842 Per Capita Ration under Slavery	1962 Per Capita Ration under Communism
	National Average	
Meat, chicken or fish	8 ounces	2 ounces
Rice	4 ounces	3 ounces
Starches	16 ounces	6.5 ounces
Beans	4 ounces	1 ounce
	(pig breeding was permitted)	(prohibition of pig slaughtering)

Scarcity and prolonged rationing have painful consequences: In the midst of an idealistic society, the Cuban New Man lives worried about material goods. In Cuba people live to acquire two pounds of lard, half a dozen eggs, and a shoe sole "because my toe is sticking out." To synthesize this unmetaphysical anguish, this modality of obsessive anxiety has been called by a Cuban psychologist "the trauma of the picadillo." Picadillo (ground meat, onions, tomatoes), Cuba's most popular dish, has ceded its name to the most popular national epidemic: the search for food. It is depressing to listen to comments such as: "This year we are going to get an extra pair of drawers," or "I've heard that at the Monaco Store we might finally be able to get sardines without our rationing book." Or the talk about where on earth you can get sanitary napkins, or whether someone has received a bottle of vitamins, or the watered-down can of condensed milk which was exchanged for the watered-down bottle of rum—a typical exchange between two dishonest merchants of the revolutionary upheaval. The worst thing about scarcity is the habit of talking about it, or of using all your energies in trying to beat the system, and the whole alienating, picaresque atmosphere that surrounds it.

While in the consumer societies young people would throw material well-being overboard and go with their guitars and frayed clothes to experience a poor and absurdly bohemian life, the Cubans, stung by scarcity, swam against the current, looking for coffee, cigars, a wrist watch, or a zipper. Fidel and his team justified the implantation of communism in Cuba as a magic formula for development. They promised the world. Domestically built automobiles in ten years, consumer goods, comforts, industrialization. A panacea. Almost opulence. "In the next decade"—Guevara said while hallucinating—"we will surpass the per capita in the United States." Twenty-three years later, if it does not rain, if there is no cold weather, if the people work, if the harvest is gathered on time, perhaps the cassava, yam, or egg quota will increase. Either the offspring of the hills or the ridiculous, which is worse and less literary.

Was there in those impudent promises the intention of deceiving the people, or just pure ignorance? I am afraid it was the latter. And I fear it because there is nothing more dangerous than euphoric ignorance. The Cuban rulers had a demented frame of reference that gave rise to giddy decisions, such as the Sierra Maestra adventure. Are we going to build cars? Of course, it was more difficult to defeat Batista, but we did that. Are we going to dry the Zapata Swamp? Of course, it was more difficult, etc. Are we going to have a 10-million-ton sugar harvest? Of course. Are we going to make a Sierra Maestra out of the Andes? Of course. The guerrilla victory against all odds—described at the beginning of this book—gave the Cuban leadership an inexhaustible confidence in their adventures. For a pistol-packing, poorly educated mentality, not given to serene reflection, realizing that it is much more difficult to build automobiles than to blow them up was impossible. Any project, any plan, no matter how complicated it might be, was easier than the "other thing." Simpler than the sect's mythology.

It has been said that poverty and rationing are arms used by totalitarian repression. There is something to that. The "trauma of the picadillo" turns man into an obsessive exhumer of bones. His only prepossessions are food and clothing. Rationing, besides, is a formidable form of blackmail. When you go with the rationing book to get your quota, you have the impression of being alive thanks to the government's generosity. It is something similar to what a poor person feels when he is given leftovers. The ration book foments the beggar's abject mentality. The government becomes a powerful entity on whose kindness our hunger or satisfaction depends. If you rebel—thousands of Cubans have lost their ration cards for different reasons—you can be left without food or clothing. If you obey, you will not be denied your quota. Enormous power emanates from the brutal fact of having and controlling the key to the cupboard, in a country in which no one can hoard more foodstuffs than are necessary for a 72-hour supply.

The above notwithstanding, the Cuban government would have given anything to avoid the slippery problem of rationing, the long lines, and the scarcity of any item—from toothpicks to ballpoint pens—which makes life more pleasant. It is very difficult to explain why coffee, cigars, sugar, or rum have been rationed in an island that used to export these items. Or the rationing, at times, of electricity or water. The unbearably long lines in front of restaurants, movies, ice cream parlors; the scarcity of rice, milk, clothing, of everything. In Cuba it is impossible to consume without patiently waiting. It takes months to repair an umbrella; a refrigerator, years. Television sets cannot be fixed. Production is a disaster, but distribution is worse. However, both look good when compared to the incredible inefficiency of the services. It is chaos within authoritarian order.

Nonconsumerism Rhetoric

Halfway along the road and in the midst of economic failure, Castroism changed horses. Originally, communism had been the perfect formula for the island's resounding development. Later, the government said that it no longer proposed to build a consumer society. Initial reaction to this public statement was good; the "consumer society" had a bad press. Among the things that are consumed in consumer societies is a good dosage of anticonsumer societies literature. It seems like a tongue twister, but it is really a paradox. What is certain is that development, progress, is nothing more than the growing list of objects, machines, and talent at man's disposal over time. Man's only real necessities are food, rest, and sex to perpetuate the species. Consumer societies started with the stone, club, fire, the wheel, and have not stopped even at spaceships. This clamoring against the consumer society might be very poetic—it seems frankly reactionary to me—but it does not fit into the history of man's cultural evolution.

There is an obvious contradiction when on the one hand the revolution's leaders frantically apply themselves to development, and on the other, state that they renounce the attainment of a consumer society. Development is only a consumer's tool, unless we have lost our minds. Only contemplative societies—Buddhist monks, Trappists—can honestly proclaim their renunciation of progress, because progress is nothing but the perfection of material goods at man's disposal. To progress is to go forward from the carriage to the automobile to the airplane. To renounce consumption is to renounce the dialectics of progress.

Naturally, this public renunciation in Cuba is the tropical version of the fable of the fox and the grapes. They renounce consumption because creature comforts are "evil." The truth is that they renounce consumption because production is a disaster. It could not happen any other way, given the few incentives the workers have, the stupidity of their leaders, and the absurd economic structure of socialism. In any case, before accepting as valid the proposal made by Castroism of creating a nonconsumer society for Cubans, somebody will have to answer the following questions:

First: In which verse of *Das Kapital* are the blessings of permanent ascetic poverty prescribed? This sounds rather like a certain renunciation of a religious caste, very close to the theology of poverty debated in the bosom of the Catholic Church, or in Oriental mystic traditions.

Second: We accept, then, that nonconsumerism is an objective alien, strange, and even contrary to the essence of Marxism, but out of what mysterious sleeve has sprung the mandate for decreeing noncommunist asceticism for Cubans? When and how have Cubans chosen austerity as a vital objective? How can a government dare decree nonconsumption as a permanent vital norm? Nonconsumption can be admitted as a passing fatality when faced with a catastrophe, but from there to establish this misfortune as a way of life is going quite far. It is likely that certain revolutionaries and cloistered monks may obtain spiritual rewards as a result of the vow of poverty, but this kind of peculiar human being is only a minimal percentage of the population and it seems total madness to convert him into an archetype.

Third: Let us admit (what difference does it make if we do not?) the imposed arbitrary action, but demanding a certain precision: What kind of consumption are we going to forbid? Will color television be forbidden, video, stereo, electronic games, pocket computers, the washing machine, the family freezer, the car, the quartz watch, the typewriter, or the electric shaver? Do you forbid soft contact lenses, cosmetic surgery of the silicon prosthesis?

Are toilet paper, deodorants, or sanitary napkins consumable or nonconsumable articles? Where is the line drawn between legitimate and superficial needs? How many shirts, skirts, jackets or *guayaberas* (typical Cuban shirts) can be had without breaking the law? Which are the forbidden articles and why these and not others? It is very easy to get out of a bind with the refrain that we are not going to build a consumer society, but this requires a multitude of clarifications that Cubans do not ask for because, I suppose, clarifications must be rationed as well.

Fourth: Whatever the articles and their manipulation that determines the contemporaneity of societies, their relative place in time, it would be interesting for Cuban civil servants to clarify to which state of development they plan to take the Cubans. I suppose the Cuban rulers have noticed that the essential difference between Londoners and Hottentots is the possession or use of certain objects and the skill with which they are used. At what exact point of nonconsumption and use of objects should Cubans remain? At what distance from the Hottentots or from the Londoners does it fall to the inhabitants of that island to exist? To what level of social complexity have they been assigned by the illustrious revolutionary leadership?

Fifth: Those who live in Spain have been able to see on countless occasions Cuban civil servants, with irrepressible greed, buying every kind of article with the aim of taking them to Cuba for their personal enjoyment. Does this mean that nonconsumption is only for the Cubans who cannot travel abroad? Who can enjoy consumer goods and why? What are the limits and the rationale of the privileges? Moreover, how should the civil servants who live abroad behave? Should they succumb to the alienation of Western consumership, or should they remain within the ethical coordinates of the island, i.e., subject to the ascetic austerity and poverty of the Spartanism proposed by Havana?

There are many more questions to ask, but I prefer to put an end to this list with a final observation: It is understandable that civil servants and partisans, always in search of alibis and pretexts, will raise high the virtues of asceticism and nonconsumption for the poverty and backwardness prevailing in Cuba, but truly serious people who inquire into the intimate nature of Cuban society should not accept this explanation without further ado. Cubanology, like any other appendix to social science, should begin by doubting the premises and axioms offered it at the outset. If Cubanologists do not do this, they will end up accepting a pig in a poke.

The Castron Bomb

Yankee engineers, as always, have gotten things the wrong way around. The Americans have built the neutron bomb, a crude artifact without imagination or class that kills people and leaves the surroundings intact. Much more subtle, diabolical, and perverse is the "Castron" bomb. Designed in Cuba by Scientist Fidel Castro, summa cum laude of Patrice Lumumba University in Moscow, rigorously tested on Havana Atoll, the Castron bomb is a terrifying device that destroys, annihilates, sweeps away, flattens, disintegrates, and pulverizes the surroundings, but leaves the people alive. Can the reader imagine such refined cruelty? A bomb that does not take lives but civilization. You are having your coffee and peacefully smoking a Havana cigar in a corner of the twentieth century and suddenly, for the next twenty years, a ceaseless bombardment of mega-Castrons falls on your head, evaporating the coffee, rationing the Havana cigars, making toilet paper disappear (something that does not prove to be too serious because food has also been suppressed); and it destroys transportation, converting any trip into a Himalayan feat. Still stunned, you discover that the few taxis that survived went mad from the effects of the radiation, and they never stop, as though they had discovered perpetual movement. Then you note with sorrow that the intense heat has destroyed the interesting films and only the armored hodgepodge of Stalinist filmmaking survives. There are no shirts, nor trousers, nor medicines, nor shoes, nor deodorants, nor bras. There is no water. Alternating current has taken its name seriously and comes and goes when it feels like it. Daily life in the twentieth century—press the button and make light, turn the faucet and make a shower, or spin a disc and talk with your distant aunt—has disappeared. What is escaping at a gallop, swiftly, is time, and the titanic struggle of the Cuban, as though it were the Mambises (Cuban separatists of 1868) against H.G. Wells, is to avoid being returned to the nineteenth century, to the burro, the candle, and muscular traction. It is a difficult battle, because it goes on beneath the murderous cornices of a Havana that is crumbling and with one foot in the court in session, while one legally tries to get a pound of picadillo to prop up a skeleton, or a homemade potion to calm the inclement fierceness of tropical underarm.

The deterioration of the Cuban economy is so severe, so profound, so unbelievable, that the brothers Castro, authors of the mega-Castron bombardment, feel like Truman after Hiroshima. It is they, now, who are trying to organize the rescue, because that is the way they are, strange. First they thoroughly club your cranium. Then they go for your throat to give you artificial respiration. But they give it badly, because the most serious problem that Groucho and Harpo Castro have is that they do not understand human beings. For example, in order to attempt to rescue the country from chaos, no other measure occurs to them but to demand responsibilities by waving the penal code. It is the angry father of "they will tell me who threw the stone or I will break their backs blow by blow." Groucho and Harpo have not lived, read, observed, or understood enough to be aware that human beings move happily with the spur of reward and pretend to move with the threat of a beating. The only unquestionable truth of behaviorist psychology is that positive effort is much more lasting and effective than negative, and that more is gained with lumps of sugar than with blows to the ribs.

Every so often, first Groucho and then Harpo jostle the microphone to denounce the chaos in which the country is submerged and to warn that heads will roll if this is not corrected. Minister Lussón was made responsible for the disaster in transportation, the Apocalypse Now of bold Cubans who dare take the Moncada of the *guaguas* (buses). A great injustice. Lussón is not to blame that the busdrivers destroy their equipment, the mechanics do not repair it, that the man at the warehouse may have sold the crankshaft on the black market, or that three-fourths of the passengers do not pay their fares. Lussón is not to blame for the longing for resistence, disobedience, and vandalism that occurs throughout the country, Lussón is only responsible—and this, now, is serious—for being the minister of a system punctiliously mistaken in its theoretical assumptions and outstandingly clumsy in its practical development.

What is happening in Cuba, from one end to the other, is a secret but total civil insubordination, a product of disillusionment, the discouragement and universal loss of faith in the economic and political direction of the Castro brothers, a spiritual mood which has produced an uncooperative attitude of every-man-for-himself in the population. Cuba today is a country of loafers who pretend to work and of cynics who pretend to agree, all skillfully concealed by a thick web of criminal complicities, alibis, and "socialism"— for "my associate," "my friend"—against which police repression can do nothing. This is not going to change. Faith in the revolution—revolutions, like mysteries, are a question of faith—simply cannot be restored. This is going to get worse. With every passing minute, the regime, the system, Fidel—all for one and one for all—are more unpopular. Power always erodes, but when it is stupidly exercised, the erosion becomes devastating. Economics—as economists say—is 50 percent exact science and 50 percent psychology. The work that one accomplishes is to a large extent, the result of a previous psychological state. In that intimate area of beliefs, an area where pressures are worth nothing, an area that determines job behavior and social conduct, the Cuban revolution is completely and irreversibly wiped out, dead, and as thoroughly flat as the encephalogram of enthusiasms.

There is, yes, a powerful army, substantial Soviet subsidies, and an apparently solid power structure, but behind this façade there exists only a rotten, disillusioned, and degraded society that will end up tearing down the edifice of power.

Summary

On 31 December 1958—24 hours before the triumph of the revolution— Cuba was an underdeveloped country, poor and dependent on sugar, secretly subject to the dictates of a foreign power, and under the control of a tyrant. Almost thirty years later, Cuba is an underdeveloped country, poor and dependent on sugar, secretly subject to the dictates of another foreign power, and under the control of another tyrant. Between one objective reality and the other, there clearly intervenes the inexhaustible Fidelist rhetoric, the lightning bolt of saliva that never ceases.

But that crushing torrent of words cannot hide the facts: In 1958, in spite of the deplorable picture described, Cuba, according to the most trustworthy economic indicators—cement, kilowatts, proteins, telephones, steel, and other mysterious symptoms per capita—was the third country in Latin America in terms of development. Today it is eighth. Costa Rica, for example, which had its revolution some years before, and did not install execution walls, nor spy networks, nor imprison thousands of dissidents, instead of creating an Afrika Korps took the healthy initiative of dismissing the army and replacing it with a bicycle-and-whistle police force. Costa Rica has progressed twice as much as Cuba in these thiry years. With schools for all and hospitals for all. But, in addition, with human rights. The flesh-and-blood reality, the observable, the relentless evidence points to a very sad truth: The Cuban way is the water's way. The revolution sank, the country sank (even further), and the hopes sank of the well-intentioned Left that dreamed and suffered for the adventure of thirty years ago.

This pessimistic diagnosis is privately shared by Fidel Castro, Carlos Rafael Rodríguez, and the very brotherly Raúl, and there is not a Cuban head with its brains intact that is able to ignore it. There is no dogma that can resist thirty years of increasing numbers of ration books. There is no stupidity invulnerable to hunger.

The consequences of this national pessimism are beginning to be seen: Cuba, thirty years later, is looking for a way to change course. It now knows that the solution (or the palliatives) to the tremendous problems the country suffers does not go through Moscow, but through Washington and the marketplace of Western capitals, a source scarcely willing to collaborate with Cuba, especially after the formal statement of bankruptcy declared by the National Bank of Cuba in September 1982. The key to this crisis can be summed up in two words: financing for future plans and refinancing the already existing debt. To get out of the mire, Cuba must go into debt in the West as it has already done in the Communist world. In 1984 Cuba must begin to pay Moscow the monstrous debt of several billion dollars with interest: a debt acquired during these tiring years of euphoria and silliness. And if a merciful deferment is not granted, Havana will be unable to fulfill its commitments to the USSR, as has already occurred with the Western countries.

It is likely that the Cuban Revolution has fallen into a secret economic mousetrap that demands much more than a change of alliances to outwit it. In the West, there is simply not the capital available that Cuba needs to stay afloat. If the capacity of Mexico, Brazil, and Argentina to pay their debts is in doubt, what can be expected of Cuba whose economic history in the last quarter century is appalling?

Nor would Washington be willing to "buy" a business as ruinous as Castro's Cuba. Those almost $3 billion that the island costs the Soviets annually will never come out of the Yankee till while the make-up of the American Congress looks similar to the one that has been seen in recent admistrations. If President Reagan had difficulties in getting Congressional approval for economic aid for barely $350 million for the *whole* Caribbean, how can it be thought that an American president is going to get the $2,500 billion needed by Cuba to keep afloat?

There is another economic road, of course, but it means the end of the revolution. It involves dismantling that monstrous centralized and inefficient holding company by breaking it up into independent units regulated by the market and far from the ill-fated influence of the commissars. Cuba has economic solutions, but all of them go by way of the end of communism and the gradual return of the country to a less rigid economic model.

Castro and his closest followers know this, but they also know that this relentless transformation brings with it the end of their political power. With some caution, Castroism tries to put into effect capitalist reforms, but immediately afterwards it crushes them without pity. Why? Because capitalism and competition generate economically powerful citizens who do not respond to the machinery of the central power. To have money is a way of having power, and this is something that communist dictatorships cannot tolerate, especially those that rely on one leader.

It is valid, at this point, to ask why a change of system can lift Cuba out of its prostration, if the island will continue to lack petroleum, depend on sugar, and be subject to a want of international capital. My answer is this: The source of the harshness of economic ills in Cuba must be sought in another, much more important, factor. For almost a quarter century the *personal* creativity of Cubans, of millions of Cubans, has been replaced by the creativity of one man, tireless and energetic but, in the end, one man, surrounded by a mediocre and scarcely educated leadership.

It seems clear—and in Cuba it has been proven again—that the Communist class is much less creative, hard-working, and efficient than the restless managerial class. Those tens of thousands of ambitious Cubans, worried about their own prosperity an about rising within the social structure, are a much more powerful propeller than the distressing civil servants of the Communist party.

Singapore, Japan, and England have been able to prove, in totally different circumstances, that certain poor islands without energy resources are capable of prospering if the population is not handcuffed with dogmatic schemes.

Cuba could be one of these fortunate islands, but, for this to be so, the creativity must be released of the millions, of the hundreds of thousands of Cubans who feel the urge to be successful, but to whose ankles communism ties an anchor.

Appendix

Animal Farm. George Orwell's political fable. An allegory on the seizure of power by Communists (pigs) who led a rebellion of all the farm animals (the people) against an unjust farmer (czarism) and the unpleasant consequences that resulted.

Orlando Borrego. A Cuban revolutionary who served as a minister in Castro's government.

Mambi. A word of uncertain origin used to designate the insurgents who fought for Cuban independence against the Spanish army.

Zapata Swamp. Marshy region in southern Cuba which, since 1976, is included in the southern part of Matanzas province.

7

Hidden Evils of Castroism

There is a Castroism universally condemned, made up of prisons, execution walls, acts of repudiation, impoverishment, and other obvious miseries. But perhaps this Castroism, in spite of its burden of abuses and brutalities, is not the worst. There are other much deeper and more lasting consequences that seriously threaten the possibility of a livable society one day being set up in Cuba. These reflections are aimed as briefly stating these prejudices, and what follows is something like a tragic and partial index of the profound evils that Castroism has injected into the Cuban social body.

The Pessimistic Idea of National Destiny

Almost three decades of Castroism have dried up the hopes of many Cubans for a successful destiny as a people. This generalized despair casts doubt on the very viability of the island as a national entity directed toward material prosperity and spiritual happiness. This pessimistic attitude is totally new in the history of Cuba, since, in spite of the errors and the political and economic catastrophes of the republic, the criterion that the island—a cork, according to a popular appraisal—would go forward in spite of setbacks always had priority. The wide-spread superstition existed that the country "was rich," that the Cuban "was clever," and that, in the long run, the nation was expecting a radiant future. This healthy optimism—undoubtedly exaggerated, but without which it is impossible to attempt a constructive national project—has given way to the most radical pessimism. The Castroist present is seen as a terrible failure, but the future is foreseen as something perhaps worse. A huge percentage of new emigrants, even before they settle down abroad, make the secret decision never to return to that land, whether it is governed by Castro or his adversaries, whether it is run by communism or capitalism. There is not even any nostalgia. Rather a certain understandable bitterness is exuded because the remembrances are connected with shocking vital experiences.

One is not dealing, of course, with "bad" Cubans. That would be an unjust assessment. One is dealing with Cubans deeply wounded, hurt, and distressed who have made forgetfulness a personal obsession.

The appearance of this pessimism in the history of Cuba is a terrible misfortune, for the first condition demanded by any kind of undertaking for its successful development is that those who attempt it believe in it. There is no prosperous and healthy society if the people who compose it do not participate in a common optimism. It is a terrible paradox that Castroism, which began with the highest rate of collective confidence in the fate of the country, has served to unroot cruelly the heartfelt hopes of Cubans. But this is the case.

The Negative Idea of One's Fellow Man

Castroism has made the crudest insolidarity widespread among Cubans. There—and in vast areas of the emigration—a fatal attitude of "every man for himself" has become established, and one treads on and tramples one's fellow man in order to save one's skin from an invisible fire that crackles everywhere. This pessimism is revealed not only in not believing in the country's destiny, but also in not believing in Cubans, in one's flesh-and-blood neighbor. The ingenuous and traditional assertion that the Cuban was noble has turned into the twisted assumption that the Cuban is evil.

The relentless model of Castro's state has converted too many Cubans into commissars, butchers, beaters, informers, humiliators of every kind, people who have mistreated their fellow man with excessive cruelty for too long. That surprising expression with which one invariably tried to settle disputes by referring to the "Cubanism" of the participants has today lost all meaning. It is natural that "between Cubans" much harm is done. The normal thing is to expect from one's fellow man some irreparable dirty trick. Not only has faith in the country as an abstract entity been lost but also faith in one's fellow countryman. One has gone from a pleasant positive prejudice to a horrifying negative prejudice. Bad clay to unite a people.

Destruction of the Ideal Model

Every time that the horrors of Castroism has made a citizen trained, educated, and developed in the life world and values of the middle class and the bourgeoisie take off for a foreign country, it has unfeelingly wasted an important part of the human capital that country accumulated. Every Cuban consecrated by technical training and accustomed to the complexities of urban life and "sophistication"—what a horrible twentieth-century word—who has been thrown out or cast aside has been a terrible loss for the whole country. It cost centuries of suffering and struggle to give that society a tenuous but growing layer of citizens—city dwellers—comparable to the leading peoples of the planet. But with great irresponsibility Castroism has steadily erased these social strata, delaying by almost a quarter century the upsurge of avant-garde elites in every field of civic activity.

How do you replace this wealth of humanity destroyed by Castroism? How do you restore to that society the vanished product of many decades, of centuries of slow cultural sedimentation? The first observation that every traveler who tours the island at these times makes has to do with the obvious degradation and vulgarity of this society. Throughout the republic one could see a sustained evolution of bourgeois values and the middle classes (the only ones that in the end have proved throughout history to be capable of creating a comfortable social atmosphere), but from 1959 up to now the country has been sliding toward the most rampant incivility. Why? Because Castroism has dissolved, eliminated, the civic layer that served as a vital model to the rest of the nation. Castroism uprooted the social fabric that slowly transformed and trained the less well brought-up and educated population of the country in the uses, customs, and beliefs of the most civilized social levels, favoring a fluid process of social migration of noteworthy efficiency. It is probable that in 1959 this middle bourgeois social strata would have included a third of the population and have made up the main social feat of the country. Castro and his incompetent followers have irreparably destroyed it with the terrible harm they inflicted on the Cuban nation by eliminating its ideal group.

The Enemy State

I have pointed out that Castroism has produced a very pessimistic change in the perception of the country's future and a negative modification in the idea of one's fellow countryman. In addition, as was to be expected, Castroism has worsened the popular conception of the state. Today the state, in any of its manifestations, is an enemy that one can—when one is able to—deceive, rob, or harm without this producing the slightest crisis of conscience in the Cuban. The state is not perceived as a common enterprise that can be perfected, but as an awkward, strange, alien, and arbitrary structure of power that provides few goods and bad services while it demands uncomfortable and badly paid workdays, and—what is worst—constant ceremonies of ideological adherence, expressed by means of parades, functions, meetings, applauses, voluntary or abject work, and frequent acquiescent smiles.

It is no surprise, given this perception of the world, that millions of Cubans deliver themselves without remorse to the task of destroying the social environment in which they live. Castroism has provoked the total alienation of Cubans as citizens, turning them into legions of destructive vandals. Scholastic centers, offices, public means of transport, rural or modern work tools, nothing escapes the destructive power of a people who do not identify with the dreadful state that day by day oppresses them and forces them to perform the most denigrating genuflections.

Owing to this, the notion of the common good does not exist. Public property is an incomprehensible abstraction. Only the individual dimension, for reasons of the most deep-seated egotism, merits care and respect. This Midas in reverse that Castro has turned out to be, tried to end with revolution the dishonesty of a handful of politicians that used to rob the state, but what he has achieved is that millions of Cubans turn into enemies and irreconcilable exploiters of that same state. He who with communism wanted to increase the cooperative conscience of Cubans, has provoked the upsurge of a fierce and ungovernable individualism that relentlessly files down and roughens any common constructive effort. When the tragic anecdote of Castroism is one day overcome, how will a minimally healthy conception of the state be reinstilled among Cubans? How do you convince millions of beings for centuries revolting against a state they abhor that living together in freedom is only possible by combining rights and obligations, by protecting the public sector with the same respect with which one protects the private one? I am afraid that these questions have no easy answer. Moreover, I fear they do not even have an answer. No formula exists for revitalizing the public conscience.

The Destruction of the Past

Not content to offer a present of privations and failures, not content with destroying the hope of a better future, dislodging from the civic heart of Cubans one of their best virtues, Castroism has also demolished the republican past, leaving the country without historic pretexts that would serve as a starting point for the task of national reconstruction. In that social ruin to which Cuba has been reduced, the notion of rebirth, that useful idea of national resurgence that serves countries in critical hours, is not even possible, because to be reborn or to resurge always implies a previous state of civic plenitude in which Cubans also do not believe. One is not dealing with the fact that Cubans hate their present or their future, but that they also hate their past, which leaves them no space to get down on their knees and support the colossal effort of binding up the wounds and trying to rebuild the nation.

Numerous countries throughout history—Japan, Germany, Spain Italy— have overcome terrible political catastrophes, but they always relied on a legendary Golden Age, with a happy Arcadia that could serve as a reference point in the search for utopia. Every country needs to be nourished with this healthy mythology in order to trace its historic course. Castroism has deprived Cubans of this vital resource.

Cuban Sovietization

It all began with the film *The Battleship Potemkin*. (This is not a figment of my imagination, it always begins with *The Battleship Potemkin*.) The expressionist classic of Russian cinematography is something like a cultural spearhead. Afterward, the other bulwarks come: the Bolshoi, the folkloric ballets, massive editions of *Ten Days That Shook the World,* a Soviet scientific exhibit, etc. Up to this point, there are no objections. A country enriches itself with this type of cultural mission. Cuba needed to hybridize its experiences with others that were not North American. It needed other influences to reinforce the enormous specific weight of the Yankees. No objections. But Cuba, in spite of everything, is a parcel of the Spanish Caribbean, assigned to the region's history, to the American context, and to the Iberian truck. To the most famous of Castro's works, *History Will Absolve Me,* a witty Cuban journalist added a phrase, partly melancholic, partly humorous: "Yes, but geography condemns you." Geography condemns us all: the Yankees in Southeast Asia, the British in the Middle East, the French in Africa. When the time comes it will condemn the Chinese in Albania and the Russians in Cuba. Ninety percent of the Russians are not very sure where Cuba is. Ninety percent of the Cubans do not know if Minsk is a Russian city or a fur that the bourgeoisie used to wear. This radical and pervasive lack of knowledge is amply justified due to the total lack of contact between both portions of the world. There are no ties. The revolution, in spite of geographical obstacles, wants to create them immediately. In one decade, Communist mythology Soviet style, with its military parades, the enormous pictures of Lenin, Marx, Brezhnev, its heroes, its cosmonauts, and its history, has surprised the startled eyes of the Cubans. What epithets would a leader from the West receive if he were to have his troops march before equivalent pictures? In Cuba there is a veritable bombardment of "Oriental" culture. The Soviet Union is something like the new adoptive Motherland; the Eastern European countries seem to be the new neighbors. In Cuba, they talk and write about North Korea as if it were next to the Isle of Pines. The leaders of Ulan Bator—capital of Mongolia (the explanation is for the 98 percent of the readers who need it)—are received in Havana with full honors; while the magazines deal with the country as if they were writing about Venezuela. There is a variation or madness in that eagerness to forget the cultural and historic surroundings of the island. Insane and alienating. Alienating because, with an obvious servility, the Russian mise-en-scéne is being copied.

The sad spectacle of the forties, in which the world saw Bolivian and Peruvian soldiers march "with a nazi goose step," is now taking place in Cuba—Soviet style. Cuba, a tropical and mulatto Caribbean island, that does not have the slightest point in common with the Slavic culture and tradition—. there are other ingredients, but I am simplifying—wants to be confused with Eastern Europe. If this is not alienating, let Marx come down and be my witness.

There are two factors that have sent the revolution down the road: first, imitation; second, the desire to erase from Cuban memory all traces of their previous sociocultural surroundings. When the United States is mentioned, it is done only to talk about its gangsters or its crimes in Vietnam. When Latin America is mentioned, it is to point out the progress made by pro-Castro groups. The rest is ignored and substituted with mysterious Polish and Bulgarian stories.

The reaction of the average Cuban is some "wonderment" in the Brechtian sense of the word. The spectacle is there, and he sees it and they tell him about it, but he is unable to awaken his emotions. What is being exhibited is a cold drama, logarithmic, cerebral, and he could care less. He ends up calling Valentina Tereskova "tres escobas" (three brooms) and making fun of the strange name.

The disconcerting experience to a peasant from Sierra Maestra, when faced with the story of Lithuanian work heroes, is something that out of elemental pity the regime should spare him. The bizarre nonsense is similar to that of the primitive natives of a village in Oceania applauding the queen of England—who has nothing to do with their paleolithic circumstances—but were it possible to imagine the situation, the Cuban circumstances are even more grotesque.

Who are the directors of this absurd montage? Is the pastiche something that Moscow demands or that Havana offers? A little of both. Havana inelegantly gesticulates to show its respect ("body language" at an international level). Moscow, for its part, is a demanding metropolis, jealous of its hierarchy. Its importance, besides, is gauged within the Communist world by the position and size of its pictures in parades, by the square centimeters of fawning press notes, and through other fastidious signals. Havana plays its game, like Germany, Czechoslovakia, or Poland. The game, of course, is not reciprocal. Brezhnev did not go around with a straw hat, nor does *Pravda* devote itself to telling the Russians everything that happens in its strange Antillean appendix. Cuba is the one that takes up the ways of the East, leaping, like an Olympic broad-jump champion, 15,000 km of real, cultural, and historical distance.

In this sense, the superstition of the international proletariat operates, but since they are going to organize Communist dictatorships anyway, respect for the cultural and historical entity of the island would have been less a delusion and more dignifying, because Soviet decor clashes with Caribbean aesthetics. All those posters, those parades, those muscular and indefatigable heroes are very expressionist, very much á la battleship *Potemkin*. To take upon oneself in one swallow all of Eastern Europe is to incur in a political "pastiche." Cuban leadership does not have (and apparently does not want) a way to disengage itself from the Sovietization in which it has involved the country without being accused of anti-Sovietism, but it is evident that of all the aggressions which common sense has suffered through these hazardous and raving years, this is one of the greatest. Let the reader imagine that tomorrow his country subscribes to a revolutionary formula of New Zealand origin, tradition and environment. Suppose that, starting tomorrow, the movie theaters, the press and the radio begin to give you, in a massive way, epic information about that remote universe. You would be left stupified. This word, of course, has the same root as "stupid" and "stupefacient."

An Asynchronic Country

Although I have determined not to use the past as reference when judging the revolution per se, in the here and now, once in a while a flashback is unavoidable. In 1959, Cuba's urban centers lived synchronized to the West's temporal system. Science, technology, aesthetic currents, literary fashions, other fashions, and music, arrived at the island rather rapidly. At times—very few—as in the case of music, Cuba contributed in addition to receiving. U.S. proximity and Cuba's porous nature were responsible for this phenomenon, but it was not any different in the nineteenth century. In his memoirs, the Italo-Cuban Orestes Ferrara tells of his surprise at finding in the Cuban jungle, during the struggle against Spain, a series of native Cubans who were perfectly familiar with the latest European books. Kant's first translator was a Cuban, for example. Rarities of an insane nature.

Cuba, then, was attuned to a Western "time flow." The fact that I am only referring to Cubans in Havana, Matanzas, Camagüey, or Santiago, does not escape me, as the peasants in Sierra Maestra lived in the eighteenth century, but these differences are to be found over 95 percent of the planet. Those acquainted with Moscow and Outer Mongolian villages know of these things. Trotsky, in his prime, wrote lucid pages that dealt at length with the contradictions between time and space. Cultural time does not exist in societies that do not change—the Bushmen—and it elapses slowly among groups that hardly change habits and lifestyles (the peasants in Cuba or in the Caucasus). Nevertheless, the United States is judged by using New York as an example and not the Apache Indians, more or less as twentieth-century man is judged by using the example of a man in Brussels and not his anachronistic contemporary.

All this verbiage—essential if we are going to understand each other—was expounded to emphatically state that the revolutionary whiplash has disconnected Cuba from its temporal system. The country lives semiparalyzed in the magic date of 1959. The invariable revolutionary mythology, the same faces, the same men, the same ideas, follow each other as in a short story written by Borges. Circular time covers the island like a pneumatic bell. I am not engaging in a literary exercise, but describing a real phenomenon. The Cubans never heard of the formidable and decisive antiauthoritarian currents of the sixties. Any residue of a positive nature that might be left in the West by the jolting hippie movement, with its demythologizing of hierarchies, order, and obedience, was zealously hidden. The significance of the French May of 1968—the last *ratio,* not the loud confusion of the barricades—is a remote event to Cubans. The relevant ideas, the knots of tension, the latest poetry, the latest movies, the latest plays, the latest literature that did not fit within Marxist rhetoric, the antipsychiatric movement, the militant feminist movement, the changes that liberated sexual behavior—sex resigned from the realm of ethics during these prodigious years—Marcuse, Watts, Goodman, Fromm, the renaissance of a certain vague religiosity. Eastern spirituality, yoga, the rediscovery of Nietzsche, Zen Buddhism, the analysis of the subculture, the counterculture, underground movies, underground literature, pornography, hallucinogenics—all that is trivial, stupid, profound, noxious, or beneficial that shapes our time has been missed by the Cuban people. The revolutionary leadership, that genial cast of supermen, has taken upon itself the task of covering up the cracks. Let no one find out anything, not even a newspaper line; stop the entry of books or records that might corrupt. Do not permit youth to deviate from Marxism-Leninism's sacred ways. To the abusive, unjust, and stupid material blockade imposed by the United States, the Cuban hierarchy has superimposed a—similarly qualifiable—spiritual blockade. They know and define what is convenient for Cubans, they decide what is good or bad, they protect the fragile neurons of the poor natives, feeble creatures incapable of value judgments.

The result of this monstrous isolation—Cuba, in spite of everything, is located in the heart of the Americas—is a disagreeable anachronistic feeling. They know that the world that surrounds the island advances at a dizzy and different time, pushed, it is true, by the United States and Western Europe, but that does not change things. Cubans are suffocating under the foolish jargon of Marxist-Leninist slang, caught among the dogmas, the prohibitions, and the theological fears of the new scholasticism. They live in a cultural time that does not belong to them nor to their geography and tradition. That pained expression, like that of a frightened child, that the Cuban émigré shows while looking at a pocket calculator, or his amazement at the brilliant ideas of Szasz, Laing, or Erving Goffman, or the silly horror he experiences before the eroticism of an avant-garde magazine, reflects his ostrich-like past in the Caribbean. He will have to reinsert himself into his time zone, "return to the world," as the cloistered nuns do when they leave the convent. He has to get on H.G. Wells's vehicle in order to fly through one of the modern world's most decisive times and reach the present, a trip that is not always successful, as man's coexistence with his time should be a natural and spontaneous process. The claustral Cubans left on the island will not even have that opportunity, unless what happened in Prague during its painfully aborted spring occurs again and someone opens the window so that fresh air blows the ghosts away.

The Shrinking of the Environment

To understand each other we will have to agree on a working hypothesis. Let us accept—it is not so arbitrary—that a measure of progress is the vital space potentially within our reach. I am referring to the prosaic possibility of displacing myself in space from the point where I am now to another freely chosen. Let us accept that the beast of burden, the wheel, the ship, the self-propelled vehicle, the plane, and the spaceship are successive milestones in human progress. Let us accept—and we are getting to the point—that insofar as man makes use of those discoveries he *enjoys* progress. It seems evident that an Englishman who spends a week in the Balearic islands or a Canadian who travels in his car to Orlando, Florida, is *exercising* progress, he is *making use of it,* much more so than a villager of the Hurdes, culturally self-confined within the perimeter of his village. There is an admiring phrase used to qualify certain people with high mobility: the "Jet Set." For the time being this summarizes the idea.

And what does space have to do with the Cuban Revolution? A great deal. A certain type of airtight dictatorship produces a type of moral suffocation. These are not just words. Why the mad stampede of Cubans toward boats, planes, lifesavers, or rustic rafts that will take them away from Cuba? For many reasons. Here is one of them: because they are suffocating and one of the causes of the suffocation is the limitation of their movement in space. The sudden shrinkage of his vital confines has produced in the Cuban a strange discomfort. The revolution, for economic reasons and its simplistic nature, has suddenly reduced the Cubans' capacity for movement. It is not possible, for example, to move freely from one province to another, and the disastrous transportation system makes the simplest trip a calamitous operation. This is a very serious problem in Havana, where some 20 percent of the country's population lives, and where, by the way, there used to be more generous movement habits. Obviously, I am not complaining about transportation. That can be more or less deficient—in Cuba it is tremendously deficient. I am referring to the claustrophobic horror of a space-age urbanite who knows that his life will softly pass between the metaphysical walls of the two blocks separating his home from his work. He knows that his itinerant autonomy has nothing to do with that of his fellow men in Caracas, San Juan, or Madrid, since the revolution—incapable of conceiving that people have certain needs not described in *Das Kapital*—has confined him to a tiny grazing field in which he can hardly stretch his legs.

The term *parochialization* will have to be added to describe the phenomenon that has taken over the Cubans. It exists and it is terrible: a form of suffocation.

These are not all the hidden evils of Castroism, but they are probably the worst because they are a crime against the very essence of the Cuban nation. Cuba is very sick. That society is thoroughly rotten and it is better to take this into account before formulating any political project. To start with, the urgent measures of any group that plans to replace Castroism must be oriented toward the restoration of the social spirit of the Cubans. It is absolutely impossible to create a livable urban space if the revitalization of civic consciousness and the return of that poor people to a certain degree of hope in their collective destiny are not produced first. It is not only a question of substituting the inefficiency of planned centralization by the agility of the capitalist model, nor of eliminating the repressive mechanisms created by Communism and of substituting them by the state of middle-class and democratic law—which is necessary—but of the titanic and much more difficult task of building a civilized and reasonably cooperative people out of a frightened mass of incredulous and cynical citizens. The only cohesive factor that Castro has left in force is fear of the state, and the only thing inspiring obedience in the country is the dread of repressive forces, in other words, exactly the elements that make the system hateful, exactly the elements that have to be erased from the face of that society if one day the difficult enterprise of living in freedom and without the contorsions of anger is attempted.

Appendix

The Battleship Potemkin. A warship of the Czar's Imperial Russian Navy stationed in the Black Sea. Her crew mutinied in 1905 in protest against the bad quality of the food. This premonitory incident inspired the film of the same name by Soviet director Sergei M. Eisenstein.

Jorge Luis Borges (1899–1987). Argentine poet, writer of "fictions," and essayist who through the literature of fantasy has ·exercised much influence throughout the entire Western hemisphere. He was also an excellent translator of works from English. In 1980, when almost completely blind, he traveled to Spain with his wife, Maria Dodama, to receive the Cervantes prize. He died in Switzerland.

Orestes Ferrara (1876–1972). A politician, essayist, and army officer of Italian origin who, along with other foreigners, fought in the 1895–98 war of independence against Spain. He reached the rank of colonel. He was ambassador of Cuba to Washington and minister of foreign affairs during the Machado dictatorship. His mansion, La Dolce Dimora, built in high renaissance style on University Hill, now houses Havana's Napoleonic Museum.

"History Will Absolve Me." A text taken from Fidel Castro's defense speech during his trial after he was made prisoner following the unsuccessful attack on the Moncada barracks in 1953. The defense speech, written by Castro himself, contains a summary of the reformist political program he then proposed.

Hurdes. A mountainous area west of Madrid.

In the Brechtian Sense of the Expression. The German playwright Bertolt Brecht (1898–1956) argued that in the West the theatre had, since the days of Aristotle, sought to involve emotionally the public in what was taking place on stage, thus bringing about a suspension of judgment. To counter this, he proposed a theatrical method that would hamper such emotional involvement so the spectator could apply his intellect to what he saw and heard. He called this the "alienation effect."

Pravda. The official Soviet daily whose name means "truth" in Russian. Its task is to relay to the Soviet people the directives of the Politburo and the Central Committee.

Valentina Tereskova. Soviet woman who was the first female cosmonaut. She was given a lavish welcome on her visit to Cuba. The wordplay "Tereskova-tres escobas" (three brooms) is impossible to translate.

The Time Machine. The novel by H.G. Wells, the well-known author of *The War of the Worlds.*

8

Freedom and Repression

Freedom

Let us not make faces. We are going to talk about freedom using the smallest possible amount of rhetoric. Traditionally the word has been a refuge for rogues and demagogues. For example, Sepúlveda the priest even invoked freedom to justify Black slavery. The Right always plays semantic juggling games with "freedom" and "licentiousness," and ends up abolishing both. The Communists know how to use an obscene language with which they establish nuances between *formal* and *real* freedom. The formal ones are not worth anything: freedom of expression, freedom to set up political parties and organize parliaments, freedom to question the state or dogmas in force. These liberties of bourgeois democracies are the *formal* ones, the ones that are not good. The *real* ones, by the way, are never clearly defined. They have something to do with proletarian dignity, but exactly what that is has remained nebulous and rhetorical. In Cuba there are no formal liberties. I do not think that any sane person would question the veracity of this statement. The regime does not believe in liberties. Let the bourgeois democracies worry about them. But neither—we shall accept the Leninist nomenclature—are there any of the other kind. There are no *real* freedoms.

Let us leave aside freedom of the press—the first that comes to mind—the freedom to organize political parties or to oppose the system, to organize strikes, etc. None of that is necessary in the worker's fatherland. Let us not touch them. They are abstractions. Let us examine the rabidly real freedoms. There is no freedom of movement because the state rigorously regulates the international movement of persons; there is none because emigration is possible only under painful and exceptional circumstances. There is no vocational freedom because higher education is a privilege for those who are integrated into the system. There is no freedom to change jobs because the state, the only employer, decides where and for how long a person is going to work; one cannot voluntarily stop working, as idleness is a punishable crime. The person who does not work does not eat and goes to jail. The citizens of the island cannot move about freely from one city to another, because the state—the only institution with the power to do this—would not give them a place to live, unless the transfer had been ordered by the state. A Cuban cannot decide how he is going to dress or eat, because economic imperatives have dictated three successive five-year rationing plans. He cannot choose his friends, because any relationship with "nonintegrated" citizens makes him guilty of the worst suspicions. He cannot choose and practice a religious belief without that "atavism" automatically stopping him from ascending within the economic and social Communist structure until he reaches his legitimate potential level. If he gets married, he cannot establish a new home, because there are no available dwellings, and there are none, because the state, without consulting him, has drawn a scale of priorities, and everybody knows that apartments are not a productive investment, which is why the construction of housing is invariably postponed in socialist economies. The right to intimacy, the freedom to set up an independent family nucleus, is limited in practice by the lack of dwellings. The same thing happens if you want to get a divorce. Painfully, the couple postpones its marriage or separation, until an independent roof will permit them to exercise freedom to decide whether they want to throw flowers or any other object at each other. What more *real* nonexistent freedoms could be asked for?

If the citizens of the "first free territory of the Americas" cannot freely choose, without any adverse consequences, their jobs, their dwellings and neighborhoods, their friends, their studies, and the studies they would like their children to pursue, the dates of their weddings or separations, their religions, their government, their political affiliations, the books they read; if they are not even allowed to emigrate with only what they have on, can anybody tell me where their freedom is to be found? Which, for heavens' sake, are the liberties that they now enjoy? The freedom to have an obligatory job, medical attention, a certain amount of clothing and food? Those are not freedoms, and let us not confuse the issue. Medicine, food, clothing, and education are the just rewards of work—that is all; the salary generated by certain effort. Freedom always entails a series of personal decisions. To assume a position and risk making decisions which directly concern you is to be free. The more decisions you may make, the freer you are. The person who, within the limits of his particular circumstances, can move wherever he wants is free. The person who rejects is free. The citizen forced to obey is *not* free. Perhaps he is happy to comply—that is another matter—but he is not free. Erich Fromm, in his book *Escape from Freedom*, effectively describes the phenomenon of the man who prefers to have his life set up for him rather than to run the risk of deciding each step of his life; that trembling animal who prefers to be assigned a job, some food, a roof, a time schedule, a life standard, rather than to make decisions that might jeopardize his small world; that poor and respectful animal ready to repay with blind obedience the security which is offered him, more or less like the domesticated dog that suffers the master's discipline in order to have its piece of meat. What doubt is there that those peculiar souls have been benefited by the revolution? But is all the authoritarian machinery justified because it takes care of the timorous and the destitute? Was it not possible to create a politico-economic structure permitting the practice of formal and real freedoms, which at the same time would have guaranteed, with a minimum of decorum, the material needs of its citizens without autonomic urgencies? Such states do exist, with a thousand imperfections. Countries in which you do not go to jail for publishing or reading a newspaper, and where the most wretched citizen has access to food, schooling, hospitalization. Communities full of structural defects, but in which people do not meekly live out their destinies, but shape them according to personal decisions. Things like that are impossible in Cuba. What is not prohibited is obligatory. Life comes in a prepared package.

Fear and Dissimulation

One always fears the state, and rightly so. It is the only plunderer authorized to kill us with one blow, to seat us in the electric chair, and to put us in a cell for the rest of our lives. It can do horrible things to us. There are very valid reasons for being afraid of facing a policeman, a judge, or the penal code. I, "who have never done anything wrong," confess my fears in front of a simple night watchman or a forest ranger, in front of anyone carrying a nightstick. Possibly, because they are capable of doing "something" to me.

The state—which is always an order, a few hierarchies, laws—maintains itself intact in all latitudes through the quota of fear distributed among its citizens. Respect for the law is nothing but a certain unpleasant pressure. The existence of official terror is probably unavoidable. I am not arguing that point. Utopias are always the foolishness of passé theorists. But there is no doubt that the smaller the quantity and density of fear, the more breathable the state's atmosphere will be. Totalitarian Marxism is not unbearable because there is no private property—who cares about that!—but because there is a lot of fear. Too much fear. The pressure is constant, could sweats are endless. In Cuba, where the revolution is young—not so much now—the government feels unsure. Due to its insecurity it kills and incarcerates more than it should. Castro and his team could permit themselves the luxury of a Cuban Sakharov or Solzhenitsyn, as the Russians do, but at the sign of the least dissident move, they overreact. They are obnoxious. No one familiar with the Cuban scene could conceive that in Cuba one of those unaccustomed protest spectacles that take place in the Soviet Union could take place. Cuban terror is far superior to the Soviet version. Fear, therefore, is more abundant. Who is afraid and why? First those who are not integrated into the government are afraid, the millions of men and women who do not sympathize with the revolution. They are afraid that they might be accused of counterrevolutionary activities, of undermining the production process, of propagating rumors, of listening to the Voice of America, of crimes against the state (?), of overstocking food supplies, of absenteeism, of vagrancy, of bourgeois habits and mentality (?), of wanting to leave the country illegally, of disabling a public telephone, or of celebrating Che Guevara's death (the latter cost a 24-year-old-man named Mateo Gavilán Cifuentes a 10-year prison sentence). They are afraid of the indiscretion of a small son in school who might tell how his parents feel about the government. They are afraid of receiving a compromising letter from abroad, they are afraid of attending religious services, or baptizing their children, or letting the government see their noncommunist nature. They are afraid—this is one of the most constant fears—of being in a place where a counterrevolutionary deed might take place, or a simple and fortuitous fire of unknown nature, and of ending up in jail because the government might be convinced that they were guilty. They are afraid to talk, and even to listen, because not to denounce someone who opposes the regime is as much as being a member of the opposition. They are afraid of irritating the man or woman in charge of the Committee for the Defense of the Revolution on their street, since, in the best of cases, he/she could make their life impossible. They are afraid of being happy and for that to be considered a sign of arrogance, or being sad and for that to be thought of as a manifestation of their displeasure. They end up being afraid of lights, of noises, like rats, because, like rats, they are always in danger of being killed by someone who relentlessly tramples on them.

Those who have become integrated, the ones who are with the system, are also afraid. They fear not making their militancy quite evident, not hanging enough pictures of Fidel or not quoting Marx as frequently as they should. They are afraid of losing the preponderance which they have won by their adhesion to the regime, they fear that some doubt—because surely they are not so stupid that they never doubt—might show through in their faces. They fear that something abnormal might happen within the perimeter of their responsibility, and that they might be accused of lowering their guard before the enemies of the revolution. They fear maintaining affective ties—which are strictly prohibited—with counterrevolutionary relatives, and they fear getting close, on a purely human level, to someone who cannot offer proof of his contributions to the revolutionary process. Besides, partisans have over their heads Damocles' machete of revolutionary goals and production quotas. They fear that it might not rain; they fear not being able to fulfill their assigned production quotas; they fear all the pressure the government applies trying to raise production. That partisan fear operates in inverse relation to the position they hold. The less important you are within the system, the more fear you have, and therefore, the more vociferous you are in order to show your political devotion.

As to the opposition—when I say "opposition," I am exaggerating; no one can really oppose anything—fear does not permit the opposition to multiply. From top to bottom, everyone is in the same situation. I am not talking about metaphysical fear, but the very disagreeable physiological symptoms which start with sweaty hands and end up with lack of bladder control: to know that your physical integrity or your family's future is in the hands of a neighbor's capriciousness or ill will. Cuban psychiatrists and psychologists have discovered, for a number of years now, an immoderate increase in nervous disorders—the only type of disorders permitted by the government. The disorders have a clearly identifiable origin: People are constantly being watched and persecuted. The weaker ones end up distorting and magnifying these police-state extremes, but in the first place their feelings of persecution were correct.

Fear's counterpart is slippery: dissimulation. Cuba is today a country of dissimulators. Everybody—except in acute cases of irresponsibility—dissimulates things. You pretend you do not see "compromising" people. You pretend to be satisfied and happy with the system, with your immediate superior. You pretend to be grateful for your small food quota, or for your voluntary work. The members of the hierarchy, who are not dumb, know that the absence of public censure or opposition *has* to be false—totalitarianism thrives in appearances, not essences. What interests them is to be able to display a photograph in *Granma* or in *Bohemia* of a one-armed worker who, while singing the national anthem, cut 25,000 pounds of sugarcane in one day. For people to complain to themselves does not bother the revolutionary leadership. Perhaps one of the ugliest consequences of the police state is the massive castration of the Cuban people. That country of obedient and solicitous marionettes used to be a land of proud and rebellious people until fear ate their guts away. The painful spectacle of a recently arrived Cuban exile, with his reflexes still conditioned by repression, who talks with a quiet voice and looks everywhere before criticizing, is a devastating indictment of the revolution. That recently-arrived person will have to learn that going around wearing a mask can become very painful. He will have to remember that it is legitimate to complain, to protest, to oppose, to give one's own opinions, to rebel and display any attitude emphasizing individual autonomy. He will have to forget the fearful days and nights.

Good Sex

Sex is not a middle-of-the-road issue. In bourgeois societies it remains on the Left; in Communist ones, on the Right. Let me explain. Those Marxists living in Paris or New York tend to be very liberal. They applaud Andy Warhol, read *Playboy*, and sympathize with the most promiscuous communal experiments. Marxists living in Havana, East Berlin, and Moscow, however, are very busily engaged in persecuting pornography, that decadent bourgeois vice. They are decidely monogamous, serious-looking, resolutely heterosexual, and prudish—real prodigies of Judeo-Christian morality.

Wilheim Reich has lucidly explained the role played by sexual repression in fascist societies. It is important that a sociologist of his stature do the same with Communist societies. Cuba, in particular, demands the effort. The Calvi(Commu)nist sect that has imposed itself on Cuba has borne a repressive lineage inherited partly through ideology and partly through tradition. There are myriad contradictions, but suffice it to say, for now, that sex is a subject that makes the Cuban government uneasy. It is certainly a touchy matter. From the beginning the state has always tried to regulate sexual behavior. Only now with Marcuse, Fromm, and other Marxist heretics—banned like demons in the Communist world because they proclaim a nonrepressive communism—has the list of prescriptions and proscriptions formulated by the state regarding sexual matters begun to shorten. The West moves toward less rigid positions, in the direction of tolerance. Sex, little by little, is disappearing from ethics. Every day, those activities undertaken south of the waistline are becoming less important to the state.

In Cuba, the virile and chivalrous Communist caste marches in countercurrent. First, a colossal drama was made of prostitution. There was prostitution in Cuba just like there is prostitution in Spain, France, Japan, or Mexico; one of the arguments often brought forth to justify the revolution (the other kind, surely, cannot be eradicated). This is as insane as tearing down half of Spain to eliminate the "costa Fleming" in Madrid, or taking over Paris to close down the Moulin Rouge. Certainly, prostitution is a social calamity, especially for its degrading effects on the participants and furthermore for nurturing a parasitic mafia. But prostitution is no worse than alcoholism and undoubtedly better than government repression. What happened to Cuba was the accession to power of a profoundly repressive sexual system directed by a sleepless team of Communists with bourgeois mentality.

After closing the brothels—something quite different from eliminating prostitution—the government closed down the *posadas* (discreet motels for furtive couples). Despite Lenin, lovers keep having intercourse, but now in dark parks, in hidden squares, in cars. The government became frightened and allowed the reopening of a few *posadas*. Lines of anguished and anxious couples soon crowded the entrances. Numbers were distributed. "Couple number 18 may now come in. Couple number 18, please." The confused lovers would rush in nervously. If they would come out shortly, the waiting line would applaud; otherwise, they would be hooted. When the scarcity of *posadas* began, as early as 1962, couples had to bring with them not only money, but also linens and soap. Adulterous or simply shy women took heroic measures: They wore caps and hoods made out of newspaper for their heads and shoulders to protect their endangered honor. What happens to kitsch has happened to the Cuban revolutionary process: Seen from outside, it seems smooth; but as soon as one comes near, the wrinkles appear. Whoever has seen in the line outside City Hall—the other City Hall—a lady disguising her identity with an eight-column newspaper headline blaring "A People United Shall Never Be Conquered" knows what I am talking about. In any case it is a miracle that sexual intercourse has not disappeared from the repertoire of Cuban customs—a miracle.

After the battle against prostitution and the *posadas*, the Bosque de La Habana (Havana Woods) was declared an area of tolerance in matters of copulation. Progress. After all it is better to fight mosquitoes than to wait in line. Later the government began hunting for common-law couples in order to marry them, a manifestation of a limited bourgeois mentality. Jubilant collective weddings were celebrated during which couples who had lived together for thirty years and who had children, grandchildren, gray hair, or no hair, were married. They signed documents and exchanged rings. Terrific. Engels must have turned over in his grave.

In matters of adultery, the party works like a kind of lay tribunal of the Inquisition. Years ago there was a famous public trial (public, of course, for the party leadership) dealing with a commonplace and vulgar love triangle involving a lady (Edith García Buchaca), a deceived gentlemen (Carlos Rafael Rodríguez), and a fiery lover (Joaquín Ordoqui, better known as "Cross-eyed"). The problem is that Communists do not go around doing such naughty things, and when they do, Rome burns. It was a prolonged and much-talked-about trial. Guillén, Blas Roca, Lázaro Peña, Escalante; they all occupied the witness stand. There were rebukes and moral sanctions. During the Castro regime, similar conflicts, but at lower levels, have been frequent. There is no worse offense a woman can inflict on the revolution than go to bed with another man while her husband is standing guard. It is bad enough if she deceives her husband for a revolutionary, but, oh, for a counterrevolutionary! She is to expect an immediate trial before the People's Tribunal, followed by strong sanctions. The revolution zealously protects the honor of Communists.

Despite the aforementioned situations, described with a certain humor because I do not believe one can talk solemnly about the funny side of things, the revolution has abstained from condemning or repressing sexual relations among young single males and females. It is even possible that such relations are more frequent today. So at least statistically, the revolution has contributed to the liberalization of sex, though still restricted compared to the situation in Western Europe, North America, and even Eastern Europe. Abortion, forbidden in the old Cuba although tolerated sotto voce, is today free, public, and available to any woman whether married or single. The same may be said of contraceptives (specifically the intrauterine device). New divorce laws have made the dissolution of marriage a simple procedure, so that divorce is now very common in Cuba.

How does one explain this strange behavior of the revolution that represses and liberalizes? The explanation is the same that lurks behind all the contradictions in the system. The Communists have built an ideal world according to the mythology of their sacred books. Such texts postulate the orthodox thoughts of the sect, and anything that does not agree with the given set of concepts is heretic and revisionist. Anything that is heretic and revisionist must be repressed so that behavior will keep up with dogma and so that practice, even if through force, will follow theory.

Accordingly, Cuban Communists conceive of sexual relations as the encounter of a mature heterosexual couple preferably with "serious" intentions—not adulterous, and discreet. Any extreme aberration from this scheme is counterrevolutionary. A Communist lady must be neither promiscuous nor lesbian. A Communist gentlemen must be neither homosexual nor a Don Juan. A revolutionary must not give himself to the pleasures of the dolce vita. There are tacit and explicit laws that condemn such behavior. Commander Ameijeiras, a veteran of the Moncada attack, a member of the *Granma* expedition, and a hero of the Bay of Pigs, is today a fourth-rate employee because he transgressed the rules. The same things have happened to journalists Kuchilán and de la Osa, as well as to dozens of other "impure" Cubans.

Bad Sex

It is an anatomical problem. In Cuba, homosexuality used to be an anal fixation. Today it is a headache: rarities of the socialist world. The reasons have been briefly explained in the preceding chapter. The revolution keeps a kind of *Manual for the Perfect Communist* from which emerges a vigorous, handsome, hard-working, patriotic, selfless, heterosexual, monogamous, and austere laborer—the marvelous new man fabricated by Doctor Castrostein. Bravo.

Certain prohibitions extracted from Judeo-Christian tradition are inscribed into the morals of this paradigmatic member of the species. One of these prohibitions is homosexuality. It seems that a good Marxist, in addition to mastering *Das Kapital*, must exhibit an impeccable endocrine system. One belongs to the party body and soul. The body includes, of course, the genitals and the anus. These comrades are fussy indeed. The Cuban Revolution is covered by a layer of hairy machismo.

Nothing makes the "great macho" more nervous than the proximity of a sexually ambiguous creature. It is as if he were afraid of being contaminated. When the "great macho" becomes leader of a revolutionary political enterprise, attitudes distant from his own pattern of behavior will be labeled "counterrevolutionary," especially homosexual behavior, so diametrically opposed to male chauvinism. It is not known exactly who began what has been called in black humor "the hunt of gays." The hormonal McCarthy of the regime is Fidel Castro himself; but Raúl, Blas Roca, Ramiro Valdés, and other big wheels have encouraged the persecution.

In 1965 purges began at the universities. Hundreds of students were accused of homosexuality and were expelled. In certain schools, e.g., literature and medicine, repression was implacable. The Communist Youth and University Student Federation directed the campaign. The accusations were incredible: "He writes weird poems," "He combs his hair in such and such a style," "The two of them always hang around together." Young men and women, at times innocent of such accusations, were expelled solely on the grounds of the biased criteria of the Leninist tribe. In certain areas of Havana, specifically in the streets known as "La Rampa," groups of adolescents, homosexuals and heterosexuals, used to gather and share their taste for rock music, poetry, art, and other features common to Western youth: tight clothes, long hair, a certain untidiness. Given macho paranoia, all this was counterrevolutionary and therefore punishable. In great haste the criminal expression known as the "social blemish" was created and camps of forced labor were instituted with all speed to "correct" such deviations, the infamous UMAP. Verbal and physical mistreatment, shaved heads, work from dawn to dusk, hammocks, dirt floors, scarce food—those were the decorations at UMAP (innocent initials of a name which leaves much unsaid—Military Units for the Support of Production). The camps grew increasingly crowded as the methods of arrest became more expedient. At "La Rampa" armed soldiers detained all youths, males and females, whom they fancied weird, then transported them to prison in buses stationed nearby.

Later, at State Security, the feared political police, a cruel spectacle, halfway between Torquemada and Beria, began. On one side the theological language of "guilt expiation," and on the other the political language of "betraying the Revolution by adopting bourgeois habits." The detainees were often young Commnists who were struck with the realization that the sexual expression and the ideology they had chosen were incompatible.

Nobody was safe from sexual espionage. The beach house of veteran Communist Mirta Aguirre was searched following an order of the Director of Culture. They were looking for proof of her deviant behavior. Alfredo

Guevara, director of the Film Institute, came under suspicion and was almost fired. He was saved by his personal ties with Fidel and Raúl Castro that went back to their days at the university. He was asked, however, to "clean" ICAIC of homosexuals and lesbians, and to adopt a discreet behavior because the revolution would be inflexible in matter of morality.

Although any single one of these outrages would merit condemnation, one must keep in mind that the homosexual population is usually estimated to be 2 to 10 percent of the adult census. Consequently this persecution terrorized hundreds of thousands of Cubans. The reactions of these men and women, harassed by the state, were varied. Among actors and actresses a protest came close to being formalized. It was never made public, although Raquel Revuelta, one of Cuba's greatest actresses (known since then as "Our Lady of the Gays"), tried repeatedly and unsuccessfully to take the issue before the government. In the circle of artists and writers, arrests and humiliations were multiple. Virgilio Piñera. Lezama Lima, Ballagas, Antón Arrufat, José Mario, Ana María Simo, Rodríguez Feo, and dozens of other poets and writers ended up in jail, some just for a few hours "to scare them"— something achieved to perfection—others for months, and still others even years. In some cases, oftentimes "unjustly" (e.g. Ana María Simo), electroshocks, in addition to threats and seclusion, were used.

Panic spread among homosexuals. Marriages of convenience were made to obscure realities, for the government was not searching for realities—it never does—but for appearances. It wanted virile men with short hair, wide pants, and unequivocal *guayaberas* (typical Cuban shirts), even if behind that appearance was hiding an effeminate creature. The important thing is to preserve the image of the revolution. There were some cases of suicide (e.g. Calvert Casey and Acosta León). Homosexuals, besieged by party cadres in work and study centers, and even in the bosom of fanatic families, adopted humble and silent attitudes so that their sins might be forgiven. Postures of abject submission (mea culpa) were expected and accepted. They were praying that the generous revolution would grant them grace as a reward for their repentance from licentiousness. Any similarity to other models of repression is not coincidental.

At a certain moment, the Cuban Revolution—its leaders who are the ones to decide and especially the leader—had to choose between either the bad international press created by its "hunts" for homosexuals, or the inevitable presence of homosexuals. Slowly and half-heartedly convinced that the "vice" could not be done away with, they opted for closing down the UMAP camps and instead maintaining a policy that excluded homosexuals from the party, universities, teaching positions, and other important posts in general.

Today, the youths who did not adapt to the rigid framework of the revolution have timidly come back to "La Rampa." Now they are not only bothered by police, but also exhibited as rare animals. One of the main points of attraction in the propaganda tours in which the government shows its achievements to foreigners is an obligatory visit to the Coppelia ice cream parlor. There, inevitably, a virile and handsome guide points toward the *raros* (weirdos) and explains to the tourists that revolutions cannot be perfect and that they have not been able to "clean the country of those effeminate animals who are there, across the street, while the rest of the country goes on building a radiant Communist future." In the meantime, these homosexual Cubans are fourth-class citizens.

Religion: Catholicism

In Cuba, priests have not been hanged from street lamps and nuns have not been raped. The revolution has limited itself to abolishing the church's influence as an institution. Religious schools and universities were confiscated, a good number of priests and nuns expelled, religious publications, radio and television time, and other means of proselytizing were suppressed. Religious processions and holidays were eradicated from the Cuban calendar. Christmas was moved to July 26 so that there would not remain even one time in the year with a religious significance. In Cuba, Christ is born in the uproar that commemorates the Moncada attack. They welcome Him with a cannon salute. The government maintains that in spite of the official census, Cuba was not a Catholic country, or that it was so only nominally, and even then only among certain sectors of the population, something like a few rich people who went to mass. There is some truth to all of this. Cuban Catholicism, in its most popular manifestations, was never more than a naive devotion to "Cachita"— the Virgin of Charity, Cuba's patron saint—and in its aristocratic expression it did not go beyond the bejeweled mendicity of the Society for the Fight against Cancer. There was no Catholic militancy similar to that in Spain, Colombia, or Chile. The ecclesiastic hierarchy hardly influenced public opinion. Neither was there any anticlericalism or militant atheism. The church had simply been losing its power and influence. An important pastoral letter, which in other countries would have shaken the government, went unnoticed in Cuba. The church was a marginal player in the national game. During the fifties it became revitalized by a certain social sensitivity, and a change began to take place. Through the Catholic Youth Workers and the Catholic University Association, the church resumed its entry into the struggle for temporal power. Had the Batista/Castro phenomenon and the subsequent rupture of institutional order not taken place, Catholic leaders would have attained power, perhaps in the sixties. Amalio Fiallo, Angel del Cerro, José Ignacio

Rasco, and other attractive figures associated with the church were moving at high speeds toward the Presidential Palace. But the insurrection against Batista stopped them cold. The church remained marginal. This explains why, unlike what happened in Poland, Cuban Communists did not have to make a pact with the church. The church lacked the spontaneous popular support capable of bringing about a serious government crisis. It also explains the church's present accommodating attitude: either it complies or it will disappear. If it wants to remain in Cuba, although it might be only on a perfunctory basis, it has to patiently accept the government's abuses.

That is what the church has lost. But believers have also lost something. In Cuba, Catholics are not persecuted; they are simply tolerated; they are considered unavoidable calamities. The revolution sees them with ironic contempt, as the arrogant Whites contemplate the natives. The government understands that it inherited some irrational tribes—and that "the believers" cannot be eliminated. So it restrains their proliferation and lets biology take its course. After all, time is the most effective mass killer. "In twenty-five years," Raúl Castro said, "there will be fewer Catholics than manatees" (the manatee is a rare aquatic mammal that can be seen off the Cuban coasts once in a while). The difference is that in Cuba manatees are considered an endangered species; the same cannot be said for Catholics. They may not be hunted but they are harassed. No one stops a person from entering a church to pray, but such an act points him out as a potential counterrevolutionary. One cannot be a Catholic and a Communist at the same time. The Communists are sick and tired of saying this unequivocally and loudly, but there are some Catholics who stubbornly think that it is possible. The charlatan fauna preaching "liberation theology" amuses itself shamelessly with such idle pursuits. In Cuba there is a small group of prorevolution Catholics that does not play that contradictory game very amusingly. The government does not incorporate them, but uses them. On a somber scale, the Nazis, while still despising them, would use Jewish thugs to terrorize their fellow Jews in concentration camps. If a Cuban manages to be Catholic and Communist at the same time, the regime will use him. He will not be singled out and praised, but used. His position as a Communist Catholic does not authorize him to criticize the government from a Catholic point of view. His only opinion is to obey. Manuel Fernández, a serious student of relations between church and state in Cuba, has pointed out how the theology of liberation becomes a farce of obedient persons unable to find an injustice to point out or a crime to denounce. Such things, it seems, only take place in Brazil or Chile, but not in the perfect island paradise. The government's plan to let Catholicism die of consumption is beginning to pay off. Church attendance is decreasing, and the most conspicuous absence is that of young people, though it is possible that this tendency has been checked by the crisis and social tensions produced after the episode of the Peruvian Embassy and the exodus from the Port of Mariel.

Afro-Cuban Religion

With less temporal power but perhaps more popular support than the church, there existed in Cuba a religious cult of African origin, almost always syncretized with a collection of Catholic saints. Saint Barbara, Saint Lazarus, Saint Joseph, and Saint Christopher were undercover agents of African theology. As time went by, Rome discovered the trick and demanded an explanation. In one of the purges carried out by the Vatican's Sacred Congregation of the Rite, almost all the deities revered by the Cubans fell. The African tradition hid behind the Catholic façade. In some measure, Afro-Cuban religion presents more serious problems to the Cuban government than Catholicism. It was very easy to say that Catholicism was the religion of the ruling class, but it would be a flagrant lie to say the same of the Cuban people's most popular religious manifestation. Besides, if it is hard to find a Communist who tolerated Catholicism, many believed in the Afro-Cuban mythology. Lázaro Peña, the Black Communist labor leader, used to go around with a "protection" in his wallet. A "protection" is an Afro-Cuban scapulary. Forty years earlier he had subjected himself to the rites of *el santo*. This is the sect's most important religious initiation. Major Vallejo, personal physician to Fidel Castro, was a well-known member of this sect. Celia Sánchez, who was at the same time Castro's Electra, Jocasta, and alienist, when things did not go well for the government placed glasses with a "magic" amount of water in front of an image of a saint to keep the evil spirits away. Juan Almeida, one of the men closest to Fidel, had—he discreetly got rid of it—in his home an altar with the required apples in honor of Saint Barbara. Both practiced Afro-Cuban religions. This is such a touchy business that the regime prefers to ignore it. However, the work of the *santeros,* the religious fraternities, and the public rites have been considerably curtailed. The Virgin of Regla procession on September 7, and the one in honor of Saint Lazarus on December 17, are intermittently interrupted by the police so that the people will lose heart. The *toques de santo,* a religious festivity that features drums and people "possessed" by saints—Freudians would diagnose this as a type of hysteria—are *sometimes* authorized as long as they take place within the intimacy of selected homes and only after having obtained clearance from the police. Magazines do not mention these religious activities, academics ignore them, and the government trusts that time and Marxist education will end up eradicating such widely extended beliefs. For the time being, the old Communist guard has been warned. For example, Nicolás Guillén has abstained from including Afro-Cuban themes in his poetry for some time. He still rhymes "palma" with "calma," but only in books of social poetry permeated with a rabid anti-imperialistic manliness. The government hopes to bury the Afro-Cuban tradition; unnoticed, it hopes to sweep it under the rug. Its hopes are not being fulfilled.

Protestants and Other Sects

Cuban Protestants were relatively few but enjoyed great prestige. They founded highly esteemed educational institutions. Whatever Protestantism there existed before the revolution, it never became a problem. In one short meal, the regime devoured its fragile apostolic organizations and hardly a protesting voice was heard. The problem began later, when Protestants insisted on continuing their evangelical work. Dramatic differences exist between the government's attitude toward Catholic and Protestant proselytizing. In the case of Catholics, their churches are closed or the people who attend mass are morally sanctioned, and consequently they are left without the possibility of recruiting new members. Protestants go after their clients from door to door, with the Bible under their arms. Seventh-Day Adventists have been an obstinate headache for the regime—the Gideons International even more so. It is an act of courage to go around Cuba knocking on doors to spread the Gospel. And these people do it in spite of the reprimands, blows, insults, and abuse they constantly receive. In the mid-sixties they were declared "social scum" and were placed in concentration camps along with homosexuals, "deviant" writers, and other "inconveniences." The *whole* Baptist seminary ended up in one of those camps. Curiously, due to the tenacious sacrifices of these combative sects, they have won the respect and admiration of many who, under different circumstances, never would have approached them. The regime sees these groups as a refuge for counterrevolutionary elements, but it is possible that in a totalitarian state, the adversaries who cannot hide, being victims of fear and loneliness, might become members of any marginal community such as Jehovah's Witnesses. In this sect's bosom there is an atmosphere of human warmth and collective activities—the only ones in Cuba—initiated by the members' own volition and which have nothing to do with official designs. The members have assumed the mystique of the first Christians; they feel like apostles. While it is true that any form of religious militancy is a subtle form of counterrevolution, the Protestant militancy, or that of Jehovah's Witnesses, are the most dangerous. The regime has found a way to eradicate Catholicism by means of a patient siege. But it is more difficult to confront religious communities unyielding in matters of evangelization. Cuba's apostolic nuncio, Monsignor Zacci, can make fawning overtures to Castro and accept a modus vivendi that permits the Catholic

Church to languish, but the other denominations, having much less to lose, employing a different style of proselytizing, and having no central power to govern them, constitute a thornier problem for the regime.

Political Prisoners

Can a political system be judged according to the treatment it gives its political prisoners? At times it appears that the answer is affirmative: Dreyfus's France, Auschwitz's Germany, Chile's concentration camps. Regularly, the choleric Left angrily denounces these deeds, and the Right shudders. In Cuba's case, the infuriated Left has become meek and domesticated. It has looked the other way, ignoring accusations. That is fine. I suspect that in an "International Bertrand Russell Tribunal" with people like García Márquez playing the role of prosecutors, Cuban political prisoners would have been condemned for not having allowed their captors to break more of their ribs and teeth. Or they would have been asked to eat less and worse in order to help the revolution. One never knows with these leftists. They become self-righteously upset when faced with Angela Davis's plight—absolved, by the way—and chuckle indifferently when they learn that for months dozens of Cuban women, on a bread and water diet, were held in unsanitary cells. The prison? Guanajay. Some names: Miriam Ortega, Esther Campos, María Amalia Fernández, Georgina Cid, Leopoldina Grau Alsina.

Castro's prisons have been an unending inferno. *I have seen*—no one has told me, I have not read it, I have seen it with my own eyes—hundreds of naked men forced together, one against the other, in the courtyard patio of La Cabaña prison, and I have seen a guard tear open with his bayonet the flesh of an old man who, ashamed, was trying to separate his body from his naked companion's. And the jailer was doing this to amuse himself. I have seen—I swear I have seen it—a jailer shout to an elderly lady and her pregnant daughter-in-law, two women who had come to prison to visit the son and husband, a political prisoner who had been executed without the government's even bothering to notify his family: "That worm was shot by a firing squad yesterday. Tell her [the pregnant wife] to find herself another husband or to see me if she needs a man." I repeat: I swear I have seen it. Monsters also live beyond the reaches of our imagination.

Cuba needs a patient Solzhenitsyn to recount the history of the Gulag Archipelago of the Caribbean. He would narrate the overwhelming stories of La Cabaña, El Príncipe, Taco-Taco, Boniato, San Severino, Isla de Pinos— terrifying human slaughterhouses. Cuba needs a great writer, who without omitting any details would narrate how Ismael Madruga died, sleeping in the upper bunk of his cell while sergeant "Porfirio" pierced his rectum and exposed the prisoner's intestines with the sharp end of a bayonet. Someone will have to reproduce his last cry and his last horrified look. Or the slow death of the student Alfredo Carrión Obeso—my poor and great friend—killed with gun-butt blows and finished off with bullets by a uniformed assasin known as "Jagüey Grande," in the concentration camp known as Melena 2. Someday a dauntless writer will revive the pain of journalist Alfredo Izaguirre Orta, kicked a thousand and one times in his eighty-eight pound body until he was given up for dead. And he did not die that time, nor the following, nor the next. In the end, a medical doctor, more of a ruffian than a physician, said that he could not permit "that sack of tumors" to be taken again to the infirmary. Perhaps the Dostoëvski of *Memoirs from the House of the Dead* missed a character in Tony Cuesta, the blind, armless, and unbending giant sentenced to thirty years in prison and released after an intense international campaign. Or in the Spaniard Eloy Gutiérrez Menoyo, systematically beaten for months until he became deaf in one ear and one of his eyes had been gouged out. How can the Cuban Revolution explain these crimes? How can it justify the torture and mistreatment of its adversaries? What does the regime gain by crushing its defeated opponents? Fidel Castro personally ordered the Isle of Pines prison dynamited during the Bay of Pigs invasion, in the event of a catastrophe for his government. The head of the prison had orders to blow up the defenseless political prisoners. Major Julio García Olivera took care of setting up the charges. If the invasion had been successful, 10,000 heads would have rolled in one mortal second. The four circular buildings were mined with hundreds of pounds of plastic explosives. These charges were left intact for months, although in some buildings, artful prisoners were able to deactivate them through difficult digging operations.

How can the revolution explain the death of Pedro Luis Boitel, the university leader of the July 26 Movement, sentenced to forty-two years in prison? How can it explain the unjustified bullet that also killed the student Paco Pico? How can a system keep Rigoberto Perera, a man who had his two arms broken, incommunicado in his cell? How could a revolution punish the poet Armando Valladares, by condemning him to live isolated in a cell on a rickety wheelchair for almost five years until, at last, international pressure forced his release? How will Major Osmani Cienfuegos answer for the prisoners he allowed to die of suffocation in an airtight truck? There were eleven dead. They were taken out of the truck bathed in sweat and violently contracted in their search for a crack that would let them breathe.

Why this contempt towards the enemy's life and suffering? In the worst days of the Batista dictatorship, after the trial of a revolutionary, the danger would pass. Fidel Castro had books, bed covers, visitors, and food. His present adversaries—some of whom were at one time his friends, or even his saviors (I submit Yanes Pelletier and Ernesto de la Fe as examples), have received nothing but blows, hunger, and distressing hardships. Of all the abuses perpetrated by the revolution, none have been as unjustifiable as the atrocities committed in the prisons.

When there were prisoners by the thousands, the regime looked for a formula which would slowly empty the prisons: rehabilitation plans. It is an old method that never fails. It is based on the premise that the enemy is permanently neutralized if he is induced to simulate behavior contrary to his ideology. It is a macabre game in which the prisoner publicly pretends to recognize his mistakes, discovers the meaning of Marxism, and proclaims the triumphal adoption of the new faith. This method was invented by Torquemada in his treatment of Jews. Castroism only adapted it. After a time of bitter dissimulation, the political convert discovers that his dissembling has cauterized his painful wound. At the bottom of his soul he repudiates the system that has him under submission, but his knees are not a good base from which to rebel. Then this marked man is turned loose. The government congratulates itself on these successful "rehabilitations." The auto-da-fé, apparently, is not yet over.

Through the years, the government has systematically refused the request of reputable international organizations—the ones that even Duvalier has permitted to visit his country—to inspect the prisons and confirm the charges. The Cuban government has been condemned by the Human Rights Commission of the OAS, but not a single voice from the Left has seconded the accusation. The guilty silence of those who should have been the first to condemn the situation—because the Left should be something like the conscience of humanity—is an act of unforgivable moral turpitude. To censure Pinochet's crimes but to forget Castro's is a demonstration of spiritual cowardice. To censure the crimes of Stalin and keep silent about those of Castro is a proof of the worst political opportunism. It is very elegant to have one's picture in the front page of a newspaper after making a passionate defense of the Chilean political prisoners who have been tortured—a cause, of course, which is urgently just—but it is compromising to timidly inquire about the fate of those in Cuba who die at the hands of a dictatorship similar in methods but different in its goals to the one in Chile. An even more painful observation: The Left is ready to support Solzhenitsyn's accusations against the Soviet Union, but about Cuba no one will say a single word. Let the little Cubans rot and die in their prison cells! They are apparently not worth the movement of a fraternal hand. It was not fashionable to extend it. Fortunately, this situation has now changed.

In spite of this selective humanitarianism, innumerable denunciations have at last opened a breach in the sanctimonious wall of silence. Andrés Eloy Blanco, a popular Venezuelan poet, described a woman who was as beautiful "as the day the prisoners were freed." The dictators are slowly opening their dungeons. Jimmy Carter's human rights campaign was partially successful, and pressure exerted by groups such as Amnesty International and publications like *Human Rights*, edited by Frank Calzón and Elena Mederos, is being felt. Accusations made by intellectuals, politicians, and labor leaders have managed to mitigate the harsh conditions of Latin America's political prisoners.

In the case of Cuba, besides the international pressures I have mentioned above, there were other factors. On 1 January 1979, the revolution celebrated its twentieth birthday, and the Cuban ruling caste decided to commemorate the date with an unexpected announcement: "The political prisons have been emptied." This is a pitiful falsehood, but undeniably, hundreds of prisoners have been freed. Castro wants to become a benevolent dictator. He would like to be loved by his subjects. He punishes them, like a stern father, not (always) to exterminate them physically, but to correct what he considers to be their bad behavior. As a result of this brutal "disciplinary policy," during many years Castro and his revolution—more or less the same thing—have had to withstand accusations by international organizations and the requests of friendly governments, two situations which are always embarrassing. This has gravely deteriorated the revolution's image, a phenomenon which explains why *Le Matin*, the French Socialist party's newspaper, recently published an article by Edouard Manet, one of the best young French playwrights, in which he directly attacked the repressive aspects of a mythicized revolution. A few years ago, *Le Matin* would not have dared publish a similar criticism of the Cuban dictatorship. When asked in an interview about the Cuban prime minister, Jean-Paul Sartre answered: "Castro? Merely another butcher." Fidel does not want to be a butcher. He wants to be a kind autocrat, who assassinates, injures, or imprisons, only when it is strictly necessary for the people's "well-being." The only inconsistency is that apparently "the people's well-being" requires an inordinately large amount of its own blood.

The Cuban amnesty is also influenced by the urgent necessity of coming to terms with the United States—one of the preconditions Washington has established before the economic blockade is lifted and full diplomatic recognition is given to Cuba is the total excarceration of thousands of political prisoners. Castro acquiesces reluctantly, but at the same time carefully cultivates his role as an indomitable rebel, refusing to talk the issue over with the American government representatives. Instead, he chooses to turn the prisoners over to an ad hoc commission of Cuban émigrés. The reasons do not matter. The day on which the prisoners were freed did arrive, and the Cuban people jubilantly embraced each other in the streets of Havana and in every corner of every city where nearly 1 million exiles have chosen to live.

Appendix

Efigenio Ameijeiras. A Cuban revolutionary who was one of the original 12 who fought in the Sierra. There he distinguished himself as a guerrilla. As the seizure of power got under way he was made chief of police. During the Bay of Pigs attack he confronted the invaders with policemen. He also fought in Algeria. Later, due to his dissipated lifestyle and his anarchic temperament, he was removed from all leadership positions. In the early 1980s, "rehabilitated by work," he was reinstated in the army with the rank of colonel.

Antón Arrufat (1935–). Cuban writer, playwright. He was editor of the *Casa de las Américas* magazine. In 1968 he won the UNEAC theater prize with his play *Los siete contra Tebas*, a work that raised some ideological hackles and earned him two decades of ostracism.

Auto-da-fe. A very brief trial by the Inquisition of alleged heretics and enemies of the Roman Catholic faith who were usually condemned to be burnt at the stake.

Manuel Ballagas. Cuban writer. He was the son of the great Emilio Ballagas, a poet of the prerevolutionary period who, together with Nicolás Guillén, cultivated Black poetry.

Bohemia. A popular Cuban magazine founded in the 1930s. It was hostile to Batista's dictatorship. The revolutionary government soon took it over and it has continued to be published to this day, but the paper used is of poor quality and the articles extremely tendentious.

Pedro Luis Boitel. A Cuban student leader who in the first FEU elections after the revolution ran against Commander Rolando Cubelas (now in exile) and was defeated. He later plotted against the Communist regime and was arrested and put in prison where he was left to die after a hunger strike.

Juan Almeida Bosque. A Cuban revolutionary who took part in the attack on the Moncada barracks and the Granma expedition. A Black of very poor family origins, he has held important posts in Castro's Cuba. He has been chief of the air force and the army. He heads the Revision Committee and the Central Committee of the Communist party and is a member of the Politburo.

Blas Roca Calderío (1908–1986). A Cuban Communist leader. He joined the Communist party in 1929 and became its secretary general in 1934. He was a delegate to the 1940 Constituent Assembly. After the revolution he edited *Hoy* from 1962 to 1965 and was National Assembly president from 1976 to 1981.

Frank Calzón (1943–). Cuban dissident who headed Of Human Rights, an organization which during the 1970s devoted itself to denouncing the violation of human rights in Cuba. He lives as an exile in Washington.

Calvert Casey (1923–1969). Cuban writer of American parentage. In the 1960s he was connected with the magazine *Lunes de Revolución* and wrote for *Casa de las Américas* but later joined the El Puente group. He had published the book of short stories *El regreso*. After leaving Cuba he settled in Rome as a translator for an international organization and eventually put an end to his own life.

Catholic University Grouping. A Jesuit-led students' union for Roman Catholic university students in Cuba.

Catholic Workers Youth. A Cuban Catholic youth organization for the working-class young linked to the Roman Catholic Church.

Angel del Cerro. Cuban political leader and teacher closely connected with the Roman Catholic movement. He fought against Batista as a member of the July 26 Movement and immediately after the revolution worked with Llanusa in the Havana City Hall. When the government turned to communism he went into exile and made radio broadcasts against the regime. At present he works with Venezuelan television companies.

Captain Osmany Cienfuegos. Brother of the revolutionary hero Camilo Cienfuegos and an influential figure in Cuban affairs. He is now president of the Council of Ministers and a member of the Council of State. He has been involved in some of the army's cultural projects. He was responsible for the suffocation to death of several detainees within a sealed truck.

Concentration Camps. The reference is to the UMAP camps established in 1965 and dismantled in July 1968.

"Coppelia" Ice-Cream Parlor. A famous ice-cream parlor in Havana located in the block at the intersection of 23rd Street and L at the start of La Rampa. It is a favorite meeting place for young people.

Emigré Cuban Commission. The so-called dialogue with the Cuban community in exile in which the Castro government participated in 1979. As a result, Cuban émigrés were allowed to visit the island to see their relatives and many recently-jailed political prisoners were permitted to go to Miami.

Ernesto de la Fe. Cuban politician connected to Batista's regime which he served as a minister. After the revolution he was involved in a plot and was jailed, but after several years behind bars he was released.

Manuel Fernández. An exiled Cuban journalist who specializes in religious issues in Cuba and has had a book about them published in Miami.

José Rodríguez Feo. Cuban essayist and publisher.

Amalio Fiallo. Cuban political leader and teacher. A Christian Democrat connected with liberal political movements of religious origin. He took part in the struggle against Batista and at first supported the revolution. He lives in exile.

Erich Fromm (1900–1980). German psychoanalyst and writer. He favored the total incorporation of the individual into the culture that surrounded him. He was persecuted by the Nazis for his ideas. His works include *Escape from Freedom* and *The Revolution of Hope.*

Gay Hunt. From the very beginning of the revolution the Castroites adopted a markedly "macho" stance and this led them to imprison homosexuals in internment camps or jails. In the 1960s were set up the UMAP concentration camps for homosexuals, dissidents, and Jehovah's Witnesses. As Sartre once said, "As there are no Jews in Cuba, they persecute homosexuals."

Granma. Official daily newspaper of the Cuban Communist party. It has been published since 1962 and replaced the daily *Hoy* of the old-guard Communists and the July 26 Movement's *Revolución.*

Guanajay Prison for Women. Prison for women located in the town of Guanajay, near Havana. It is notorious for the treatment meted out to some of the women interned there.

Gusano (Worm). The insulting epithet Cuban Communists apply to the regime's enemies.

Havana Wood. A wooded area used as a city park. It is divided by the Almendares river which joins the El Vedado and Kohly barrios. Havanans go there to relax.

Homosexuality Banned. A statement by the First Education and Culture Congress, held in April 1971, reflects accurately enough the feeling of ruling circles toward homosexuality: "The social pathology of homosexual deviations was defined. The militant principle that these manifestations and their propagation must be rejected and not admitted in any form was made clear. . . . The Congress discussed fully the origins and evolution of the phenomenon as well as its present extent and the antisocial nature of this activity and the preventive and educational measures that must be implemented. The cleaning up of outbreaks and even the control and relocation of isolated cases."

ICAIC. Cuban Cinema Art and Industry Institute, a state organization headed after 1959 by Alfredo Guevara and then by Santiago Alvarez. Its job is to make films, both long and short, for the Cuban revolutionary state.

Isle of Pines Prison. A model penitentiary built on the Isle of Pines (renamed Isla de la Juventud—Youth Island) to the south of Havana province where one of the many prisoners to spend time there was Fidel Castro himself. He was released when Batista pardoned him in 1955. It has been preserved as a museum for pilgrims wanting to see the place where Castro was imprisoned.

Alfredo Izaguirre (1938–). A Cuban journalist who spent more than 20 years in jail. He became a legend among the prisoners because of his courage in resisting the torturers. He now lives in exile in Miami but is in poor health following two embolisms.

Jehovah's Witnesses. A Christian sect with many adherents throughout the world. It is intensely persecuted in Cuba and other authoritarian countries on account of its refusal to recognize the state, salute the flag, or do military service. In Cuba Jehovah's Witnesses have been repeatedly jailed.

La Cabaña Prison. A prison for men the Castro government located in the old colonial fortress of La Cabaña, situated on the far side of the canal at the entrance to Havana bay. The prison has an evil reputation on account of the many cases of torture and frequent shootings registered there.

Angel Acosta León (1932–1964). Cuban painter who studied in the San Alejandro art academy. His first personal exhibition was in the Lyceum in 1959. He won a prize in the Second Inter-American Art Biennial in Mexico. His best-known works are *Carrusel de la paz* and *Yunque.*

José Lezama Lima (1910–1976). An internationally known Cuban writer. After the revolution he was a director of the National Culture Council and deputy president of UNEAC (Cuban National Writers and Artists Union). Later he was associated with the Literature and Linguistics Institute of the Academy of Sciences. His most important works are, in prose, the polemical *Paradiso* and *Oppiano Licario,* and in verse, *Enemigo rumor, Muerte de Narciso,* and *Analecta del reloj.* In his final years he was an "inner exile" in Cuba.

Herbert Marcuse (1898–1979). German philosopher and sociologist belonging to the Frankfurt School. In 1933 he fled the Nazis and lectured in several universities. He is regarded as a Marxist philosopher and his books had great influence on the hippie and student movement that culminated in 1968. His best-known works are *Eros and Civilization* and *The One-Dimensional Man.*

Mariel Exodus. The mass exit of about 125,000 Cubans that was organized following the incidents in the Peruvian Embassy. The people who left Cuba were transported in small vessels from Key West and Miami which took them on board in the Havana port of Mariel. In an effort to discredit the refugees, the Cuban government included among them common criminals and the mentally ill.

José Mario. Cuban playwright and poet now in exile. He is the author of *La profunda raíz de tanto daño.*

Elena Mederos. Social welfare minister in the first revolutionary government. In the early 1960s she went into exile and founded in Washington the society Of Human Rights. Since the 1930s she was considered an exemplar of public spiritedness in Cuba. She died in exile in the late 1970s.

Ramiro Valdés Menéndez (1932—   ). A Cuban revolutionary who took part in the attack on the Moncada barracks in 1953 and later accompanied Castro on the Granma expedition. Since the revolution he had been among the most radical Cuban leaders. During his long years as interior minister he had been in charge of the repression of those hostile to the regime. One of his slogans was "A mistake is counterrevolutionary; we can all commit mistakes." He had been one of the stalwarts of the Castro regime, until he was fired and ostracized by Castro.

Yañes Pelletier. A soldier in Batista's army who in 1953, in Santiago de Cuba, transported the prisoner Fidel Castro in his jeep after the attack on the Moncada barracks. He handed him over to the judicial authorities and thus prevented him from being "shot while trying to escape." Later, Yañes was himself made prisoner but he was released and now lives in Cuba.

Lázaro Peña. Cuban Communist labor leader. He lost his influence when power of the labor unions waned in the 1960s. But as Castro wanted to revive them after the failure of the "10-million-ton harvest" in the hope they would act as a "transmission belt" between the party and the workers, Lázaro Peña was brought back from obscurity and told to get on with the job. Shortly after his reappearance he died of cancer.

Virgilio Piñera (1912–1979). A Cuban writer and playwright who lived 14 years in Buenos Aires working in his country's embassy. He headed the Ediciones R publishing house in Cuba and in 1968 won the Casa de las Américas literary prize. In 1961 he was jailed as a homosexual but influential friends secured his release. His principal plays are *Aire frío, Electra Garrigó, Dos viejos pánicos,* and *La boda.* His short-story collections are *Cuentos fríos* and *Cuentos completos.* He also wrote poetry.

La Rampa. An area of El Vedado at the end of 23rd Street that stretches from L to the sea. It has many cinemas, shops, cafés, offices, and a commercial center. It is a favorite meeting place both by night and by day. Police and similar units have staged roundups of "antisocial elements" there.

Roman Catholicism versus Communism. In his conversations with frei Betto (a Brazilian theologian of the Dominican order) published in Betto's book *Fidel and Religion* of 1985, Castro declines to say outright whether a Roman Catholic can be a member of the Communist party, although he does hint that this may be possible. The entire book represents an attempt to narrow the gap between Marxists and Christians. The main objective is to harness the revolutionary potential of the Roman Catholic masses of Latin America rather than to help Cuban Roman Catholics.

The Saint. An ecstatic trance brought about by drums and alcohol in Afro-Cuban rites. After hours of dancing the person affected loses consciousness and starts to scream. This is attributed to the spirit that has possessed him and is speaking through his mouth.

Saint Beats. Special beat for bongo and the horizontally played *batá* drums in Afro-Cuban rites which is supposed to induce the "saint" (spirit) to come down to one of the participants.

Saint Christopher, Saint Barbara, Saint Lazarus, and Saint Joseph. Saints recognized by the Roman Catholic Church which Black religious cults identified with African gods and worshipped.

Santero. A believer in an Afro-Cuban religion brought in by African slaves in the eighteenth and ninteenth centuries. A kind of medicine man.

Father Sepúlveda (1490–1573). A Spanish churchman, chronicler of Charles V. In his writings he justified the conquest of the New World by the Spaniards and Portuguese.

He opposed the ideas of Las Casas and Vitoria, arguing—unlike them—that the American Indians were inferior to Europeans.

Ana María Simó (1943–   ). Cuban writer of poems and short stories. She was first published in the magazine *Lunes de Revolución* after its appearance in 1959 but then joined the El Puente group which had no official backing. She now lives in exile in New York. Among her published works is *Lydia Cabrera: un retrato íntimo* of 1984.

Tomás de Torquemada (1420–1498). A churchman from Castile who in the fifteenth century became famous in Spain for *autos-da-fé* and the burning at the stake of heretics. He was the chief of the Spanish Inquisition and became a symbol for intolerance, harshness, and cruelty.

UMAP. Unidades Militares de Apoyo a la Producción (Military Production Support Units), a euphemism for the sinister internment camps for homosexuals, political dissidents, Jehovah's Witnesses, *batiblancos*, and other religious minorities. Most of the camps were in Camagüey and this earned the province the epithet "the Siberia of Cuba." After an international campaign, this notorious institution disappeared.

Virgin of Regla. The image of the Virgin Mary in a church in the village of Regla on the far side of Havana bay. Blacks and Whites who practice some Afro-Cuban cults venerate her as manifestation of one of the gods of the Yoruba pantheon.

9

The Revolution and the Intellectuals

The revolution was born with an ugly original sin: It was extremely uneducated. Fidel and his cohorts had read a few bad books. I keep a naive letter written by Castro to Mañach in which he enumerated the books he had read and had also made the men who attacked the Moncada read out loud. They are *The Decline of the West* by Spengler, *Introduction to Philosophy* by García Morente, and a few other papers written forty years ago by reactionary junior college graduates. During the struggle against Batista, with the exception of Baeza Flores, Leví Marrero, Jorge Valls, Carlos Franqui, and some others, the revolution barely managed to recruit a single intellectual or artist. This is not strange, as intellectuals carried hardly any weight in the life of the country.

To write in Cuba was not exactly the heart-wringing affair it was in Larra's Spain, but it was an effort similar to playing the fool. The same with painting, or trying to make movies. They were tasks for madmen. The Cuban bourgeoisie was profoundly ignorant. Before the revolution, writers of stature such as Virgilio Piñera, Lydia Cabrera, or Lezama Lima were practically unknown. Novás Calvo or Gastón Baquero, resigned to being journalists, were able to arouse some interest in that nonsensical and superficial atmosphere. The insensitivity of the bourgeoisie toward intellectuals was shared by the political parties. Only the Communist party made any substantial effort to win the adherence of creative men and intellectuals, but it was not very successful. Marinello was still promising at eighty. Nicolás Guillén—"Guillén the Bad One," as Neruda used to say, comparing him to Jorge, the great Spanish poet—at the end of forty years has left only half a dozen poems of any literary worth. The rest is a farce: Félix Pita, José Antonio Portuondo, and a collection of mediocre personalities only capable of writing Cuban peasant rhymes, with folk music as background, styled after the famous "controversies" staged between "Fathead" Raúl Ferrer and Naborí, "the Indian."

Fidel did not even count on that. His initial political clientele were rough people. Furthermore, there exists a positive correlation between degree of ignorance and Fidel's esteem. The first circle that surrounds Castro is formed by people as incompetent as they are loyal. There is not a single intellectual in the inner circle. There has never been one. Fidel does not feel at home with people who speak a language he does not understand. His iron guard is made up of peasants from the Sierra incapable of thinking for themselves. The nearest thing to an intellectual that has been close to him is Carlos Franqui, who ended up exiled in Europe. Franqui—I insist elsewhere in this book— with the help of his collaborator, Vicente Báez, is responsible for a state of affairs in which a revolution carried out by uncultured people ended up becoming the point of attraction for intellectuals from all over the world. Through the newspaper *Revolución,* managed by Franqui, writers such as Cabrera Infante or Virgilio Piñera were recognized and given backing. For the first time, officially, intellectuals, artists, and creators of all kinds began to play an important role. Franqui was generous and did not demand from Carpentier a retraction for services lent to the dictatorship of Pérez Jiménez, nor from Carpentier or Lisandro Otero that they justify the sinecures they had held during Batista's regime. Retamar did not have to justify his apathy during the struggle against Batista. Franqui opened the door and the happy troop poured in. Invitations were sent out to everybody. Cuba became full of prestigious travelers who returned to their country committed to the defense of the revolution. Suddenly it seemed that Castro's Havana had become a Medici Florence of sorts. More creative fiction was published than before; there was talk of Cuban cinematography as an immediate project. Painters were asked to make large murals. There was, in the fashionable jargon of the early sixties, a genuine "cultural escalation."

All this cultural explosion was undertaken without consulting the Communist party, a situation that made the old comrades nervous, but it was also undertaken without consulting "the leadership," a situation that made Fidel nervous. It did not take long for problems to appear. The first serious clash took place between Castro and the young cinematographer Orlando Jiménez Leal, director and screenwriter of an excellent documentary titled *PM.* Jiménez Leal's film served as a pretext for the old Communist party to attack the staff of the newspaper *Revolución,* as Sabá Cabrera Infante, Guillermo's brother, had collaborated with Jiménez Leal in the production of *PM. PM* was the alibi the party used to disband the intellectuals who were beginning to constitute an uncontrollable pressure group. Castro, not having intellectuals among his intimate followers, then placed the cultural machine in the party's hands. In practical terms and with few exceptions the old comrades' power has never gone beyond the cultural sphere. Fidel, of course, took precautions. He planted Haydée Santamaría, who had nothing to do with culture but a lot to do with Fidel, which is what interests the Maximum Leader. The old party—a group that can read and write without stumbling too often—now dispenses culture. And Fidel controlled it through the services of the good lady who one day, tired of contradictions, put a bullet in her head.

Aesthetic Freedom?

In Cuba—how could it have been avoided?—a polemic also took place dealing with socialist realism. Did Portocarrero have the right to paint his mulatto women and cathedrals, or should he dedicate his talents to painting happy and muscular workers? Could Lezama dedicate an ode to an unfathomable donkey or should he compose an epic poem to the Bay of Pigs victory? Fidel hurriedly ended the polemic with a phrase that became famous by virtue of its universal doltishness: "Within the revolution, everything; outside the revolution, nothing." This was interpreted as a pat on the back to creative freedom, when it only meant that the artist's one indispensable requirement was his political militancy. Castro, after all, could care less if Mijares painted strange blue dolls, or if poets like Arcocha and Palenzuela subscribed to surrealism's tenets. Strictly speaking, Castro does not perceive any differences between elitist fantasy and socialist realism. He has never believed in the *usefulness* of painting or in the *efficacy* of a poem so to him one thing was as unimportant as the other. He was wrong. As the years passed, Fidel would discover that aesthetic freedom entails a risk for the totalitarian state. Following the thread of aesthetic freedom one always arrives at the critic's ball of yarn. It is inevitable. The principle that in a collectivist and communitarian society some persons might enjoy the privilege of creating for a few others, ignoring the masses' tastes, immediately ends up being a counterrevolutionary premise. The uproar and polemic began to intensify in the intellectual world. First, some of them were detained for "homosexual behavior," later others for taking the liberty of criticizing, even though it might have been only a symbolic gesture on the part of the intellectuals. And finally the "Padilla affair" came to the fore. Castro lost patience and decided to put that restless universe in order. As a temporary measure he punished the writers. The revolution from then on would permit creative publications only in small doses. Public education would have absolute priority. The "culture's sorcerers" were again "left out of the game," but in worse shape than before. Now they could publish their works neither at their own expense nor abroad. Reynaldo Arenas almost went to prison because he published *El mundo alucinante* in Mexico. Only the *unconditional* followers, who wrote *obviously* pro-Castro works, would have the *right* of seeing them published. This was a short-term measure. On a long-term basis, the revolution has imposed on itself a more terrifying task: to eradicate "intellectualism." That is, to eliminate the elite that defines what is and is not culture, what is a valuable creation or a simple invention. The role, played in the past by the intellectual elite, in the future, according to Fidel's plans, will be played by anonymous masses. There will be neither famous painters nor writers who might turn into deities, but hundreds, thousands of aficionados that will create their own works under the revolution's watchful stimulation. In any case, Fidel maintains that the revolution can do without the cultural elite. As a final resort, he lucidly reasons, if the bourgeois state subsisted while completely ignoring the intellectuals, certainly the revolution, with all the resources at its disposal, can do the same. Deep inside, it is a settling of accounts between Fidel and a group of men for whom he felt a bitter hatred and a certain rancor. Finally, intellectuals find themselves in an unbearable position. There is no more vulnerable group to the police's harassment, because in addition to dissembling in their behavior, they have to feign in their art, and the second is almost always more difficult than the first. The consequence of this tension is panic. There is no other group in Cuba more nervous than intellectuals. Supporters vehemently gesticulate so that they will not be confused; adversaries are scared to death. In the midst of the Padilla affair, the distinguished British critic J. M. Cohen made the naive mistake of writing a letter to his friend Lisandro Otero asking him to intercede in Padilla's behalf. Otero became afraid that the letter might have been opened by State Security and panicked. The answer he sent to the well-intentioned Cohen is an incredibly vile act and an outright show of fear. Otero made copies for the State Security Department, the National Writers and Artists' Association (UNEAC), Casa de las Américas, and all other organisms that might demand proof of the most submissive loyalty. Those copies were circulated in Cuba.

Foreign Intellectuals

In the beginning, when Havana was a fiesta, Cuba became a kind of baptismal Jordan for intellectuals from all over the world. Much in the spirit of a zoo outing, Sartre and Beauvoir arrived. Later others followed, and it appeared that the flux would never end. Castro, who does not read fiction, who despises poetry, who does not understand painting and much less sculpture, who does not know about music, who only tied and gagged would see a ballet or listen to an opera, realized the importance and enormous weight of "intellectuals" in the shaping of public opinion currents. He launched a recruitment campaign, through Carlos Franqui, editor of *Revolución*. He would later entrust that task to Haydée Santamaría, an appointment that would end up costing her her life when she could not continue to support the contradictions.

The pact between the intellectuals and the revolution was simple. Cuba would invite them to participate in an updated version of radical tourism—the regime would bolster them within and outside of the island—and the intellectuals would simply support the revolution. This agreement had the virtue of making the intellectuals into a cohesive group as it made them coincide in their loyalty to the revolutionary process, which at the same time strengthened the group's capacity for pressure. As Vargas Llosa and Donoso have acknowledged, the "boom" was possible, in great part, because the revolution turned out to be a collective catapult. They offered their talent, and the revolution guaranteed their success.

For Castro, the intellectuals' support was especially useful. Cuba, unlike Albania, was not resigned to carrying out its revolution solely within the country's borders; it wanted to become a "beacon of the Third World" and "the first free territory of the Americas." Cuba wanted to be a paradigm, and it needed spokesmen, "relaying stations," echoes, mirror games, and other tools that would multiply its voice and image. The intellectuals were good for this. A political statement from Leonard Bernstein—a musical virtuoso but ignorant in political matters—would be valuable because of his musical talent, not its political content. A document supporting the revolution signed by writers and artists of the first order was a valuable boost. But what the regime stupidly ignored was that the same document, if written to condemn the revolution, would have a great negative impact. Intellectuals were useful but dangerous.

The pact had several insurmountable flaws. The first and definitive one was that most of the intellectuals were not disciplined Communists but progressive and liberal gentlemen who possessed a degree of critical sense. As soon as it became evident that Cuba was taking a Communist course, a certain timid murmur began to be heard. Havana—unwilling to permit fickle behavior—censured Carlos Fuentes for writing in *Life* and Neruda for attending a Pen Club meeting. The criticism was written by Roberto Fernández Retamar, a second-class poet who came from the ranks of Catholicism and became a wrathful cultural commissar and inquisitor of democratic witches—perhaps because of his shameful abstinence during the struggle against Batista.

The rupture between the leftist intellectuals and Castro was only a question of time. In their trips to Cuba, Fuentes, Vargas Llosa, Goytisolo, and Cortázar not only had established contacts with the abstract revolution, but also with Cuban intellectuals, such as Cabrera Infante, Heberto Padilla, Lezama Lima, and Virgilio Piñera. As soon as the revolution conflicted with the critical intellectuals who had remained in Cuba, their foreign colleagues were faced with an ethical dilemma. To keep silent and continue supporting the revolution was an acceptance of the abuse to which their Cuban friends had been subjected. Mario Vargas Llosa was the one whose conscience bothered him the most in all this murky business. Already in his Rómulo Gallegos Award acceptance speech, which he had painfully titled "The Writer as Spoiler," he proclaimed the irrevocable critical mission of writers, and later mentioned Cuba as an example of Latin American liberty. Later it was Vargas Llosa—the intellectual most committed to Cuba but also perhaps the most intrinsically honest of all the writers—who unleashed the clamor raised apropos the Padilla affair.

Heberto Padilla had written a book of poems entitled *Out of the Game*, which received an award in a contest sponsored by the National Writers and Artists' Association (UNEAC). Since the book contained several critical poems, UNEAC accepted them for publication only after a prologue had been appended to the book in which the author was accused of being a divisionist and a counterrevolutionary. Something similar happened to the dramatist Antón Arrufat and his play *Seven against Thebes*. José Antonio Portuondo, an old Communist party militant and staunch defender of Stalinist orthodoxy who writes in *Verde Olivo*, the magazine of the armed forces, was the author of both prologues. As long as the incident was kept under UNEAC's lid, Havana was able to keep it under control, but as soon as the political police intervened, the international uproar started. Padilla was arrested by the dreaded State Security agents and a few days later he sent from his prison cell a statement of self-condemnation and regret which will become part of the universal history of infamy. The servile document, read in a session of UNEAC, in a large room full of writers and artists fearful that Padilla might mention them, constituted a depressing spectacle that further angered foreign intellectuals who had asked for Padilla's freedom. Havana's reaction was not long in coming. It accused its ex-supporters of being agents of imperialism and pseudorevolutionaries who had taken advantage of the revolution to secure fame and fortune. Vargas Llosa bore the brunt of the most virulent attacks, but the same resentment, expressed by Cuban Communists, was directed against Goytisolo and Octavio Paz. Within Cuba, the writers felt symbolically protected by the forceful action of their foreign colleagues and secretly wished for the offensive to continue. Two important defections were ably exploited by Havana: Cortázar, who retracted his words and wrote an incredible poem asking for forgiveness from Haydée Santamaría, from Casa de las Américas, and from Fidel and "his sip of coffee"; and García Márquez, who stated that he had never approved of the document that asked for Padilla's freedom, and much less of the one censuring the autocritical farce. No less useful to Havana was an open letter by Alfonso Sastre, decidedly identified with Castroism's political police and brashly siding with repression. Nonetheless, in *Triunfo*, the Spanish journal where Sastre's letter appeared, a note was published criticizing Castroism's coercive methods.

Within Cuba, the harassed writers and artists considered the attitude of Cortázar, Sastre, and García Márquez as repulsive treachery that facilitated and scantified police repression used against them. The consequence of the collision between the revolution and leftist intellectuals was the indefinite cancellation of this kind of public relations work. Fidel, who has always maintained a spiteful attitude toward intellectuals—among other things because they speak a language he does not understand and that also irritates him—took advantage of the opportunity to dispense once and for all with the costly services they offered him. The revolution has lost a good ally in that strange and incessant struggle to project a beneficent image, but its leaders, guerrillas in power without any spiritual refinement, feel freer and less inhibited, now that they are outside the field of vision of foreign intellectuals. After all, the revolution is closer to Caligula than to Sartre, as surely Castro would like to have said.

The Cuban Intellectuals

Haydée Santamaría, the most important civil-service employee for culture in Cuba, put a bullet in her head around 26 July 1981. The date is important. She did not kill herself in March or in December. She shot herself in July, probably on the night of Saturday the 26th, though they did not report it until the morning of Monday the 28th. Twenty-nine years later Haydée Santamaría wanted to join the dead of the Moncada. She wanted to combine her luck with that of Boris, her fiancé, with that of her brother, Abel, with that of a handful of heroic and idealist youths who died in time, amidst the odor of illusion, with their last gaze fixed on the dream of a democratic and free country. Haydée Santamaría killed herself out of faithfulness to her dead. She killed herself as Félix Pena, the commander of the Sierra Maestra, did, and as did Alberto Mora, the commander of the Student University Directory, because political suicides kill themselves to warn and censure. They kill themselves, like Eddy Chibás, to give a last, energetic knock in the sleeping conscience of the people.

Regarding the question of suicide, Cuba has the highest rate in America, with a figure of 21.3 per 100,000 inhabitants, and it is the first cause of death among people ages 15 to 49. By contrast, the suicide figures in other countries of the Americas are eloquent: United States, 12.5; Mexico, 1.8; Costa Rica, 4.4.

Haydeé Santamaría killed herself for clearly political reasons. If her motives had been of another nature, no one would have been more interested than the Cuban government in revealing them. Why did Havana not publish the letter written by Haydée Santamaría to Fidel Castro? If the contents of the letter had been exculpatory, if it had said, like so many suicide notes, "Let no one blame himself for my death," it would have appeared on the first page of *Granma,* and Castro, touched, would have given the funeral farewell speech. But that letter surely says, "Blame my deep and unbearable disillusionment for my death, blame the bad conscience that obsesses me because I belong to the unstable group of the oppressors, blame the brutal fact of some cruel political prisons, blame the disturbing spectacle of 11,000 unhappy Cubans crowded together in an embassy to escape from the society I helped to build. Blame our mobs for hitting, spitting, harassing, mistreating, and—at times— even killing those who want to leave the country. Blame my aching heart, unable, any longer, to bear the weight of the reality of Cuba."

Suicide is always a gesture of mistaken interpretation, but if one constant exists among those who decide to take their lives, it is that terrible conviction that there will be no restorative and bright tomorrow. Suicides do not believe in tomorrow. A little before his famous shot, Mariano José de Larra, the Spanish romantic writer, wrote a singularly heartrending article, and in it he said that, looking at his heart, he could write, "Here lies hope." That is what Larra died of. That is what Haydée Santamaría died of; hope lay immobile in her heart before the final shot.

The suicide of Haydée Santamaría should not greatly surprise us. The perception of the failure of the Cuban revolution is much more acute among cultural circles. The National Writers and Artists' Association, the Cuban Film Institute, the Office of Publishing Houses of the Ministry of Culture, and the Casa de las Américas are breeding grounds for badly controlled inconformity. It is the intelligentsia that best perceives the brutal distance between Cuban reality and revolutionary rhetoric. Those sad spectacles of rebellions and retractions, of dissidences and mea culpas, are the result of the fatal coincidence between lucidity and fear. This is the terrible situation of Cintio Vitier, of Eliseo Diego, of Antón Arrufat, of Luis Agüero, of Miguel Barnet, of Jesús Díaz, of Silvio Rodríguez, of Pablo Milanés, of Fina García Marruz, of Pablo Armando Fernández, and of dozens of other Cuban intellectuals and artists, too intelligent to be dogmatic and too well informed to really subscribe to the barbarous model of society laid down by the Castroist group. Poor Cintio Vitier, or poor Barnet, or poor Arrufat and Agüero, will have to say what the Ministry of the Interior demands that they say, but these declamatory exercises cannot hide the radical incongruity between what they are and really believe, and what they have to pretend and show that they believe. This sham should not shock anybody. Nobody, apart from being a poet, is obliged to be a hero like Valladares or like Angel Cuadra. As Reynaldo Arenas is brilliantly accustomed to saying, within socialism one only saves face by using a mask. Shortly before Haydée Santamaría's suicide, masquerading as a representative of Cuban intellectuals, Benítez Rojo, the author of *Tute de Reyes*, arrived in Paris. He went specially on Haydée Santamaría's recommendation. In Paris, Benítez Rojo decided to take off the mask and he asked for political asylum.

Education and information are incompatible with Castroist militancy. Castroism, after almost thirty years of notorious practice, can only recruit followers from among the less educated strata of the country, areas in which emotion substitutes analysis, and superstition objective judgment. Not even the Marxist intellectuals escape this predicament. How is one to believe in Jorge Ibarra's Castroism? How can one believe that Carlos Rafael Rodríguez does not feel sick when, in the name of Marxism, some poor workers who want to emigrate from the country are hit and spat upon in his presence? How can Alfredo Guevara's unconditional support for the Cuban revolution be believed? Alfredo Guevara is astute, intelligent, and mordant. He was a Marxist when Fidel was nothing but a troublemaker. Yet he was never a Marxist of slogans and stupidity, but a critical spirit who found a method of analysis in Marxism. Alfredo Guevara does not need to forswear Marxism in order to condemn the fascism of the Left that has taken over Cuba. Castroism is certainly blameworthy from a liberal point of view, but from a Marxist analysis as well. How can Alfredo Guevara, thirty years after the triumph of the revolution, continue to maintain that the monstrosities of the system are mistakes that can be corrected in the future? The inefficiency, the outrages, the abuses of the system are not phenomena alien to the essence of Castroism, but the natural consequences inherent in the model chosen. It is absolutely irrational to hope for the modification of that system. For this reason Haydée Santamaría killed herself: because she lucidly understood that there was no space for hope.

The divorce between the Cuban intelligentsia and the Castroist regime involved a paradoxical irony. No government in the whole history of the republic has done more to promote Cuban culture. But also none has done more to repress it. The republic that disappeared in 1959 had ignored cultural activities. The government did not bother to publish a book by Cintio Vitier, but neither were they worried about what Cintio Vitier could say in his books. It was the revolutionary atmosphere that gave national stature to Heberto Padilla (independently of his unquestionable talent), but it was also the revolutionary atmosphere that imprisoned him and forced him later to undergo a shameful ceremony of self-humiliation.

Why should we be surprised that Eliseo Diego looks back without anger and remembers the peaceful days when the Orígenes group, without a subsidy but without a master, met in the presence of the mysterious magisterial manner of Lezama to comment on a *pájina* (incorrect spelling of *página*—"page") of

Juan Ramón, sprinkled with impertinent *j's?* Was the Havana that scorned all that it did not know better than the Havana that keeps an eye on all that it suspects? The answer is obvious: Nobody had to leave that Havana. In that uncultured and scornful Havana, Labrador Ruiz produced his innovative work. In that Havana Novás Calvo, Montenegro, and Lidia Cabrera wrote their masterly stories. That Havana was not generous with Brull, with Loveira, with José Antonio Ramos, with Mañach, or with Varona, but it neither demanded from them a particular political devotion nor pursued them for the ideas expressed in their works.

The Cuban revolution has provoked the mass exodus of its intelligentsia. Today in Puerto Rico, alone and full of patriotic fervor, Leví Marrero is writing the best social and economic history of Cuba ever produced. This monumental work should have been done in the National Library of Cuba and with the grateful aid of his country, and not in a nostalgic and wounded corner of emigration. It is in Paris and in French that Eduardo Manet today carries Cuban theater to its highest expression. In Cuba he could not do so. Some years ago, "with eyes crying hard," he had to leave Cuba, just as a few months ago Reynaldo Arenas and Armando Alvarez Bravo had to leave, or a few years ago, Pío Serrano, the terse and vigorous poet discovered by the Spaniards. Castroism, which understands nothing, supposes that the universe is divided into people that support them and people that condemn them, into Cubans that go and Cubans that stay. Castroism does not understand that the intellectuals that desert, that escape by whatever means, do so with the deepest sorrow and clearly do not flee from material discomfort, but from the ubiquitous presence of the police and from the moral bankruptcy of a system in which they once believed. They flee from necessity and from repression, not from poverty, because they have arrived at the painful conclusion that the rending of exile is better than the tragedy of him who does not go, like Retamar, but who would like to go and lacks the strength to make the decision.

For this reason, nobody should have been surprised when César Leante, national adviser for literature of the Ministry of Culture and author of eight noteworthy books, in 1981 remained in Madrid, on a technical stopover during a flight bound for Bulgaria. The newspaper headline said, "César Leante seeks asylum," but it could have said, "Roberto Fernández Retamar seeks asylum" or "Cintio Vitier and Fina García Marruz seek asylum." Or even "Lisandro Otero remains in Madrid accompanied by Eliseo Diego, while the deserters, Antón Arrufat, Pablo Armando Fernández, David Buzzy, Norberto Fuentes and Miguel Barnet follow their example," (all of them in Cuba—still) because among Cuban intellectuals not one of them is known to support really, without reservations, that now quite old nonsense known as "the Cuban Revolution."

From here one could go, if it were possible, even to Nicolás Guillén, were he not senile, because one is no longer dealing with Marxisms more or less, political systems more or less, but with the fact that that society has entered a stage of corruption, inefficiency, despotism, arbitrariness, lack of solidarity, and abuse that is almost unbreathable for anyone, much less for the intellectuals condemned to exercise the "fatal mania of thinking."

To be a bricklayer in Cuba is difficult, to be a doctor or a teacher is lamentable, but to be a writer is absolutely tragic because the constant demand for loyalty can leave the thorn in raw flesh. A bricklayer does not have to lie with the plumb line, nor is a doctor—heaven forbid that it might occur to him—obliged to interpret an X-ray from a Marxist perspective, but the poor hacks have to make sonnets in tribute to the current power, write "dialectical" novels and contribute with words to the glorious adventure of building the radiant future of humanity. But apart from that terrible task—jealously watched over by a legion of censors, inquisitors, and policemen of every appearance—writers are treated as sumptuous objects in Communist societies, something like luxury florists who are displayed in order to demonstrate the quality of the little world built by the commissars and the popular backing which the governments enjoy.

In bourgeois societies the trick is to portray the leader with the bishop, or with the powerful foreign investor: In the Communist society that role of endorser, of guarantor, is played by the intellectual but in an involuntary way. Either he obeys and applauds or he goes to jail, or—in the best of cases—he disappears from the official literature, as occurs to all those who desert. For in the next edition that the unhappy Salvador Bueno does of his *History of Cuban Literature,* he will not be able to include Leante, nor Benítez Rojo, nor Cabrera Infante, nor Labrador Ruiz, nor Heberto Padilla, nor Severo Sarduy, nor Reynaldo Arenas, nor Hilda Perera, nor Virgilio Piñera, nor Pepe Triana, nor Gastón Baquero, nor Luis Ricardo Alonso, nor Armando Alvarez, not even the foolish Edmundo Desnoes, nor Eduardo Manet, nor Juan and Pepe Arcocha, nor—of course—Armando Valladares, Angel Cuadra, or the half a dozen good writers who languish in prison in Cuba, and it will be interesting, at least, to see how the history is going to be written of a literature that has to do without its most notable writers. But so much for Salvador Bueno with his problem, which perhaps is not so much of one if he too—as he surely dreams—takes a powder and rewrites his book in some sunny place in exile. In the end, the intelligentsia of the island today meets in exile because of the stubborn stupidity of Havana. Four congresses of dissident Cuban intellectuals have already been held (Paris, 1979; New York, 1980; Washington, 1982; Madrid, 1986). Each time they are more substantial and representative. In the decade of the 1980s, as in the decade of the 1880s, Cuban culture once more blooms in emigration. This sad phenomenon is now an internationally recognized fact. The great literature, science, thought, music, films, and theater of the Cubans takes place abroad. The talent—still a lot—that remains in Cuba cannot grow. They will not let it. That is the panorama of Cuban culture today. A sad thing.

Appendix

Amateurs. The status to which, according to Fidel Casto, all writers and other intellectuals will be forcibly reduced. He predicts they will be eradicated, with their role being taken over by the masses.

Reynaldo Arenas (1943–   ). Cuban novelist, short-story writer, and poet. In 1962 he became a farming accountant and attended the university in 1964. He was jailed as a dissident in the El Morro prison between 1974 and 1976. His works were published abroad before they appeared in Cuba. He went into exile from Mariel in 1980. His publications include *El mundo alucinante, Celestino antes del alba, El palacio de las blanquísimas mofetas, El central,* and *Arturo, la estrella más brillante.*

Gastón Baquero (1916–   ). Cuban poet and journalist who wrote for *Diario de la Marina* before the revolution. He went into exile, settling in Spain. His works before going into exile were already volumnious. At Santander's Menéndez y Pelayo Univeristy he taught a number of courses and worked for years at the Institute of Hispanic Culture and Ibero-American Cooperation. He is now retired and lives in Madrid. His works include *Poemas escritos en España, Memorial de un testigo,* and *Magias e invenciones.*

Lydia Cabrera (1900–   ). Short-story writer and expert on folklore connected to Cuba's Black cultures. She lived in Paris in the 1920s and 1930s, returning to Cuba at the outbreak of World War II and dedicating herself to anthropology and ethnology. In 1960 she went into exile, settling for a time in Madrid and then moving to Miami. In 1977 she received a doctorate honoris causa from the University of Denison. Her publications include *Cuentos negros de Cuba* and *Refranes de negros viejos.*

Lino Novás Calvo (1950–1983). Cuban novelist, short-story writer, dramatist, poet, and essayist who arrived from his native Galicia, Spain, at age seven. In the 1930s he worked as a journalist for Spanish newspapers. He returned to Cuba in 1940 and two years later won the Hernández Catá prize for his short story *Un dedo encima.* From 1947 to 1960 he was professor of French at Havana Normal School. In 1960 he went into exile in the United States where from 1967 to 1974 he was professor of Spanish at Syracuse University. He is best known for two works, *Maneras de contar* and *Pedro Blanco, el negrero.* He has translated works from English and French into Spanish.

Alejo Carpentier. An author who died in Paris in 1980, the year after he won the Cervantes prize, Spain's most prestigious literary award. He often said in his French accent: "A writer, if he wants to be published, cannot afford to part company with the Left."

Casa de las Américas. A cultural organization formed by the Castroite authorities with the aim of encouraging those Latin American writers who were violently Communist. An annual prize carrying the institution's name was awarded a work considered committed.

Eduardo R. Chibás (1907–1951). A Cuban politician who founded and led the Cuban Revolutionary party (Orthodox). In 1939 he became a representative and in 1944 a senator. He won fame as a fierce foe of president Batista (1940–1944), president Grau

(1944–1948), and president Prío (1948–1952). When Prío was in power he accused education minister Aureliano Sánchez Arango of corruption and illicit appropriations but he had no hard proof of this and in August 1951, while making a dramatic radio speech, he shot himself, dying a few days later. This left the Orthodox party leaderless and opened the way for the coup d'état Batista staged within eight months.

J.M.Cohen (1903–198?). A British critic and translator whose crowning achievement was the translation of *Don Quixote* into English for Penguin Books. In the 1960s he had a sharp exchange of letters with Lisandro Otero and was brutally insulted by him.

Julio Cortázar (1914–1985). An Argentine writer who lived many years in Paris where he died. There he worked as a translator and edited publications for international organizations. From the very beginning he was an unconditional supporter of Fidel Castro's government and backed all his actions. His main works are *Rayuela, Octaedro, Historias de cronopios y de famas,* and toward the end of his life *Los autonautas de la cosmopista.*

José Donoso (1925–   ). A Chilean writer and, in his country, a professor of English literature. His best-known works include *El obsceno pájaro de la noche* (1970) and *Casa de campo* (1978).

Alberto Baeza Flores (1914–   ). A Cuban writer born in Chile. He has written poems, short stories, essays, biographies, and journalistic pieces under the pseudonym Carlos Flobal. He settled in Cuba after arriving there on an official mission from Chile. After working for the National Popular Libraries organization he left in 1960 for Mexico, proceeding to Paris a year later. He is an expert on Martí.

Carlos Fuentes (1928–   ). A Mexican writer who has held diplomatic posts and taught at Princeton University. He became famous thanks to his novel *La muerte de Artemio Cruz* of 1962. His initial enthusiasm for the Cuban revolution has waned but he has recently been flirting with the Sandinistas who rule Nicaragua.

Fuera del juego (Left Out of the Game). A play on words alluding to a collection of poems of the same name by the Cuban poet Heberto Padilla. He wrote them in Cuba and won the UNEAC prize when it was published, but the award was given with considerable reluctance as some poems criticized the negative side of the revolution.

Juan Goytisolo (1931–   ). A Spanish writer, one of the best prose writers of the postwar years. He wants to bring Europe closer to Arab culture and for that reason lives in Marrakesh, Morocco. His principal works are *La resaca, Campos de Níjar, Makbara, Crónicas sarracenas,* and *Paisaje después de la batalla.*

The "Indian" Naborí. A popular Cuban poet who, to the dismay of many writers, has kept his faith in the revolution.

Guillermo Cabrera Infante (1929–   ). A Cuban novelist, essayist, and film critic. Before the revolution, he was the film critic of the magazine *Caretas.* In the 1950s, he was one of the founders of the Cuban Film Library. After Castro took power, he edited the literary magazine *Lunes de Revolución.* But when the newspaper *Revolución* was closed and *Lunes* folded, he was sent to Belgium as cultural attaché, a job he held from 1962 to 1965 when he went into exile in London. He still lives there and has acquired

British citizenship. Among his works are *Tres tristes tigres*, which won the Biblioteca Breve de Seix Barral prize, *Así en la paz como en la guerra*, *Un oficio del siglo XX* (film criticism), *Vista del amanecer en el trópico*, and *La Habana para un infante difunto*. He recently published a book about tobacco, his first written directly in English, titled *Holy Smoke!*

Latin American Literary Boom. The flourishing of creative and publishing activity by Latin Americans in the 1960s and 1970s was a reaction against the appalling socioeconomic problems faced by the region.

Orlando Jiménez Leal (1941–   ). A Cuban filmmaker who after the revolution produced shorts like *La tumba francesa* for ICAIC together with Nestor Almendros, who twice won an Oscar for the best photography. In 1961 he codirected *PM* with Sabá Cabrera Infante, but it was banned by the regime's censors because it showed Havana night life as it really was. In exile in the United States he has produced *El Super*, which won a prize in the Mannheim festival, *La otra Cuba*, and *Conducta impropia* with Nestor Almendros as codirector. This film was awarded a prize at the Festival for the Rights of Man for drawing attention to the plight of homosexuals in Cuba.

Mario Vargas Llosa (1936–   ). A Peruvian writer initially sympathetic to the revolution but, like Octavio Paz, able to see the dangers Communist authoritarianism held for Latin America. He soon rejected the Castroite solution to the evils affecting the hemisphere. His works include *La ciudad y los perros*, *La guerra del fin del mundo*, *Historia de Mayte*, and the play *La señorita de Tacna*.

Jorge Mañach (1898–1961). Cuban essayist and academic. As a journalist, he wrote for *El País* and *Diario de la Marina*. He took part in the struggle against Machado and in the 1930s was a professor at Columbia University. In 1940 he became professor of history at Havana University. He joined the Cuban People's party (Orthodox party) and was moderator in the "Meet the Press" television program which enjoyed considerable success in the 1950s. He was an expert on the works of Martí. In 1960 he went into exile and died a year later while he was a professor at Río Piedras University, Puerto Rico.

Gabriel García Márquez (1928–   ). A Columbian writer who was awarded the 1982 Nobel prize for literature. He has traveled throughout Europe. In the 1960s he worked for Prensa Latina in its Havana office and as the agency's correspondent in New York. He has been such an unrelenting defender of the Cuban Revolution that he can be described as a collaborator. His main works include *Cien años de soledad*, *El otoño del patriarca*, *El coronel no tiene quien le escriba*, and *Los funerales de la Mamá Grande*.

Leví Marrero (1911–   ). Cuban historian, geographer, and educator. Before going into exile in 1960, he was professor of Cuban economic history at Havana University. Later, in Puerto Rico, he taught geography at the Humacao Regional College before retiring in 1972. His most important works are *The Geography of Cuba* (1966) and the 12-volume *Cuba, economía y sociedad*, published by Editorial Playor in 1972.

José Mijares (1922–   ). A Cuban painter who studied in the San Alejandro academy and became a member of the group of 10 Cuban concrete painters. He has taken part in several biennials and was notable for works like *Landscape* of 1946 and *Ink*.

Manuel García Morente (1886–1942). A Spanish philosopher with the well-known Free Education Institute. He was a professor at Madrid University and, between the wars, a follower and collaborator of José Ortega y Gasset. He is known for several works, among them *Introduction to Philosophy*.

Pablo Neruda (1904–1973). A Chilean poet who was openly Communist and won the Nobel prize for literature in 1971. His real name was Ricardo Eliezer Neftalí Reyes. When Salvador Allende was in power Neruda held official posts in Paris. He traveled throughout Europe and the Americas giving poetry readings. Despite his ideological allegiance, he was not well received in Cuba because he demanded to be paid in hard currency and he had given a lecture in the United States Pen Club. His main work is *Canto General*, an ode dedicated to America which contains extravagant praise of Communism, and the famous *Veinte poemas de amor y una canción desesperada*.

Lisandro Otero (1932–   ). A Cuban writer and journalist who studied at the Sorbonne between 1954 and 1956. He wanted to fight alongside the Algerian forces in Algeria but was unable to do so. When the revolution succeeded he got the job of news editor of the newspaper *Revolución* and became secretary of UNEAC. From 1963 to 1968 he edited the magazine *Cuba*. He has held diplomatic posts in the Cuban embassies in Chile and Great Britain. His works include *Pasión de Urbino* and *La situación*.

Octavio Paz (1914–   ). Mexican poet, essayist, and journalist who is in many ways the unofficial conscience of his country. He was a sympathizer of the Spanish Republic during the 1936–39 Civil War. As a convinced liberal he soon saw the Cuban Revolution as a negative incursion into authoritarianism. He has never belonged to Castro's clique. He has recently written scripts for TELEVISA. In prose, his best-known work is *El laberinto de la soledad*, and in verse *Pasado en claro* and *Ladera este*. For 10 years he was Mexican ambassador in India but in 1968 resigned because of the Tlatelolco massacre of students.

René Portocarrero (1912–   ). A Cuban painter whose first exhibition was held in 1934 at the Lyceum. He specialized in murals, drawings, and watercolors. He took part in the Venice Biennial with his multiple work *Variations on a Single Theme*, a series of portraits of women. Other outstanding works were *The Witchdoctor*, *The Cathedral*, and *Color in Cuba*.

Roberto Fernández Retamar (1930–   ). A Cuban poet and academic who was professor of linguistics at Havana University. He completed his studies in Paris and London and later at Yale and Columbia universities in the United States. After the revolution he became cultural atttaché in the Cuban embassy in Paris. He has been editor of the *Casa de las Américas* magazine. His works include *Patria*, which won the national poetry prize, and *Orbita de Rubén Martínez Villena*. He supports the Castro regime and lives in Cuba.

Rómulo Gallegos Prize. A prize for literature created by Venezuelan cultural organizations in honor of the former president and author of works such as *Canaima* and *Doña Bárbara*. It is open to writers from all Latin American countries.

Félix Pita Rodríguez (1909–   ). Cuban writer and journalist who in the 1930s traveled as a foreign correspondent in Europe and Morocco. In 1937 he participated in the Second Intellectuals' Congress in Valencia during the Spanish Civil War. He continued writing on his return to Cuba in the 1940s and joined the Communist Movement, writing for the daily *Hoy*. In 1946 he won the Hernández Catá international prize for his short story "Cosme y Damián." In the 1950s he was well known as a radio and television scriptwriter. Since the revolution he has traveled to all the Eastern bloc countries and was named president of UNEAC's Literature Section.

Haydée Santamaría. A Cuban revolutionary who was with Castro in the attack on the Moncada barracks in 1953 and later joined him in the Sierra. After the revolution she was the head of Casa de las Américas but in the early 1980s committed suicide for reasons that were never made public.

Alfonso Sastre (1926–   ). A Spanish writer and playwright connected in his own country with the Communist Left. He visited Cuba in 1968. His main works include *El pan de todos, La taberna fantástica, Escuadra hacia la muerte, La mordaza, El cuervo,* and *La sangre y la ceniza*.

Jorge Valls (1933–   ). A Cuban poet, playwright, and short-story writer jailed in Boniato prison for interceding on behalf of a condemned man. In prison he wrote poems on toilet paper. In 1982 he received, together with Angel Cuadra and Armando Valladares, a prize from the Association for Hispanic-Puerto Rican Culture. In 1983 he was awarded a Dutch prize for poetry. When freed in 1984 he went into exile.

10

Voting with Their Feet: Those Who Choose Exile

Only those who know how to swim will save themselves.—Cataneo, watching television, January 9, 1959, date of Fidel Castro's first speech in Havana after the triumph.

If one says "emigration" it sounds like a work stoppage, a customhouse transaction, and currency payment, all irreproachable and civilized, although painful affairs. That is not it. If one says "diaspora"—and it is said at times—it sounds like a story from the Bible—the story of a people persecuted by another. It is not that either. The people of Cuba are persecuted so that they will not leave. It is the reverse. Perhaps "exodus" or "exile" are the closest words to the phenomenon of mass exodus of almost a million Cubans on board anything that floats or flies.

What are the Cubans running from? Let us take one group at a time. The first group—January–February 1959, hardly 3000—were mostly running from revolutionary justice. The second round—the rest of 1959 and beginning of 1960—went after their money, which was in unquestionable danger due to the system about to be put into practice. (Money has the most delicate sense of political smell.) In the third big wave—1960–62—half a million Cubans were running away from the implantation of a Communist dictatorship. This flux would not have stopped in October of 1962 if the "missile crisis" had not taken place. The exodus of Cubans toward American soil was stopped as flights between the countries were interrupted. The *legal* exodus was practically terminated.

Then the other one increased: Cubans fled in yachts, in boats, on rafts, or simple life preservers. As stowaways they fled also on merchant ships and planes. The embassies that granted political asylum were virtually flooded. Venezuela had 400 and some overcrowded into three family residences. Uruguay about the same; Honduras, Brazil, Argentina, Colombia, the same.

137

Hundreds of men and women, disguised as street vendors, as pharmacy delivery boys, as physicians, as policemen, were able to clear the guard houses outside the embassies and breathe at ease. The government decided to stop the exodus with bullets. One bloody afternoon, seven corpses were left at the entrance to the Ecuadorian Embassy. The government forces began to fire against the clandestine emigrants. American coast guard patrol boats would find the remains of machine-gunned whole families dead from hunger, too much sun, or bullet wounds. A poor wretched man had to throw overboard one by one the dead bodies of his children; and finally his wife's. He eventually drifted alone and insane into an American port in the sixties.

Neither the vehicles' unrealiability nor the fear of the regime's murdering patrol boats—which fired first and asked questions later—were able to stop the families that took to the sea. More than 10,000 persons reached the American coast, Yucatán, Gran Caimán. A similar number, according to the gringos, who compute and average everything, died in the stretch. The Florida strait began to be known as Death Strait. There were episodes of incredible solidarity, such as the young shipwrecked man who, while clinging to a board, kept an elderly lady from death by holding her in his arms for several days until an unexpected ship picked them up. But there were other unspeakable acts, such as the story of the Swedish ship that returned to Havana four electrical plant workers who had shipwrecked while trying to flee the country. The government executed three and sentenced the fourth— Alberto Rodríguez Vizcaíno—to thirty years in prison in January 1961. I was in prison with him.

Cuban embassies and consulates saw their staffs reduced due to the sudden resignation of ambassadors or other minor officials. Commerical, athletic, and artistic delegations, fishermen, dancers, buyers; any opportunity to leave the country served as an alibi to go into exile, even within the Communist world. The trick was to get first to Yugoslavia, then to Italy, and there one was free. The government trained its sleuths to detect possible defectors. At times there was an agent for each athlete; half the personnel at the embassies belonged to State Security, but the exodus continued pertinaciously.

Two Cubans, who knew nothing about physiology or aeronautics, hid in the landing gear of an Iberia Airlines plane. One fell; the other, Armando Socarrás Ramírez, a 19-year-old, was able to hold fast and miraculously hibernate during the trip until he reached the Barajas airport, tumid and numb. He pulled through it and now lives in New York. Doctors cannot explain it yet— nor can Castro's police. The government, however, benefited from the exodus. First, through that irrefutable saying of "providing a silver bridge to an enemy in flight"; then by providing housing for those who remained, as the housing shortage is one of the country's most acute problems. But the repugnant slaughtering on the coasts was becoming a source of discredit to a revolution obsessed with its image.

One day in 1965, Fidel decided to permit the Cuban exiles to pick up whomever they wished at Camarioca port. In Cuba and the United States madness was organized. The trips began, in the other direction, to fetch relatives and friends at Camarioca. In twenty-four hours the government realized the enormity of its mistake. Thousands of Cubans, poor, middle class, ex-rich, massed together at the beach while everybody in the island became aware of what was going on. From the eastern provinces, farthest from Camarioca, the caravan toward the "free port" began. In Miami and Key West, against the will of the United States Immigration Department, horrified by this unprecedented and illegal situation, hundreds of boats were crossing the strait. State Security officials—the Cuban Gestapo—were stunned at seeing how the children, brothers, and sisters of the hierarchy were fleeing the country. In a week, they halted the exodus. The government realized that the prolongation of Camarioca would have been the disorderly depopulation of the island. The last straw came with the news that some exiled Cubans were in the process of renting a ship capable of transporting 2,000 persons and making a round trip every twenty-four hours. Everybody was leaving the country. The exodus was then regulated.

Two flights a day would be permitted to the United States in what became known as the Freedom Flights, in addition to the two weekly flights to Spain. Interminable waiting lists, which never shrank because of the incessant incorporation of new names, were compiled. The government then decided to punish the emigrants in a way that has never been seen in the modern history of civilized nations. First, it was decided that males between the ages of fifteen and twenty-seven would not be allowed to leave the country, as they were subject to compulsory military service. This tied down the parents of young men within that age bracket, as they would not want to abandon their sons.

As soon as a formal request to leave the country was made, the family would be considered an enemy of the fatherland. Young people in the family would have to abandon their higher studies, the parents would be dishonorably fired from their work centers and sent often like prisoners to work at agricultural tasks in the most remote sections of the country. There they would work from dawn to dusk, and if they met their quotas, if they respected the unquestionable and always insolent authority of the guards, they could, once a month, visit the family. Any rebelliousness or infraction of the camp's rules would mean the cancellation of the departure permit, which would automatically make the punished person a pariah in his own country.

Women who wanted to leave the island were not better treated than the men. In a number of cases female prisoners had to placate the ire of the guards by submitting to their sexual advances. The alternative was to be unable to depart with their husbands and children who were in other camps.

The government did not spare any harshness to discourage the exodus. The wait in forced labor camps lasted an average of two years, although many

Cubans spent five or six years there before receiving permission to leave the country. What atmosphere can the Cubans be breathing when there are hundreds of thousands ready to go through three, four, five years of forced labor, miserable food, family separations, dog-like treatment, in order to get out of the country and start the always hazardous life of an exile? There is something no one remembers: Cuba is an island but—it has a border: to the U.S.'s Guantánamo base. Many Cubans tried to escape through this route, and many succeeded, but there was also an extremely high percentage who were either shot down by frontier guards (as in Berlin, they shoot to kill), devoured by the sharks when they tried to escape swimming across the Guantánamo Bay, or blown to pieces, because there is a mined stretch of land surrounding the base.

The government itself investigated this situation. It had its Pavlovian psychologists find out the reasons for this apparently suicidal decision. In the end, the psychologists kept their mouths shut and the government slammed shut its floodgate. Again, the Camarioca picture prevailed. Two sisters of Raúl and Fidel had left; also a sister of Major Sergio del Valle, the next in command; the whole family of Major Piñeiro, better known as "Red Beard," a nephew of Nicolás Guillén; brothers of Celia Sánchez, of Armando Hart. They did not see a limit nor an end. The Camarioca episode repeated itself in 1980, but now at the Port of Mariel. Some 130,000 Cubans managed to embark before the American goverment forbade entry to refugees, the result, perhaps, of an alarming fact: Taking advantage of the massive exodus of opponents, Castro decided to take several thousand hardened criminals or chronically ill people from prisons, insane asylums, and hospitals to send them to the United States in the midst of the migratory wave.

But in 1980, as in 1965, as in 1961, not only those who had been ruined by the revolution were leaving the country, but also many who benefited: the government's own people, the family of the new class. This had never been seen even in walled Berlin. Chernienko's brother is not exiled anywhere, nor Den Xiaoping's son nor Jaruzelki's nephew. It is false that the exodus was the refuge strictly of those people ruined by the revolution. It is also false that the blockade's deprivations pushed many to exile. The Cubans were a domestic fauna, island-loving animals. In the horribly lean years of the thirties, the population census hardly changed. Besides, the revolutionary government has always guaranteed work and a minimum amount of food. These are the two factors that generate economic emigration around the world. Spaniards who have seen poverty-stricken Cubans making keys at Puerta del Sol plaza cannot believe that these people have emigrated in search of fortune. They have left for reasons of political ecology. You cannot breathe in Cuba. For those who might doubt this last statement: Odón Alvarez de la Campa, a major who lost his sight and arms as a consequence of a bomb explosion in the struggle against Batista, went into exile. What could he gain by exiling himself, poor and mutilated as he was? He forsook the protection of the revolution, the honors that were being offered him, the very high position he held. It is a mean falsehood to characterize the three-quarters of a million Cubans who have been able to flee the country as "stampeded bourgeoisie," "exploiters," "whores," or "drug traffickers." They really are a cross-section of Cuban society, with the stress on the middle social levels, but with thousands and thousands of representatives of the lowest economic extraction. This can be easily confirmed among Florida fishermen and many of the peasants who have made the sugarcane industry prosper in the southern part of the United States.

The gringos who, as we already know, measure everything, before the Mariel exodus had concluded that the Cuban emigration was the group that showed the lowest crime index in the United States, lower than the American average. This figure may have varied with the inclusion of two or three thousand delinquents criminally "exported" by Castro, but the forecast is that in a few years statistics will again reveal the virtues of the emigration. A million Cubans is too large a group for them not to constitute a valid sample of the whole society, or to be characterized with a number of easy prejudices. In Cuba's vineyard, there was a little of everything, and all (that could) took to their heels.

To discredit the mass exodus, the government has come up with the most absurd arguments. It has said that something similar happened to Puerto Rico, with a million Puerto Ricans now living in New York. If the Cubans had fled toward Moscow, the reasoning would have made sense; but it is a mockery if we realize that the flight has been to Havana's adversaries. Another time, stretching his imagination to the limit, Fidel compared his countrymen's flight with the one that took place in the United States during the War of Independence. Another bit of foolishness. Neither Washington's sister nor Jefferson's aunt desperately fled in a boat. British nationals left the ex-colony as in Cuba, at the beginning of the century, several thousand Spaniards emigrated when Spain was defeated. This had nothing to do with the impressive Cuban phenomenon. There are no convincing arguments to explain why almost a million persons fled their country, knowing that the fare costs not only a lot of money, but also years of hardship and deprivation. There is no acceptable reasoning that might clarify why a sane and responsible family head would put his wife and children in a raft in order to venture across "Death Strait."

If one could maliciously speak of those who have been "hurt" by the revolution, what can be alleged about the diplomats, dancers, writers, officials, cinematographers, relatives who have been *benefited* by the revolution and yet have opted for exile? It seems obvious that the Cuban atmosphere is totally unbreatheable. Neruda, after an unpleasant visit to Cuba, made the following painful and melancholic confession to Miguel Angel Asturias: "What a pity, Miguel, we spend our lives defending countries in which we couldn't live." The only valuable proof the revolution could offer to show the support it really can count on would be to open the airports and seaports. But the regime has already faced reality twice. Everybody leaves the county. Cubans, apparently, do not take to paradise. Lenin once said that "exiled persons vote with their feet." That is what the Cubans have done every time they have had the opportunity. Nostalgia is better than moral suffocation.

But in Cuba not only Cubans are exiled. Exiles are also exiled, as happened with the majority of the Spanish Republicans and, later, Chilean exiles who arrived fleeing Pinochet's fascist repression. The experience has been fateful for the Chileans. Although they are ideologically in agreement with theoretical Castroism, in practice it has proved unbearable. Practically all of them left Cuba. After the suicide of Allende's daughter in October 1977, and his invalid sister years later, the government allowed them to depart little by little, to avoid negative propaganda. If the Chileans had read *Persona non grata* by their countryman Jorge Edwards, the first diplomatic envoy Allende sent to Havana, they would have chosen another country. If they had been aware of Eldridge Cleaver's experience, the head of the Black Panthers who abandoned Havana, or had heard the tales by grieved air pirates who opted for turning themselves in to the FBI rather than remain in Cuba, they would have thought twice. They now know that Pinochet is no worse than Castro, just another variety of barbarism.

The Peruvian Embassy

In April 1980 (to quote a revolutionary song) "the commander arrived and ordered a halt" to the horror in order to punish the Peruvians. That is to say, he removed the guard that prevented access to the diplomatic precinct, and 10,000 Cubans—the Anabasis, the apocalypse, the hullaballoo—rushed the Peruvian Embassy in order to punish the commander. (As the waltz says, "Let me tell you, girl from Lima, let me tell you my sorrows.") For a few hours, Cuba had its open territory, its free port, to flee with what you had on you from that monstrous, cruel and foolish thing which the commander invented twenty-one years ago and which with surprisinig doggedness, had not ceased to get worse.

The whole world knows the story up to this point. There are other details less well known, and sadder, like the ones of the other thousands who did not fit inside, were taken prisoners, beaten, and spat upon by the Castroist mobs, motivated, as their commander, by a rabid pride. More horror, and with more rage, fell upon the unhappy ones who arrived late to their square centimeter of freedom.

In addition—what is more serious—the rage fell upon the people of Cuba, because from this unusual episode Fidel Castro did not draw the conclusion that the people rejected the regime because it had been thoroughly disastrous; on the contrary, he thought that he had been too "soft," that the Defense Committees "had let their guard fall," that the revolution had been too tolerant. Castro's conclusion to this episode was that the revolution must be saved with a stick and a doll that bounces back. That the screws must be tightened. Out of the moving event of "The Ten Thousand of Havana"—as the *New York Times* called it—came more firing squads, more repression, more misery for a poor and crushed people.

But this is only the next stage. In the long run, "The Ten Thousand of Havana" may be the starting point for a larger youthful rebellion, for the desertions of civil servants, for future military conspiracies. Suddenly, the deep suspicion, shared by 10,000 people, was hopelessly confirmed; Cubans are overwhelmingly against the system. This is the symbolic meaning contained in "The Ten Thousand of Havana." Before the events of April 1980, this belief was only a reasonable hypothesis ineptly proclaimed by the enemies of Castroism and always ably answered by his supporters. Before "The Ten Thousand of Havana," inside Cuba and out, the suspicion hovered in the air that Castroism, despite its errors, had the support of the people. This idea ended both inside and out of Cuba. It ended for the opposition and it ended for the sympathizers.

Now there is no alibi. Now there is no crowded Plaza of the Revolution to belie the staggering plebiscite of those thousands of hasty, early-rising citizens. When the lamentable history of Castroism—however long it lasts— is written, historians will be able to point out that the stampede of April 1980 was the beginning of the end.

Why Young People Desert

The final count of the last wave of Cuban exiles produced a significant fact: a very large percentage were less than thirty years old and many of them had not reached twenty. What has happened? In the 1980s it would be absurd to call the recently arrived anti-Castroists "bourgeois exploiters," and nobody moderately serious can believe that one is dealing with the lumpen, prostitutes, and drug addicts. Obviously, one is dealing with a proportional sample of the Cuban people. What has occurred? Let us consider.

Cuban children no longer sing children's circle songs. Now, in their games, instead of "Cheer up, cheer up," they entone, "Reagan has no mother because he was born from a monkey." And later they silently go back home where the grandmother tells them fantastic stories about countries where the children do not have to hate or learn foolish rhymes in order to go out later and sing them in chorus at demonstrations: "Fidel, you're the guard,/ Hit the Yankees plenty hard." Or that other obscene, foolish one: "Carter, you old cuckold,/ You forgot what Bay of Pigs told."

The revolution for Cuban children is not a game, an amusement, or a delight, but a responsibility, a political commitment, a total contradiction between a home where the system is hated and a society that demands the emotional tension of having to pretend all day, at all hours, always. Nobody can know that the mother hides a Sacred Heart of Jesus in the wardrobe. Or that at night, in secret, the family listens to the Voice of America. Or that the father studies English with the obsessive hope of being able to flee the country. At school another face has to be shown. One has to smile without wanting to, collaborate without wanting to. For children the revolution is not a happy experience, but a monstrous rhyme, repeated ad nauseam throughout the whole length of an endless avenue. The revolution is poverty and slogans. Fear and slogans. Shamming and slogans. But altogether, it is incomprehensible and always painful.

The greatest miseries, however, begin with adolescence. After all, children less than twelve years old do not go to prison in Cuba. That will come later when they are men and women; but the dress rehearsal begins at puberty and is called "the field school." Three months of the year adolescents are separated from their families and are taken to the sowing and harvesting of crops. During that time, living a semibarracks routine in large unhealthy cabins, improperly fed, the young people must submit to the superstition that farm work purifies, ennobles, and makes better citizens. The regime, which is apparently as simplistic as its jingles, wants to break the supposed tendency to form social classes. It wants to destroy the family influence. But the only thing that the regime manages to do is to bore the adolescent, annoy him for several precious months of his life and convert him into a permanent critic of a system that forces him to lead an unpleasant life without any rational justification.

At this stage—the slender one of from thirteen to seventeen years—life has become even gloomier than in childhood, because the demand for submission and commitment has been increasing with the years. More responsibilities are necessary, more obedience, more pretending, more submission to the arbitrary rules of the state. If he has been "good," if he has shouted enough slogans, if he has signed for the political youth organizations, if he is manly enough, if he wears his hair short, if he has rejected blue jeans and rock, if his parents are "integrated into the historical process," then he may be able to gain access to a university faculty—"the university for revolutionaries," as Fidel has said— not to study the career indicated by his vocation, but rather that which is assigned him by the state.

Strictly speaking, the life that awaits him is sad. He lacks the articles he longs for. He cannot choose his fate. He cannot dream of being a pilot, a doctor or an adventurer. (He will be what the state allows him to be.) He cannot read the books he wants to. He cannot manifest his peculiarities or his extravagances, because to distance himself from the conformist and disciplined archetype is a counterrevolutionary act. He cannot reject or make fun of the official truth. He cannot protest against the absurd African adventure. Life now, and forever, is an inability to carry out a freely chosen personal project. Is it any wonder that thousands of youths brought up by the revolution ran to the Peruvian Embassy or to the boats in the Port of Mariel? Faced with this horror, there is only one answer possible: flight.

Return of the Exiles

Silently—as silently as it is given to Cubans to be—thousands of exiles traveled to the island. They were brief, intense, and devastating visits. This tourism from exile brought about an irreparable erosion at the water line of Castroism. The exile who left because he could not stand the intolerance and inefficiency of the Castroist collectivity and who returns after a number of years to tell about the battle for the Cadillac, the house on installments financed by the FHA, the trip to Europe—"they outdid themselves in the Louvre, ole pal"—and the boy who studies at Yale and has had a car since he was sixteen, are an irrefutable demonstration that the only wise, prudent, and advisable thing to do under Castroism was to clear out. Clear out and return later—because of the question of homesickness—as a "member of the community abroad" to show that to belong to the community is much more intelligent than to belong to Communism.

To Cuba the members of the community take underpants, blue jeans, watches, a girdle for the grandmother so her cellulitis does not run off with her, a Polaroid—"Look, look, look how it's coming out . . . Mister, these Americans are the devil's own!"—socks, shoes and ball-point pens. (Some day, somebody will have to explain the incompatibility between Communism and ball-point pens.) Communism, on the other hand, is the war in Angola, volunteer work, guard duty in front of the dry cleaner's so they do not rob the coat hangers, and the raffle for the right to buy a refrigerator when the rains and the price of sugar coincide on the astral chart of a five-year plan. Communism is a drag. And a boring drag, monotonous, inefficient, gray, foolish, and wordy. Ah, this the Cubans suspected, but now, with the fugitive return—from flight—of the exiles, they have had the pathetic confirmation of the suspicion. Because Yeyo, who was an idiot, who left school because he could not roll a ball of clay, and who was a bus driver, a parking lot attendant, or a rascal, has come back to the neighborhood, wrapped in a radiant cloud of polyester, like an infallible prophet from the legendary kingdom of Union City, land of El Dorado and overtime. There is no communist manifesto, dialectical materialism, appreciation in value, or alienation that can resist the impressive reputation of Yeyo's victorious return; he, his little self, with his gold tooth, his old flattery, and his ironic little smile saying, "I told you so, brother; one had to go."

But it is not only this. The endless trail of exiles brought unknown information back to Cuba. They returned to tell, not to be told. For almost twenty years this poor country has had to suffer the lethargic tales of *Granma*, *Bohemia*, and other similar horrors. The exiles who returned contributed to the patriotic labor of sobering up their fellow citizens by offering them another version of the facts, another interpretation of the real situation abroad. For almost twenty years Castroists have been devoted to stifling, censuring, and blocking all information contrary to the official dogma. This gigantic effort of manipulation is being destroyed beneath the merry pace of the "community."

And furthermore: Several hundred young exiles had become Castroists in the uprootedness and mythification of a Cuba they did not know. The clash between the fantasy—the *exilium tremens*—and the flesh-and-blood Cuba has been decisive. And the personal recognition of error is frequent: The imagined Cuba was not that. It is true: One *had to* leave. This, sadly, has been confirmed even by a good part of the Maceo Brigade, that Castroist phalange which Cuban Security has organized abroad.

The Maceo Brigade against the Machos

As is known, there are a number of children of exiled Cubans who are Castroists, travel to Cuba, and keep certain lines of communication open with the Cuban establishment. These young people, in accordance with the militarist spirit that reigns in the island, have formed something called the Maceo Brigade. Splendid. Anti-Castroism—without trying—is able to adopt the most paradoxical attitudes. (At times I suspect that life is stubbornly anti-Castro.) Well, the brigaders, in spite of the ideological boasting, are contaminated by the incurable liberal virus, even when they recite verses learned in *Granma*.

They are people who, at a rather high price, have been exposed for two decades to the commotion of the free democratic discussion. They are people accustomed to the gesture of protest at universities (almost all of them are university students). They are people who "necessarily" subscribe to militant feminism and the free expression of sexual preferences. They are people scarcely superstitious about the question of drugs. (Many of them smoke or have smoked marihuana.) They are people accustomed by the gringos to repudiating inefficiency and for whom dogmatism—at least that of others—is repugnant. They are people so given to rebellion and nonconformity that they have fallen into the curious foolishness of becoming Castroist against all the warnings of common sense. That is to say, they are a people fatally against the system, because the system—rhetoric apart—embodies the model of robotized society in which it would be totally impossible for them to live. Havana knows this and shrewdly advises them to "keep working" in exile. This the brigaders know, and they do not insist too much on remaining in the Cuba of their dreams because it is better to dream about Cuba than live in it. It is preferable to travel there once in a while, enjoy the glorious solidarity of the "persecuted sect," give the ego a pleasant sensation of heroism, play acting in the catacombs, but without abandoning the much more comfortable American society.

Why do these boys, in spite of their background, join Castroism? In truth, they only join it for a time. Or for a few trips. Sometimes a single contact is enough to do away with the strange devotion. Sometimes a brief conversation with the frightened cousin who stayed in Luyanó, condemned by Castroism to a shack, poor in blessings and spirit, sad, desolate, vulgar, and hopeless, is enough for the brigader to reconsider his position. These stories told in a tone halfway between frustration and shame I have heard dozens of times.

On one of the Brigade's trips, a revealing incident occurred. One hundred and twenty brigaders traveled to Cuba. Out of this number, some twenty-five were homosexuals and lesbians. The most conspicuous of the homosexuals was a youth named Roca, an activist in American gay groups. I do not know how one can be a gay militant and a Castroist militant at the same time, but I suppose that Mr. Roca has some secret ideological key beyond poor Cartesian reasoning. In any case, the contradiction of Mr. Roca and the twenty-some homosexuals and lesbians is of little importance. One has seen too many anti-Semitic Jews and racist mestizos to be alarmed. What was truly noteworthy is that Mr. Roca, in public, in an open discussion with a group of young Communists, put forth his lacerating dilemma: Why could he and his colleagues not be homosexuals and Communists at the same time? Mr. Roca and his nervous colleagues wanted to hear a reassuring answer, or at least the minimal excuse of a courteous host, but Mr. Roca and his friends heard the frank and brutal ratification of the official Cuban position on the business of hormones: "Homosexuals are sick men produced in the bosom of bourgeois societies, and fortunately in Cuba"—the commissar stressed "fortunately"—"the species will soon die out." Mr. Roca was overcome by an access of wrath. Another gentleman had a nervous breakdown (that is, a fainting fit) and he was checked into a Havana clinic.

The audience was immediately divided. There was applause for the combative Mr. Roca and applause for his very macho opponent. There was whistling for some and whistling for others. For a fleeting and grotesque minute, on a tiny scale, there was an embryo of ideological pluralism and a diversity of opinions. Excellent. There, through those cracks, the discredit and destruction of Castro-Stalinism. "The dawn that will dispel the monsters," as the poet Palenzuela would say, is being woven like a fabric of painful confrontations similar to the one starring Mr. Roca. The protesters of tomorrow are perhaps today scholarship holders in Prague, Warsaw, or Moscow, exposed to the phenomenon of the dissidents and spending the last cartridges of hope. It is these gusts of information that will end up sweeping away the system. It is the debate that the Cuban delegation witnessed at the destalinizing congress of the Spanish Communists. It is the impact that Cuban fishermen receive when they dock in Western ports. It is the melancholic admission on the part of Cuban economists, in exchanges with their colleagues in exile, that Cuba is the country of the Americas that has grown least in the last two decades with the exception of the chronically ill of the continent: Haiti, Bolivia, and Nicaragua. It is the therapy of the "mirror," of the clash with reality, that will end up doing away with the system.

Appendix

The Absurd African Adventure. The first complete Cuban military units to be sent to Angola arrived in November 1975 when Portugal pulled out. Since then, as Castro himself has said on several occasions, hundreds of thousands of Cubans have performed their "international civilian and military duty" there. General Rafael del Pino, who defected from Cuba on 28 May 1987 and had been Cuba's military aviation chief in Angola, revealed that at the time of writing the number of Cuban troops stationed there was over 40,000 and that casualties due to deaths in combat, disease, wounds, and missing in action came to about 10,000.

"A ... portion of the Mariel refugees are under 18 years of age (20.1%) ... and ... the median age of the Mariel arrivals tends to be ... young ... with 68.5% below 36 years of age." J. M. Clark, J. I. Lasaga, and Rose S. Reque, *The 1980 Mariel Exodus: An Assessment and Prospect* (Washington, D.C.: Council for Inter-American Security, 1981), p. 7.

Miguel Angel Asturias (1899–1974). A Guatemalan writer who won the Nobel prize for literature in 1967. In his youth he went to Europe, settling in Paris in the 1920s. In 1927 he translated into Spanish *Popul Vuh*, the sacred book of the Quichés of Guatemala. When Arbenz was in power he served as a diplomat, but on Arbenz's overthrow he was obliged to seek asylum in Argentina. In 1966 the Soviet Union awarded him the Lenin prize. His literary works are examples of Latin American magical realism as in the case of *Hombres de maíz*, or political protest as in his trilogy about the banana companies, *Viento fuerte, El papa verde,* and *Los ojos de los enterrados.* His best-known work is *El Sr. Presidente*, about the dictatorship of the Guatemalan leader Estrada Cabrera.

Comandante Piñeiro (Barbarroja). Cuban revolutionary fighter. For several years after the revolution he held the second spot in the Interior Ministry under Ramiro Valdés. He is married to an American woman. He is in charge of spying and the penetration of Latin America by the America Section of the Central Committee of the Communist party.

Breakdown of the Exiled Population by Occupation

Professionals, semiprofessionals, managers	22.2%
Salesmen and employees	27.8%
Services	8.7%
Workers (skilled, semiskilled, unskilled)	35.3%
Farmers, fishermen, miners	6.0%

Source: J.M.Clark, "The Exodus from Revolutionary Cuba (1959–1974): A Sociological Analysis," Ph.D. dissertation, University of Florida, 1975.

Odón Alvarez de la Campa. Cuban labor union leader and revolutionary who lost both his arms in a bomb blast. After several years with the CTC (r) labor union organization he sought political asylum in Canada and now lives in Miami.

Eldridge Cleaver's Experience. The Black Panther leader visited Cuba on several occasions but later broke with Castro and Communism because he did not think Marxism would bring about the liberation of Blacks in the United States.

Armando Hart Dávalos. A Cuban revolutionary and a founding member of the July 26 Movement. He fought against the Batista dictatorship after he was arrested in 1954. On 30 November 1956 he took part in the Santiago de Cuba uprising. He was taken into custody and made a spectacular flight during the trial but was recaptured in January 1958 and held until the success of the revolution brought him freedom. From then until October 1965 he was education minister. During that period he married Haydée Santamaría whom he later divorced. At present he is a deputy in the People's Power Assembly, a member of the Council of State, and culture minister.

Jorge Edwards (1913–   ). Chilean novelist and essayist born into a leading Chilean family. He is a member of the Chilean Academy. In 1970, he was the first diplomatic envoy sent by Salvador Allende's government to Castro's Cuba to reopen relations years after they had been broken. But he had several confrontations with Castro due to his concern for human rights and freedom of expression and was eventually expelled. His vicissitudes at this time are narrated in *Persona non grata.* His works include the novels *El patio, El peso de la noche, Los convidados de piedra,* and the essay *Desde la cola del dragón.*

Comandante Sergio del Valle Jiménez. A revolutionary military chief who for a time was interior minister replacing Ramiro Valdés. In the 1980s he was a member of the Council of State and public health minister. He is one of the pillars of the revolution.

Luyanó. A working-class, industrial neighborhood in Havana.

The Peruvian Embassy Incident. On 1 April a few people forced their way into the Peruvian Embassy. Cuban guards fired on them from several sides and one of the guards was mortally wounded. Even though the individuals seeking asylum had been unarmed, Castro accused them of murder and called on Peru to hand them over. The Peruvians refused. On April 4, Castro withdrew the guards from the embassy in accordance with a carefully prepared plan. In 1978 and 1979 Castro, who desperately needed to revive the Cuban economy, had stopped calling the émigrés "worms" and allowed them to visit their relatives in Cuba as "members of the Cuban community abroad." Within a few months 100,000 exiles brought in over 100 million dollars. But their appearance had a devastating effect on the Cuban population who compared their own situation to that of the visitors and started giving vent to their discontent. As in the 1960s, acts of sabotage occurred and police repression intensified. Castro started looking for a safety valve so the unrest, spurred by economic problems, a labor surplus, and social agitation could spend itself. He had already done this in 1965 when he managed to engineer the exit of hundreds of thousands of Cubans. The Peruvian Embassy incident gave him the pretext he needed. Later, as the daily *Granma* put it, "the cyclone would blow where it has to blow" or, in other words, the Mariel exodus would head for the United States. A few hours after the Peruvian Embassy guards were withdrawn its grounds had been invaded by 10,800 Cubans of all social classes and ages and from all parts of the island. They were so tightly packed there was no room for them to sit down. Some countries, moved by their plight, offered them a certain degree of asylum and the people granted it began to leave. But Castro was obsessed with the desire to punish the United States and the Cuban émigrés. He announced that Cubans living in the United States could come and take out relatives who wanted to leave the country. Thousands of vessels converged on the port of Mariel. Castro pushed so many people onto these vessels that the crossing was made extremely dangerous. Many were drowned. Cruelest of all, Castro only let go some of the relatives the vessels had come to pick up and pressed the people sailing them to take aboard refugees from the Peruvian Embassy, saying, "their lives are in danger because the Cuban people are very angry with them." But after 125,000 had been taken by the flotilla from Mariel to Key West, the operation was halted on 2 November even though there were still 1,000 people in the Embassy. These, for some reason or other, were not being allowed to leave the island. Eight years later, a small group of these still remained.

Plaza de la Revolución. A huge esplanade located in the geographic center of Havana and flanked by many modern buildings. Its most striking feature is a gigantic monument to José Martí made from gray marble from the Isla de Pinos. It was built under the Batista dictatorship and was then given the name Plaza de la República. It is now used by Castro for mass rallies.

The Refugees' Prison Record. "Much has been said about the extremely high percentage of Mariel arrivals with a criminal record. Official figures appear to contradict that common belief. According to Immigration and Naturalization Service (INS) figures, a total of 1,761 persons, representing 1.4 percent of the new immigrants (in 1980), were classified as felons (convicted of murder, rape, or burglary)." Clark, Lasaga, and Reque: *The 1980 Mariel Exodus.* These are the prisoners who, on the announcement in November 1987 of the resumption of the U.S.-Cuban immigration agreement, feared they might be returned to Cuba after having been in American jails since arriving in 1980. They mutinied saying they preferred a U.S. prison to the freedom Castro had promised them in Cuba.

11

Anti-Castroism

Earliest Anti-Castroism

Anti-Castroism began before Castro became "Maximum Leader." I am not referring, of course, to Batista's armed forces. Batistaism was never specifically anti-Castroism. Batista—his subordinates—confronted the July 26 Movement with the same brutality and inefficiency with which they confronted other sectors of the opposition. It is very difficult to assume that Castro would have come to power without Batista's tenacious elimination—worthy of psychoanalysis—of the remaining options. Systematically, the former sergeant destroyed all the political options with one purpose in mind: that his declared enemies, the Orthodox and the Authentic, would not be able to supersede him. On 31 December 1958, the date he chose to flee the country, the opposition's conclave had already selected its pope: Fidel Castro. Thus, secretly Fidel had much to be grateful for to Batista. The old and corrupt dictator held the burning candle in his hand until the exact second that his substitute did not have any visible rivals. Then he blew out the flame and left the country. Fidel, in that euphoric moment, became the idol of 90 percent of the Cuban people. Who was not fidelista that first dawn of revolutionary triumph? Let us sidestep Batista's meager partisans. Anti-Castroism began among the group that had carried out the revolution but mistrusted Fidel and his previous background. First, the old Communist party (PSP). The Fidel they remembered was the student leader, militant in UIR (Revolutionary Insurrectional Union, an impetuous anti-Communist action group) and candidate for Congress from the Orthodox party, another anti-Marxist entity. On the other hand, the strategy of the insurrection departed radically from the classic procedural manual. There were no class struggles to be found here, no proletarian strikes, nor the rest of the Leninist recipe's seasonings. A petit-bourgeois elite had assembled a number of peasants in the rural areas and students and professionals in the cities. That was all. The Communists, flooded by the Marxist-Leninist insurrectional mythology, could not accept Fidel. Neither his pedigree nor his methods had anything to do with the missal of their sect.

Neither, but for other reasons, could the Authentic or Orthodox Castroists accept him. The Authentic, because after the scant cannon smoke had cleared, Castro was pro-Chibás and repeatedly anti-Authentic, with a past history as a member of the university's gangster groups. The Orthodox leadership did not support him because Castro was a second-class leader of the party, who had never enjoyed the sympathies of Eduardo Chibás. Chibás considered him a "trigger man"—yet Castro had ended up by seducing the party's membership without taking the leadership into account.

The Revolutionary Directorate and the Second Front of Escambray, two insurrectional groups of the same origin that challenged the July 26 Movement's claims to leadership in the anti-Batista struggle, could not be pro-Castro, due to Fidel's divine attitude. Several quarrels developed, augmented by Fidel's criticism of the attack on the Presidential Palace (Batista's official residence) which had been the work of the Revolutionary Directorate, and later, by Che's undiplomatic behavior toward the guerrillas in Las Villas province, which had as a consequence the appearance of a feeling of jealousy and hostility toward the caudillo of the Sierra Maestra.

Anti-Castroism existed, then, on January 1, 1959, the date of the revolution's offical debut—an anti-Castroism incubated during the struggle, but only at the leadership level. The masses—Orthodox, Authentic, students— were delirious followers of Fidel Castro.

Second Anti-Castroism Wave

The year 1959 began with the news that Fulgencio Batista had left for Trujillo's fiefdom. Cuba experienced an outburst of joy unlike anything seen in the island since it achieved independence in 1902. Castro entered Havana in the arms of the multitudes. He was the unquestionable but not unquestioned leader. A few days later the Revolutionary Directorate announced that it would not turn over the Presidential Palace nor the university to the forces of July 26. Fidel attacked them with a terrible and unheard-of weapon: a two-hour televised speech. The members of the terrified Directorate surrendered and turned in their weapons.

A few weeks later, the Communist party (PSP), horrified upon discovering that Fidel was planning to establish a personal dictatorship, organized a public demonstration in front of the Presidential Palace asking for elections. Secretly, Carlos Rafael Rodríguez notified the party not to be foolish, that the business about the dictatorship was true, but that there was a strong possibility that it would be a Communist one. The party was again able to breathe with ease and began to scream the slogan of "Elections, what for?"

There were no other notable incidents during the first few months of Castro's government. There was, however, criticism of the revolution's judical procedures. Among the country's educated sectors a certain repugnance arose in the face of the obvious arbitrariness of the revolutionary tribunals. The country was accustomed neither to summary trials nor to massive executions. It was not that the crimes committed by the previous government thugs were not condemnable, but simply that on many occasions their trials were not convincing. Fidel publicly asked for a new trial to convict a number of pilots in Batista's air force who had been previously found innocent by a revolutionary tribunal. After a second trial, the pilots were given a 30-year prison sentence; Félix Pena, commander of the Sierra and president of the tribunal, committed suicide, and here Fidel's public image suffered its first serious blow. Almost everybody knew that "a person cannot be tried twice for the same crime."

The first polemics with the Communists erupted. The liberal and conservative press began to criticize the government. The anti-Batista groups that were not part of the government—the Triple A of Sánchez Arango, the Authentic party of Tony Varona, the Second Front of Escambray, certain leaders of the Revolutionary Directorate— began to show nervous symptoms. There were two hypotheses circulating: The optimistic one believed that Fidel was going to implant a terrible personal dictatorship; the pessimistic one was convinced that the dictatorship would be Communist. Toward mid-1959, there were still no formal conspiracies, but sounding-outs, conversations, and exchanges of ideas. The July 26 party itself was divided into two clearly defined wings throughout the years of struggle. The urban 26—"the plains"—essentially made up of students and professionals, constituted the organization's Right; the rural 26—"the Sierra"—blindly followed Fidel, and set off with their leader on the Marxist adventure.

In July 1959—hardly seven months after the triumph of the revolution—the flagrant desertion of Major Díaz Lanz, commander-in-chief of the air force, took place. In his signed resignation, broadcast by the United States, Díaz Lanz stated that Castro had every intention of establishing a Communist dictatorship. President Urrutia confronted the Communists and Castro forced him to resign. A short time afterward, Luis Conte Agüero, a journalist and political leader, initiated a polemic with the Communist party which involved the whole country. Castro, contrary to everybody's expectation, intervened, attacking the journalist. Public opinion again became divided over the "Huber Matos affair." Matos was a very popular major who had won his stripes in the Sierra and who resigned from his position as military commander of Camagüey province, after sending a confidential letter to Castro in which he expressed his reservations regarding Communist machinations within the revolutionary ranks. The moment he was notified of the dissident's resignation, Castro answered publicly, accusing Matos and his commanding officers of treason. The Cabinet itself became divided over this patently unjust and excessive accusation. Several ministers, among them Manuel Ray and Manuel Fernández, turned in their resignations. Faustino Pérez refused to sign a public statement against Matos. Manuel Fernández, an old pro-Guiteras revolutionary, fought a tremendous battle while trying to preserve the freedom of the labor unions. During the Ninth Congress of the Cuban Labor Federation (CTC), the union leaders refused to collaborate with the Communists. Castro personally attended the congress and demanded that the members of the Communist party be accepted. There was a degree of resistance, but David Salvador, the July 26 labor leader, ended up by submitting under enormous pressure. At the University of Havana the Communists had hardly any power. The two leaders disputing the elections were anti-Communists: Pedro Luis Boitel and Rolando Cubela. Cubela won, but years later he and Boitel ended up in prison at the same time.

The "Díaz Lanz," "Urrutia," "Conte Agüero," "Huber Matos," "university," "CTC" events slowly opened Cuban eyes to the Communist twist that Castro had given the revolution. Anti-Castroism turned from barbershop discussion to full-blown conspiracy.

The Conspirators

Anti-Castroism, as seen through propaganda's eyes, appeared to be the refuge of Batista's henchmen and millionaires, but essentially it has only been the continuation of the anti-Batista ideology scheme based on a deeply rooted liberal tradition: reformist currents directed by men from middle social levels. The pro-Batista people—as a group—have practically not intervened in the anti-Castro struggle, and the large economic interests have done nothing but lament their woes. The truly original element in the anti-Castro struggle has been the appearance of rural guerrillas, who operated autonomously, without the leadership of the urban elite. Another new ingredient in the struggle was contributed by the apostolic character that some groups, openly oriented by Jesuits, wanted to lend their conspiracies. For the first time in the history of Cuba's domestic struggles one could hear the rather exotic shout of "Long Live Christ the King," a shibboleth, by the way, that was a portent of bad luck among the Mexican *cristeros* of the twenties.

The Heirs of the Revolution against Batista

The most vigorous anti-Castro groups were formed by revolutionary dissidents. The Revolutionary Movement of the People (MRP), led by engineer Manuel Ray and an eminent group of men from the ranks of the urban July 26 party—Emilio Guede, Reynold González, Enrique Barroso—

were able to bring together a good portion of the social democratic revolutionaries who opposed the implantation of a Communist dictatorship. The moment Ray turned in his resignation as a minister of public works—in October 1959—he feverishly proceeded to organize the resistance. Toward mid-1960, the MRP was an impressive clandestine network, but very vulnerable because of it vast dimensions. The Castro intelligence apparatus had been able to infiltrate it at different levels.

The November 30 group (named after the date of an aborted uprising against Batista) was another important anti-Castro movement directly conceived by the revolution. Its chief coordinator was David Salvador, president of the Cuban Federation of Labor. The November 30 membership consisted almost wholly of proletarians. Its leaders were at the same time leaders of various syndicates, and its action cadres were nurtured by dissidents from the July 26 Movement.

The Liberal Political Tradition

The Authentic party, overthrown by Batista's 1952 coup d'état, created two insurrectional groups to combat the usurper: the Triple A, led by Aureliano Sánchez, Mario Escoto, Pepe Utrera, Mario Villar Roces, and other revolutionaries of the thirties, and the Authentic Organization. These two groups opposed Castroism as soon as the communist direction of the political process became obvious. The Triple A, which had close ties with the Latin American democratic Left, was able to replenish its cadres with university students attracted by Sánchez Arango's honest background. The Authentic Organization disappeared, reemerging as a movement called Rescate (Rescue), founded by Tony Varona (in light of the discreet withdrawal of Carlos Prío, who as a former president of Cuba was the natural head of the Authentic party). Rescate's cadres and membership were recruited among the members of the old structure of the Authentic party, with a few exceptions among the youth.

A Rare Anti-Castro Element

If the previous groups answered to easily indentifiable roots, the appearance of the religious factor gave origin to an anti-Castro community without historical precedents: The Movement of Revolutionary Recuperation (MRR) and Agrupación Católica Universitaria (ACU) under the leadership of the Jesuit Llorente, had created a kind of Catholic masonry very similar to the methods and objectives of the Opus Dei, Father Llorente wanted the "agrupados" to become an elite capable of controlling economic and political power. ACU's most daring and persuasive leader was Manuel Artime, and during the dictatorship's last few months, Llorente himself—a friend of Fidel

Castro and his spiritual advisor during Fidel's years as a student at Belén Jesuit School—succeeded in incorporating Artime and Emilio Martínez Venegas into the guerrillas of Sierra Maestra. Soon after the triumph of the revolution, Artime was named director of an agricultural development zone in Oriente province, a project under the umbrella of the National Institute of Agrarian Reform (INRA). Artime, who had imagination, dynamism, and a certain charisma, then organized the Rural Commandos with his comrades from ACU. Later—while conspiring against the government—Artime and his followers would take possession of the incipient MRR. The student sector of that movement became the Revolutionary Directorate, a group whose connection with its namesake which had fought against Batista was only nominal.

The MRR, an organism without historical tradition, without effective ties with the noncommunist faction of the power structure at that time, turned into the center of the anti-Castro struggle by virtue of the special support it received from the CIA. The American intelligence apparatus had better relations with the Catholic youth group than with the MRR, the November 30, or the Second National Front of Escambray. The basis for the collaboration between the CIA and the anti-Castro groups was established by Juan Antonio Rubio Padilla, prominent member of the Agrupación Católica Universitaria. The CIA, in its search for docile elements, forgot that a political conflict such as the one taking place in Cuba could not be shouldered by a group which was hardly representative and totally foreign to the country's revolutionary tradition.

The Bay of Pigs

The idea of the Bay of Pigs—like the support for the MRR—was an erroneous, sectarian, and selfish prolongation of the CIA's viewpoint. The CIA not only sought to overthrow Castro, but was also careful to install a substitute docile to Washington's command. Before the invasion was launched, men whose job was to control and direct the clandestine movements were sent to Cuba. These men had at their disposal sufficient economic resources, equipment, and training to take control of the anti-Castro apparatus. Only the peasant guerrilla groups who had emerged in the Escambray mountains, in Las Villas province, remained independent. Since these were not groups which could be controlled, the CIA preferred to passively contemplate their extinction.

The German writer Hans Magnus Enzensberger provides a negative portrayal of the Bay of Pigs invaders in a particularly valuable book, *El interreogatorio de La Habana* (The Havana Inquiry). He is mistaken when judging anti-Castroism by the socioeconomic composition of participants in the invading brigade. Possibly, the Bay of Pigs was the least representative episode in the history of the struggle against Castro. A human mosaic like the

2506 Brigade—the name of the invading army—was able to materialize only by virtue of the enormous resources of the CIA, placed at the service of a debatable objective: to overthrow Castro in order to implant a government that would strictly obey the United States. There would be few objections to the Brigade's individual members. With the exception of three dozen of them— there were almost 1,500 men—the members of the Brigade were well-intentioned persons who could claim unstained antecedents. Yet the Brigade was not a revolutionary organization with a determined political projection, but an army arbitrarily recruited by the CIA for a strictly military battle. Later, it would serve as the power tool of a movement without minimum popular support (the MRR), ascribed to an exotic, confused, and sectarian brand of militant Catholicism.

One of the most incomprehensibly stupid aspects of the Bay of Pigs invasion is the fact that the CIA chose a conventional battleground while at the same time depriving its forces of air cover. Even without the support of public opinion—which was very much divided in April 1961—the Brigade, solely by force of arms, could have maintained control of a beachhead and a few square miles of territory for several weeks if the awaited air cover had impeded the Brigade's supplies from turning into target practice for Castro's intact air force. Those weeks would have sufficed to provoke a coup d'état from within Castro's army—also very much divided at that time—or the ample recognition by other countries of a belligerent government located on the beachheads and in towns controlled by invaders.

The 2506 Brigade's defeat—its triumph would have meant the end of an independent and nationalist anti-Castroism—marked the end of a certain kind of anti-Castroism, chiefly for one reason: The repressive apparatus of the government took advantage of the situation and in forty-eight hours dismembered the clandestine networks of the opposition through the massive detention of half a million persons in one of the largest police operations in history. Sports stadiums, government buildings, and schools served as temporary prisons that housed any citizen who was not a manifest adherent of the regime. After the triumph, and not before carefully sifting the release, the majority of those detained were set free.

After those disastrous days of April 1961, the anti-Castro movement, disorganized and defeated, with its leaders either having been granted asylum in embassies, herded into prisons, or executed, did not again have real possibilities of success.

The Anti-Castro Guerrilla Struggle

The government called them "bandits" and created some "battalions to fight the bandits." They were not bandits, but viscerally anti-Communist peasants. Only very tough peasants were able to survive in the Escambray mountains, facing constant siege by tens of thousands of men. I quote the *Granma* newspaper (May 25, 1970): "Following Eisenhower's orders—as he himself would confess—a few days after the triumph of the revolution, the CIA began to organize counterrevolutionary bands in our mountains; in our country's six provinces they existed, spread out over different periods. And finally, there were 179 guerrilla groups simultaneously razing the Cuban countryside, 179 guerrilla groups which were composed of 3,591 bandits who had risen up in arms and been given weapons by the CIA." The figures may be accurate. What is not true is the CIA's role in the affair. Of those 179 guerrilla groups, hardly a dozen of them had even sporadic contacts with the CIA. The government called them "bandits" and not "guerrillas" to conceal the evident fact that there was a tenacious and bloody peasant opposition that moved Raúl Castro to exclaim, reflecting on the government campaign to eradicate the insurrection: "What price did it cost us? What is most valuable above all: nearly five hundred lives of our young combatants, some almost adolescents? How much did it cost us in material resources? There were years in which the struggle against the bandits cost us nearly 200 million pesos, and it is not an exaggeration to say that altogether it cost us between 500 and 800 million pesos."

Why the guerrilla explosion, who were their leaders? To understand this long, internecine, and heroic—why not?—episode of the anti-Castro struggle, one must take into account certain regional factors that developed at the time of the struggle against Batista. Fidel Castro had chosen the mountains in Oriente province to conduct his guerrilla war, a stretch sufficiently rough and extensive to operate in with a certain degree of impregnability, but Eloy Gutiérrez Menoyo, Faure Chomón, and Rolando Cubela—the first a leader of the Second Front of Escambray, and the latter two from the Revolutionary Directorate—had taken a more daring step by creating a guerrilla nucleus in Las Villas province, in the middle of the country, in a mountainous zone, much smaller and more accessible to Batista's troops than Sierra Maestra. When Fidel Castro started his invasion headed toward the Western part of the island, led by Che Guevara and Camilo Cienfuegos, what he sought was not to widen his military front, but to take away from Menoyo guerrillas and the Directorate's men, the revolutionary leadership of the central region of the country. Fidel Castro's fear of the Second Front of the Escambray and of the Directorate's activities was so great that his decision to pact secretly with the Communist party was probably a result of this consternation. The CP was able to organize two small guerrilla nuclei in Escambray, one under the command of Félix Torres, the other under the leadership of Armando Acosta, both party veterans. What the CP offered Fidel in Sierra Maestra—the party was convinced of Batista's eventual defeat and was fearful of the anticommunist feelings in the Directorate and the Second Front—was those two guerrilla groups that operated in Escambray and which permitted the July 26 Movement to place a foot in Las Villas mountains while Che and Camillo undertook their difficult journey.

When Che and Camilo arrived in Las Villas, they were greeted with open hostility by the Escambray men, with cordiality by the Directorate, and with enthusiasm by the Communists who had been keeping their beds warm for the July 26 Movement's newcomers. The area's peasants, massively, were partisans of Gutiérrez Menoyo. This small, thin revolutionary— born in Spain and exiled when he was a small child—was one of the bravest and most imaginative guerrilla leaders in the struggle against Batista. His charisma did not depend on political training or on his leadership qualities—which he lacked—but on his legendary physical courage and his extraordinary ability to carry out daring guerrilla actions.

It is in the Escambray context, where the figure of Gutiérrez Menoyo stood out, and in which Fidel Castro did not leave his military imprint, where one has to begin explaining the surge of the anti-Castro guerrilla activities. Almost all leaders of the anti-Castro guerrillas were local caudillos who in the struggle against Batista had taken to the hills, and now were contemplating the communization of the country as the work of people for whom they felt an old rivalry. This was the case of Osvaldo Ramírez—a legend among the peasants and the only guerrilla leader to whom Castro offered a truce and amnesty if he would lay down arms. This was also the case of Porfirio Ramírez, president of the Students' Federation at the University of Santa Clara (executed), of Luis Vargas, Evelio Duque, Edel Montiel, César Páez, Ramonín Quesada, Thorndike, José Andrés Pérez ("Cloud Tail," a nickname given him because he always had a swarm of militiamen pursuing him), Plinio Prieto, Vicente Méndez, and other guerrilla leaders.

What the government called the "Escambray cleanup," an operation led by majors Tomasevich and Victor Dreke, was a bloody war in which the government's brutal excesses were many. Having decided to stamp out the establishment of guerrilla groups at all costs and conscious of the sympathies with which the peasants of the area received the insurgents, the government had whole towns moved, using tactics reminiscent of the massive reconcentration of Cubans carried out by Valeriano Weyler during the colonial wars of the past century.

The Castro government's military strategy was as primitive and costly as it was effective: Rings of soldiers combed the area inch by inch, shooting on the spot any rebel they found. Helicopters from Russia and dogs from East Germany were used. The captured insurgents were executed on the spot, frequently without the useless procedure of a summary trial, and immediately turned over to the coroner, to learn through an autopsy what kind of food the guerrilla fighters had ingested. This small detail—corn, sugar, pork, beef—

could be useful in tracking down the survivors. On one exceptional day, the coroner at Topes de Collantes Hospital had to perform thirty-eight autopsies of young peasant insurgents whom he had seen arrive at the hospital that same morning alive and well.

The Escambray cleanup, the Bay of Pigs invasion, and the intense days of the October crisis have been the fundamental milestones in the elaboration of Fidel Castro's mythology after the revolutionary triumph. Part of the military hierarchy that later perfected its skills in Czechoslovakian and Russian military academies, received its baptismal fire in Escambray. Of that silenced episode there are hardly any chronicles left, aside from the triumphant and distorted versions of the Cuban press. Two valuable books by the *Granma* correspondent on the front, the young writer Norberto Fuentes, in those years decidely pro-Castro, are the exceptions. The author had sufficient honesty and did not hide his admiration for hundreds of forsaken men, tenaciously idealistic, surrounded by a very powerful army, but incapable of giving or asking for a truce. The books are entitled *Cazabandidos* (Bandit Hunters) and *Los condenados del condado (The County's Condemned)*. Norberto Fuentes would end up, of course, discredited and finally pardoned.

Last Operations

After the October crisis (1962), with the United States committed to coexistence with Castro and with the clandestine organizations that operated inside the country practically destroyed, some groups from abroad began to prepare commando raids. The "Commando L," under the leadership of Santiago Alvarez and Tony Cuesta, an ex-captain of the July 26 Movement, were able to seriously damage the Soviet oil carrier *Bakú*. Alfa 66—the cryptic name adopted by Gutiérrez Menoyo and his men—carried out several raids against coastal installations. The Students' Revolutionary Directorate, in a raid directed by Juan Manuel Salvat, the most combative of its leaders, machine-gunned from the sea a hotel frequented by the Soviets.

After Manuel Artime and the Bay of Pigs invaders were set free, in 1963 the CIA organized several commando raids, but months afterwards, the plans were cancelled due to international pressure following the attack which took place against the Spanish cargo ship *Sierra Aranzazu,* when the commandos thought it was the *Sierra Maestra,* the flagship of the Cuban merchant marine.

Three men, among them a few with a long guerrilla warfare history, insisted on returning to Cuba to organize another guerrilla uprising: Eloy Gutiérrez Menoyo, Vicente Méndez, and Amancio Moqueda, known as "Yarey." Gutiérrez Menoyo landed with three of his men in 1966. Putting up strong resistance, he was captured one month after his landing. Yarey, due to his multiple clandestine landings and departures from Sierra Maestra, had become a legendary figure among the peasants of Oriente province. His execution was made a public affair with the object of *proving* the death of a man who appeared to be immortal in the naive eyes of Cuba's rural people. Vicente Méndez, after years of difficulties and failures, was able to return to Cuba with a guerrilla group of several men, only to die fighting a few weeks later.

There is in the lives of all these men an inexplicable spirit of sacrifice that transcends any reckless adventurism. The biographies of all of them can be reduced to one word: struggle, a struggle that began in their adolescence, first against Batista's regime, and later against the Communist dictatorship. The spectacle of half a dozen men merely armed with rifles, joyously undertaking a trip to an almost certain death, is genuinely distressing, but that episode, repeated a thousand times during the past century and a quarter, appears to be the inevitable fate of Cuba.

Appendix

Agrupados. A colloquial name given to members of the Roman Catholic University Group (ACU).

Luis Conte Agüero. A newspaper and radio commentator connected to the Orthodox party and stepbrother of Batista's candidate for the 1958 elections, Andrés Rivero Agüero. In the early stages of the revolution he supported the July 26 Movement and Castro, but later went into exile.

Aureliano Sánchez Arango. Cuban politician linked to the Authentic party who played a part in the struggle against Machado during the 1930s. He was education minister in President Prío Socarrás's cabinet. The Orthodox leader Chibás accused him of embezzlement. After Batista's coup d'état, he opposed him from exile with his organization known as the Triple A. Later he opposed Castro's Communist regime.

Manuel Artime. A Cuban revolutionary and student leader who fought in the Sierra Maestra. He was a member of the Roman Catholic University Group. After being sent to a farm development zone in Oriente, he went into exile in 1960 but returned the following year as a leader of the 2506 Brigade which landed at the Bay of Pigs and was taken prisoner. After being tried and condemned along with his comrades in arms, he was allowed to go back to the United States in exchange for arms and foodstuffs.

Cristeros. Roman Catholic combatants in the civil war that broke out in Mexico between 1926 and 1929 in reaction to the anticlerical legislation of President Plutarco Elías Calles. The fighting was on occasions extremely fierce and the conflict destroyed completely the already fragile Mexican social and political order.

The Escambray "cleanup." The fighting that took place in the Escambray range until 1963 when a large number of peasants and other insurgents waged guerrilla warfare against the government in opposition to the arbitrary measures in the area of the National Agrarian Reform Institute.

Mario Escoto. A Cuban revolutionary who was a member of Aureliano Sánchez Arango's Triple A. He died in exile in the United States.

The freeing of the 2506 Brigade. After the failure of the Bay of Pigs invasion, the survivors were tried and sentenced, but after long talks the U.S. government agreed to ransom them for about $60 million. On returning to Florida they were welcomed by First Lady Jacqueline Kennedy, who received them with an emotional speech delivered in Spanish.

Norberto Fuentes (1943–   ). A Cuban writer. In 1965 he experienced the campaign against "bandits"—in fact, insurgents—as a war correspondent. He then wrote *Los condenados de Condado* which won the Casa de las Américas prize. He has also written feature articles for the newspaper *Hoy* and the magazine *Cuba.*

Granma. The name of the yacht in which Fidel Castro and his 82 men set sail from Yucatán in late November 1956. After overcoming considerable difficulties, the yacht took them to the southeastern coast of Oriente province, a swamp-filled area. The official Communist party newspaper takes its name from that of the yacht.

INRA. National Agrarian Reform Institute, a "superministry" set up after the revolution. Its headquarters was in the old mayor's palace facing the Plaza de la Revolución, nowadays occupied by the Ministry of Armed Forces. It coordinated everything connected with agrarian reform, a traditional demand of the revolutionaries.

Pedro Luis Díaz Lanz. The first chief of the Revolutionary Air Force. He carried arms to the Sierra while Castro was fighting there. In the summer of 1959 he fled to the United States because of increasing Communist penetration and returned to Havana aboard a B-26 from which he scattered leaflets. He was fired upon from the land and the bullets caused several deaths when they fell back to earth. These deaths were blamed on Díaz Lanz who was accused of bombing Havana. He lives in exile in Miami.

Manuel Urrutia Lleó (1901–1981). A Cuban high court judge who ordered the release of anti-Batista revolutionaries whom he considered patriots and was in consequence expelled from the judiciary by the dictator. After the revolution, Castro chose him to be transitional president but he soon found himself at odds with the Communists who were penetrating the new government and the country's insititutions. In 1959 Castro cleverly engineered his resignation. Shortly after, President Urrutia sought asylum in a foreign embassy but could not leave it until he received a safe-conduct in 1963.

Father Llorente, S.J. A Spanish Jesuit who in the 1950s was the spiritual director of the Roman Catholic University Group and knew Castro when he was a pupil of the Jesuits.

Amancio Moqueda ("Yarey"). A Cuban revolutionary who returned with Eloy Gutiérrez Menoyo in 1966 to start guerrilla operations in the Escambray range. A month after landing he was shot in public to put an end to the legend that he was indestructible.

Opus Dei. An international Roman Catholic organization of a decidely conservative nature which was founded by Monsignor Escrivá de Balaguer and has branches throughout the world.

Juan A. Rubio Padilla. A Cuban physician and member of the Roman Catholic University Group. He was the first middleman between the anti-Castro opposition and U.S. government agencies.

Revolutionary Insurrection Union (UIR). A revolutionary political organization set up on paramilitary lines which acquired a markedly gangsterlike character. Fidel Castro was a member for a time in the 1940s.

Mario Villar Roces. Cuban lawyer, writer, and member of Aureliano Sánchez Arango's Triple A. At present he is deputy secretary of CID.

Juan Manuel Salvat. A Cuban student exiled in Miami and linked to the Roman Catholic University Group. Soon after the revolution he participated in anti-Castro incursions. In one of them he machine-gunned from a high-speed launch the Hotel Rosita de Hornedo, on Havana's sea front, where the Soviet technical aid delegations were lodged.

José Utrera. A Cuban revolutionary and student leader belonging to the Triple A. He died in exile in the United States.

Valeriano Weyler (1838–1930). A Spanish general who has an evil reputation in Cuba where he was military governor toward the end of the nineteenth century. He waged an extremely harsh war against the insurgents and relocated peasants far away from their natural environment, sending them to towns and villages where, landless and penniless, thousands suffered hunger and disease. The objective was to deprive the *mambises,* as the rebels were called, of support. Weyler was finally replaced as a result of international pressure. In 1909, when he was captain-general of Catalonia, he organized the crackdown that brought about Barcelona's "Tragic Week."

12

Cuba and the United States

Every so often Cuba comes on heat and makes signs to the United States. The United States wags the tail of the Department of State and then makes a gesture of drawing near. They sniff each other, there is something like some little growls, it seems like the thing is going to start, but suddenly, at the halfway point, an uproar of barkings and bitings ensues, and discord starts up again. Why?

Basically because Fidel Castro is kind of political animal who is completely incomprehensible to his Yankee interlocutors. The Yankees give the negotiations an institutional character and that is the way they conceive of them: as business, as nonleisure, as nonsport, as nonbattle. Negotiation is, on the other hand, a give and take of common interests. With Fidel the opposite occurs: Negotiation is not a business but a sport he is going to win. It is his favorite sport. Because Fidel does not negotiate but argues, and his greatest pleasure as a sophist is to defeat his adversary. Fidel goes to the negotiations not with the spirit of interchange but with that of conquering and seducing. His ideal formula for "settling" the problem of Cuba versus the USA lies in shutting oneself up in a room or going on a shark hunt with the Yankee chief and Indian wrestling like two old savage leaders until one of the two gives up. From this comes his capacity for seduction in certain areas of the planet. From this, his easy dialogue with the little tyrants of the Third World. Fidel wins them over by means of histrionic gestures, affectionate expressions, infinite curiosity, and the shyster logic of his reasoning.

These "virtues" become defects in his negotiations with Washington. He wraps his pettyfogging in a skein of sophistries. Why, if the Yankees have the right to intervene in Vietnam, does he—Cuba, I mean—not have the same right to intervene in Angola? Why, if the Yankees have a base in Puerto Rico, is he—Cuba, I mean—not going to have another in Jamaica? Why, if the United States has bases in Germany, and even in Cuba itself, cannot the Soviets have their base in Cienfuegos? Fidel, when it suits him, does not understand history or the existence of a particular political logic that deposits in some countries certain responsibilities corresponding to their potentialities, histories, origins, and all the ingredients that enter into the game of designing international politics.

Fidel cannot understand the legitimate astonishment of Kissinger when he asked what the little Cubans were doing sending their armies hither and yon, because Kissinger has a keen perception of the political fabric while Fidel cannot give up the most elementary pettyfogging schemes. Fidel begins with the strange legal superstition that Cuba is as much of a country as the United States, and he as much of a president as the Yankee. His bad habits as an inveterate sophist have not allowed him to discover that the equality of nations is nothing more than a crude extension of equality among men, a piece of nonsense that resists analysis. It is very likely that the only thing that a Hottentot and a Belgian have in common is the necktie, i.e., the kind of civilization. And surely that Hottentot, transferred to Brussels, can be a doctor or an effective teacher, or the Belgian, in the jungle, can turn into a magnificent hunter, and so one proves that a potential equality exists among men. But from this to proclaiming the equality between Pago-Pago and France there is a gap that is bridged only by courtesy or sophism. Burundi and England, or Cuba and the United States, are clearly not equal, but Castro does not understand this.

Anchored to his pettyfogging schemes, to the fiction of international justice—an abstraction foreign to politics—Castro is not even capable of understanding that if tomorrow a cyclone wiped every vestige of Cuban society off the map, it is probable that the planetary consequences of the catastrophe would scarcely be perceived in the supplying of maracas to tropical combos, while if the same thing happened to the United States the planet would be snowed under.

Fidel is accustomed to saying that in thirty years he has gone from being a revolutionary to being a statesman. False. These thirty years have only served to convince him that he had not the slightest idea of what it means to run a country. Maybe in the next thirty years he will manage to understand Cuba's exact dimensions, his own, and the low specific weight that befits his country given the extension, population, history, and underdevelopment of the natives. Maybe then he will have learned to negotiate realistically.

The Falklands Case

As proof that Castro continues to be Castro, one has to refer to the Falklands episode. It was perfectly foreseeable: Castro wanted to send his regiments to the Falklands. Castro is capable of fighting against the elements and then shooting them. No war is sufficiently alien or remote to this tireless Napoleon of the Caribbean. It makes no difference whether it is Ethiopia, Angola, Southern Yemen, or the most distant archipelago. For Castro the world is like a machine to kill Martians and his personal function is to press the buttons until no one is left alive.

It is naiveté to suppose that the Cuban presence in this embroglio was by order of the Soviet Union. There was no time to coordinate that sort of thing. The shots rang out and in Havana the madhouse was unleashed. The smell of war drove them crazy. Castro took part because a Latin American war in which Cuba did not participate was absolutely inconceivable to him. It was all the same to him that in the Falklands he accepted what he is fighting against in Belice, or that his arms went to the aid of the Argentine "disappearers" of men. Any sign of ideological incoherence will always be less than the irrepressible urge to play soldiers that this restless warlord suffers from, to waste Cubans (or their opponents).

It is good for this to be known, because apparently Castro is a tool of the imperial designs of Moscow, when exactly the opposite happens: Moscow is the tool of the imperial (or hormonal) designs of Castro. Without Moscow there is no protagonism on a planetary scale, and Castro does not conceive of life without protagonism. It is Castro who summoned the USSR to the massacres in Angola and Ethiopia. It is Castro who, faced with the cool caution of the USSR, joyfully offered his Migs for the war in the Falklands. Before Castro, Moscow had no African or Central American policy based on the violent seizure of power. Now it has. Castro proposed it.

The gringos have never understood the warlike dimension of Castro. To seduce Castro one did not have to offer him credits or petroleum, but a historic role in which he could exercise his hero's vocation. In 1959 it probably would have been possible, in exchange for headlines in newspapers, to recruit Castroism for pro-Yankee adventures. Castro might have been a democratic pistol if Kennedy had contracted him, say, to overthrow Trujillo and Somoza on behalf of the Latin American democracies. Perhaps Castro would have preferred to make use of Washington before Moscow for his imperialistic designs, but within the mechanics of American foreign policy the mischievous complexity of a person as complicated as Castro is not conceived. If one personality repugnant to the values of Yankee society exists, it is that of this visceral, talkative, emotional, tactile, chaotic, sweaty Castro. The dialogue was absolutely impossible.

Three decades later all attempts at a rapprochement between Washington and Havana continue to fail. Neither one opposing party nor the other explains for sure why the negotiations fail, but the key is this: Washington does not offer Castro a role. The Yankee presidents maintain the rare superstition that the Cuban president is a president like them, made of flesh and blood, worried about balancing the budget and reducing inflation. A gross mistake: Give him a horse, a Winchester and a number of Indians for target practice. Then he will be utterly happy.

The Blockade Affair

As is known, the United States, in different ways, economically blockades, or has blockaded, Rhodesia, Chile, Cuba, and Argentina. But it is the blockading of Cuba, for being aimed at a Communist country, that excites the greatest number of rebuffs. Cuba fosters these condemnations because it ardently desires relations with the United States. That is the obsession, the mania, of the Cuban leaders. In that country, thoroughly mistaken, the leaders have ended up clinging to the delirious consolation that relations with Washington will alleviate the economic situation and end up by bringing a new prosperity.

Those poor, desperate people assume that the end of the blockade will be like a magic kind of Leatril that will cure the cancer of scarcity, the chaos and the domestic inefficiency, by virtue of some mysterious and unexplained beneficial properties. Those poor people have not stopped to think that where 8 million dollars a day in Soviet aid have not been enough, plus the overpricing of sugar, plus the subsidy for petroleum, plus Eastern European aid, plus credits, sometimes generous, from Spain, Canada, France, Japan, Argentina, Mexico, Algeria, and Libya, plus COMECON, plus the hiring of thousands of Cuban technicians and soldiers by pro-Soviet Arab countries, the ending of the blockade will mean very little because, frankly, Cuba has nothing to sell to the United States, and it has very little funds to buy from it.

What does Cuba expect, then, from the end of the blockade? A shower of manna? Perhaps the possibility of going a little further into debt on the American financial front? Issue some bonds for the Yankee market, as it did in a bankrupt way in Switzerland, with pitiful conditions? Funds from the AID and the World Bank? Whatever it manages to get—20, 30, 100 million dollars—will scarcely be enough to face the huge economic catastrophe. They are homeopathic doses for a generalized and incurable infection. That is to say, Cuba needs to be exploited and the United States refuses to exploit her.

And if this is the case, why does the United States not lift the blockade and put an end to the last alibi of the Cuban regime? There are several reasons. The first is almost a law of political behavior: Inertia is more powerful than the will to change. The blockade is the policy that exists, that is there, the modus vivendi that Americans have grown used to without serious obstacles. Nobody feels the need to lift it because nothing substantial is at stake by doing so. To lift it, however, is to stir the wasps' nest of moderate political forces, go against the lobby of the companies damaged by the nationalizations of the revolution, add an issue to the political cockpit that will not bring votes to the one who proposes it, and maybe will take them away. In other words, there are no practical reasons for ending the policy of blockading Cuba, even if that policy makes little sense.

In the beginning, for Kennedy, the blockade was the alternative to war. An energetic gesture that meant that the United States was ready to fight. Later he maintained it while he had secret plans developed that would put an end to Castroism. What at the outset was only a bellicose language, later remained as the visible framework of hostility in which the CIA carried out its attempts to overthrow Castro by means of assasination or conspiracies. The capitulations that put an end to the October crisis explicitly excluded conventional war, the landing of Marines or OAS forces, but not clandestine conflict. Kennedy renounced intervening in Cuba with his army, but not liquidating the Castro regime. With these aims in mind, it was absurd to lift the blockade. The blockade has remained as a sign of belligerance, the ensign raised on the tallest mast.

What will happen, then, with the blockade? Objectively, it is all the same whether it exists or is eliminated. But it has an enormous symbolic value for Fidel and his followers who are used to evaluating all events as "battles" that are "won" or "lost." To harvest 10 million tons of sugar, which was a simple agricultural question, in the hands of our eponymous heroes became a frenzied "battle" for dignity and "against imperialism." The epic of now, the Moncada of these times, is to force the United States to lift the blockade. Fidel now wants to defeat imperialism in the diplomatic category as he had already overthrown it by arms in the legendary battle of the Bay of Pigs, the Thermopylae and Lepanto of the underdeveloped Cuban mythology.

From this fact, the American government is not far wrong in demanding of Cuba parallel "defeats" as a condition of lifting the blockade. If it is Castro who raises his battle against the blockade to the category of a fighting symbol, he should be made to pay a high symbolic price to obtain his objective. Let him, for example, withdraw from Angola and Ethiopia. Let him stop meddling in the affairs of Central America, Puerto Rico, and Jamaica. Or if he gives none of these concessions, let him remain sighing for the end of the blockade. If Rhodesia was forced to modify its policy in exchange for lifting the blockade, there is no reason for not doing the same with Cuba. In the end, Castro will have to learn sometime that in negotiations, even if they are symbolic, the essence of the affair consists of giving and receiving.

The CIA Affair

In 1959, the Central Intelligence Agency began to harass Castro as a reply to the aggresive anti-Yankeeism shown by the Cuban leader. It will never be possible to determine to what extent Castro's surrender to Moscow was partially motivated by fear of Washington's attacks, although today I believe—with Thomas—that Castro deliberately provoked them. The one attacking, of course, was the CIA, at times directly, at others through the services of anti-Castro Cubans. For each step the CIA took against him, Castro would answer by moving left. This radicalization of the Cuban revolutionary process crudely showed its dialectic mechanism on April 16, 1961, twenty-four hours after the beginning of the air attacks that preceded the Bay of Pigs invasion. Fidel felt compelled to declare that the revolution was socialist and that he himself, since his student years, had been a Communist, but had hidden it for strategic reasons. To the push and shove in the CIA efforts that culminated with a picture-book invasion, Castro responded with the culmination of the radicalization process. Obviously, Fidel was trying to protect himself under the Soviet umbrella. The same mechanism that made him overcome his repugnance toward the Cuban Communist party (PSP), making use of the party's cadres in the island's interior to resist growing pressure of the opposition within the revolution's own ranks, operated in the international sphere when he aligned himself in the Soviet orbit with a deceiving declaration of Communist militancy. In reality, it was a pact between opportunists. Fidel contributed the revolution and Soviet Communism would protect it. Fidel would keep the undisputed power in his hands and Moscow, the ideological orientation.

CIA Influence

Washington served both as the paradoxical catalyst of Cuban Communism and the clumsy organizer of anti-Castroism. At times the United States even served as an obstacle to independent anti-Communist groups. The CIA's first blunder was to deal with the "Cuban case" in accordance with some models which had been successful in the "Guatemala case," without realizing that the time, men, and circumstances were drastically different. Castro was not Arbenz and Cuba was not Guatemala. The CIA, with a long series of successes in Latin America, underestimated Castro's capacity for maneuver, and dusted off the cover of the operations manual for banana republics. The result was one of its most resounding failures, the Bay of Pigs invasion, and the beginning of its liquidation as an omnipotent organism. Since then it has had to submit to increasing vigilance by the committees of the United States House of Representatives. Until the Bay of Pigs, the CIA had been an impressive club that the president of the United States kept in his office and used at his pleasure. Afterward it was to be less a private instrument operating with almost total impunity.

The CIA did not invent the anti-Castro movements, but found them organized—in an embryonic state—since the end of 1959. At the end of that year, a large sector of the forces that participated in the struggle against Batista was taking the first few steps in the struggle against Castro and the Communists. Curiously, it was the revolutionary elite which started the long march. The CIA, having decided to overthrow Castro, began its recruitment then.

The CIA's Men

The CIA was looking for—and found—pliable people. It did not want independent-minded persons, but obedient "boys" with a certain tendency toward corruption. For an opposition which was beginning to actively plot against Castro, the eruption of a powerful and mythical element such as the CIA would end up by impairing everything. They bought men and groups with money or military equipment. There were meager means—as always—at the disposal of the clandestine struggle. The CIA had them all: explosives, electronic detonators, communication systems, conventional arms, and all the money in the world. Money, besides, was very difficult to find outside these foreign suppliers, because the high Cuban bourgeoisie did not defend itself. It sank, passively, playing canasta.

This anti-Castro recruitment campaign had fatal consequences. The CIA began by deforming the ideological profile of the anti-Castro movement and by giving the upper hand to an organization engendered in one sector of militant Catholicism: the Agrupación Católica Universitaria (ACU), a group that took to the struggle as a kind of religious crusade which in no way corresponded with Cuban reality. Besides, the CIA got along better with the young bourgeoisie recruited in Havana's exclusive clubs than with the peasants who started to take to the hills, or with the working-class cadres that were beginning to show discontent. A question of affinity, I suppose. Undoubtedly, the "Agency of the Americans" ended up being a factor in the weakening of anti-Castroism, due to its corrupting money (which made salaried agents of hypothetical patriots), with their preferences (which had nothing to do with Cuba's most desirable destiny but with Washington's interests), and with the absurd pretention of creating a counterrevolution with methods extracted from espionage manuals. Neither can the fact that some Cubans sought the CIA's help be interpreted as a kind of obscure treason. In 1959 one lived according to schemes fathered during the Cold War, in which "the free world" and "Christian Western Civilization" were articles of faith. The United States was the head of the "free world," but that head needed a sledgehammer to guard its defense perimeters. That sledgehammer was the CIA, and it seemed logical that the "free world Cubans" would look to the CIA for support. When this matter was presented as an ethical dilemma in the midst of a babbling opposition, the previous behavior of the Communist paradoxically served to justify the alliance. European resistance movements during Nazi occupation, especially French resistance—an epic four years during which thousands of Communists and noncommunists participated—did not have any scruples about accepting the help and technical direction of the American agents of the OSS (an organism which gave birth to the CIA) to face the German invaders and the Pétain French. There were no other viable alternatives, as Maurice Thorez once commented to justify himself. As a consequence, many Cubans reached the conclusion that, in the face of the Soviet support Fidel was receiving, the opposition did not have any other option but to get under the protective wings of the Americans, especially after seeing that the democratic Latin American republics were not willing to stir a finger for the freedom of the island.

However, in the first stage, the Yankees did not *exactly* want the Cubans to free themselves of a Communist dictatorship that was beginning to take roots, but wanted Fidel and his team to be replaced by docile and submissive Cubans who would guarantee American investments in the island. Later, when pacts with the Soviet Union froze plans to overthrow the regime, the CIA directed its efforts toward keeping the United States government informed of all that was happening at the military level.

For almost ten years reconnaissance planes overflew the island and hundreds of Cubans were sent on more than 1,000 missions in search of military information useful to the Yankee defense establishment. This unknown CIA story had its most important successes with the recovery of fragments of the U-2 plane shot down by Havana during the missile crisis and with photographs of several secret bases operated by the Russians taken by a Cuban agent able to gain access to them using false Russian documents.

For those who are unfamiliar with Cuban history, this political promiscuity between the United States and Cuba, characterized by the Yankees' violent interference in Cuban affairs, perhaps might appear strange, but it has been an unhidden truth for the past century and a half. There were periods in which the island's annexation to the United States appeared imminent, and times in which illustrious Cubans wanted and asked to become part of the great American nation. This situation, a little strange, has been frequent in the Caribbean. The Yucatán Península, the Dominican Republic, and Puerto Rico have gone through similar phases. It is necessary to remember that the United States was in the past century the most admired nation in the world. Even in faraway Spain, the Cartagena region verified that such a cherished sector of the country would ask for "secession from Madrid" in order to become part of the United States.

Appendix

Cartagena region. Incredible as it may now seem, in 1873 this region wanted to break away from the rest of the country and become part of the United States.

Maurice Thorez (1900–1964). A French politician, leader of the French Communist party, and one of the men responsible for France's Popular Front of 1936. He spent World War II in exile in Moscow. In 1945 and 1946 he was a minister in General De Gaulle's government and on several occasions was a deputy in the French National Assembly. He died on the ship *Litva* en route to Odessa.

13

Destiny of the Cuban Revolution

The One in Charge of Cuban Affairs

I intend to make a little future telling about the Cuban Revolution. I will not state, as I do not know, what is going to take place, but what *could* happen in the next few years. These predictions are subject to a few decisive variables. For example, Castro's death, or the permanent increase of the price of sugar to more than thirty cents per pound, or the breaking away of a Soviet satellite in Eastern Europe, or a Cuban defeat in Africa, at the hands, let us say, of South Africa. And, of course, the start of a third world war. These variables, and many others, could noticeably affect the turn of Cuban events; thus this precarious guessing exercise should be undertaken with reserve. Political prediction is neither a science nor an art; it is only a shaky agreement between common sense, the information available, and the deep understanding of the main characters in the plot. To me—and I am very distant from any deterministic interpretations of history—the first factor to take into account is the last: the principal characters in the plot. And among them, of course, the key figure: Fidel Castro. Fidel is Cuba's factotum. He is the leader of those in power, the leader of the opposition—when he turns into the critic of his system—and soon, if he skillfully rations nostalgia's spigot, he might be able to become the leader of part of the emigration. Nostalgia, when it is well administered, can perform miracles. But let us not get too far ahead. Let us continue with the working hypothesis.

An Inventory of Beliefs

If Fidel Castro is the person who changes at will the turn of Cuban events, to understand what has taken place in Cuba, it is necessary to know what Fidel Castro thought in 1959 and what he believes almost three decades later. Without a minimum inventory of the beliefs, fetishisms, and superstitions implanted in the head of the Cuban president, it is useless to try to understand Cuba's recent history. One is to assume that his behavior, in some manner, reflects the theoretical frame of his convictions. In 1953, when Castro attacked the Moncada, in the manifesto which he himself wrote, he declared that the revolution "makes its own the revolutionary programs of the Young Cuba, the radical ABC and the Orthodox Party of the Cuban People." But in addition to seizing these debatable analyses, Castro shared two popular beliefs of the fifties with respect to Cuban society and economy: (1) Castro and half the country thought that Cuba was a potentially rich country; (2) Fidel and a substantial part of the Cuban "political class" thought that the country was kept in poverty due to the politicians' pillage and exploitation by foreign companies.

The legend of Cuba's potential richness was based on the fertility of the land and on some mythical deposits of uranium, oil, and gold, which, together with the nickel and iron mines in Oriente province, could transform Cuba into a rich state. The decade of the fifties was particularly fertile in this type of false information. The other causes of poverty—supposedly—were also easy to eradicate: By sweeping away administrative corruption and by nationalizing certain foreign companies an enormous quantity of monetary resources would be made available to the country. Castro, in this sense, inherited beliefs that have been widespread since the time of Chibás and Guiteras, political opinions that he sustained since his restless youth. Let us take a look at other popular superstitions related to the sugar industry that were subscribed to by Fidel:

1. Sugarcane was responsible for the sad state of Cuban agriculture. This inveterate single crop closed the door to a healthy diversification of agriculture, leaving the island's economy at the mercy of the international market's fluctuations.
2. The sugar quota with which the United States favored Cuba was really a trap, as it gave impetus to the single crop, served to enrich American sugar companies in Cuba, and maintained the high prices of the beet sugar industry in the United States. The suppression of the quota, in the short run, would favor Cuba, but in any case, it was the United States who needed it and not the reverse, for if Cuba did not sell, the United States would have to ration its sugar.
3. (And here is the origin of the 1970 sugar harvest.) If Cuba were to produce 10 million tons, it could cause a lowering in the price and consequently ruin other producing countries in order to later acquire a larger share of the world sugar market and then set the price. It was the dumping theory.

This extraordinary stupidity was part of the sugar strategy that the Cuban revolutionaries used to outline in all the island's barbershops since the fall of the Machado dictatorship (1933). The 10-million-ton sugar harvest had been a naive obsession for the past thirty years. Fidel picked it up and thus caused considerable damage to the island's economy, because the total mobilization of the country's resources destabilized the rest of the production process.

In matters of finance and foreign commerce, key elements in the economy of a country, Fidel fancied an obviously unjust picture dictated by imperialism's cruel hand.

Symptom: A chronic deficit in the balance of payments; Cuba imported more than it exported.

Bad Remedy: To fight this evil, Cuba became indebted with foreign loans, which were paid at usurious prices and thus contributed to sinking the economy even further.

Diagnosis: The one responsible for the deficit, the loans, and the ruin was the United States, which sold at high prices, monopolizing, in addition, 80 percent of Cuban exports and imports. We depended on one market and a single supplier.

Castro's prescriptions to end Cuban evils were no different—we are talking about 1959—than what is frequently found in the political programs of all of Latin America: (1) agrarian reform and liquidation of large ownership; (2) nationalization of foreign monopolies, the banking, insurance, and transport industries; (3) diversification of the economy to eradicate the single-crop economy; (4) industrialization to replace imports; (5) opening of new markets to end dependency on the United States.

Beliefs Crumble

Broadly, that was an important part of Castro's ideological equipment on the day he entered Havana surrounded by cheers, applause, and partisans. With those ideas encrusted in his brain, Castro resolved to change the Cuban situation. Upon initiating his magic reforms, but for different reasons, Castro chose to realize them through Communism. Communism was going to be the theoretical (and police) framework from which the revolution toward development would start. In other words, leaving aside the Napoleonism of Fidel Castro, the Communist revolution was being carried out for the development of Cuba, a country which had always been exploited by foreign empires, corrupt politicians, and local gamblers. This Communist expansionist revolution was going to turn Cuba into the ideological beacon of the Third World and serve as a new model for economic development. The ethical basis of the revolution, for many years, was the search for the material well-being of the Cuban people and the general development of the island. Authoritarian excesses were justified by these lofty goals. What has changed in the economic picture of the island in the time since Castro's glorious entrance into Havana?

Today Cuba is still an underdeveloped country with one crop depending on the Soviet sugar quota and further depending on Soviet subsidies, munificence, and conditioned generosity. Cuba is still without industries, indebted on all financial fronts—East and West—and on top of that, Cuba has developed less in the two past decades than its Caribbean neighbors. For example, in these past years, in terms of increase of the gross national product, Cuba grew at a rate of 2.5 percent, while the Dominican Republic—in the midst of civil wars, coups d'état, and the worst unrest—averaged a 6 percent GNP increase.

After three decades and after paying a very high price, Fidel Castro has learned a very important lesson: What he identified as causes of Cuban poverty, what he thought were the origin and reason for underdevelopment, in the end turned out to be only partially true. Even worse, the easy solutions he had learned while chatting in the porticoes of Paseo del Prado, in the *tertulias* of Plaza Cadenas, or in the gatherings at sidewalk cafés or at the intersection of 12th and 23rd, ended up being totally ineffective as solutions that would overcome the everlasting underdevelopment of the country. When Castro thought that he was making a profound analysis, he was in fact repeating naive beliefs which history would later discredit.

New Beliefs

The revolution was carried out. After modifying the whole production plan, receiving the financial and technical support of the Eastern European countries, and the assistance—when necessary—of Western European countries, Cuba continues to be an impoverished Third World nation. There no longer are large landed estates, multinational corporations, nor exploitative capitalists. Nor is there any plausible excuse for the present situation (I do not believe that anyone talks seriously about the "American blockade"), and yet, the objective picture remains the same: a single-crop economy, dependency, underdevelopment, and poverty. Why? The answer which Fidel Castro gives himself is that there are no economic solutions for Third World countries lacking abundant raw materials as, for example, oil. And there are no solutions—I am following his thinking—because the international terms of trade are dictated by the big capitalist powers, and these norms have been conceived in order to perpetuate the dependency and servility of the Third World. While industrial products' prices skyrocket, the raw materials or crops of the Third World each year are worth relatively less. This means that at present Castro is not a developmentalist revolutionary. The thirty years Castro has spent exercising absolute power have tired his willingness to transform Cuba into a rich country. He no longer believes in that possibility. He does not think it is possible to achieve it, unless the definitive collapse of capitalism takes place. Only—Castro believes—when the international terms of trade are dictated within a worldwide Communist order, only then will the redemption of the Third World take place, since sugar in the angelic gathering of nations will not be priced according to supply and demand, but according to the effort it took to produce. Oil, sugar, gold, machinery, or fruits will not be—in this just world—valued according to capitalist laws, but according to socialist justice.

Consequences of the New Beliefs

Thirty years later, Fidel Castro has substituted one utopia for another. He has changed a few naive beliefs for other equally naive ones, which would not be especially risky if this new system did not necessarily entail an adventurous and aggressive attitude. Castro has not patiently sat down to wait for the revolutionary universal Armageddon to take place, but has given military aid to countries going through a revolutionary process in order to harass the weak flanks of imperialism. The function Castro has imposed on the Cuban people is that of the catalyst of the revolution in those countries and territories where the hand of the United States and Western Europe is unable to detain the advent of Communism. Revolutionary Cuba, due to its obvious failure at becoming a developed country, has changed its raison d'être; it is no longer a showcase. It is now an armed branch of "Internationalism." An international knight-errant. A socialist spearhead of the Third World. This is the Cuban rationalization for getting involved in Angola, Ethiopia. Shielded behind this scheme of reasoning, Fidel Castro will send his legions every time the situation is favorable.

At some point the new system of beliefs will begin to weaken. That logical edifice sustains itself on two blurry and complementary premises. First, Communism will inevitably impose itself on a worldwide scale. Second, until that day arrives, until the Communist countries dictate just terms of trade, Third World countries will not be able to develop. At some point that reasoning will begin to break up.

Cuba versus the Soviet Union

It will be reasonable to expect serious conflicts between Cuba and the Soviet Union. The conflicts will probably start not due to the master's tight leash, but to its free rein. There is a fundamental difference between Moscow's and Havana's perspectives: Moscow follows its national hegemonic designs, while Havana sets forth to the conquest of the planet according to

Fidel Castro's personal and urgent scale. Even Gorbachev does not dream of seeing the planet's total Communization, while Castro has no other vital objective than to be a witness to that shaking event. Moscow's deliberate march, the march of an old imperial power, with remote and negotiable objectives, will clash with Castro's hurry and improvisation (an impetuous man if there ever was one). It is possible, for example, that the arms race between the Soviet Union and the United States, or the treaties, or the grain needs of Eastern European countries might lead, through agreements, to a reduction of Soviet involvement in Africa. That would contribute to alienating Cuba from the Soviet Union.

In the next few years, another anti-Soviet uprising is expected in Poland, Czechoslovakia, or East Germany. In order to crush it—as occurred during the Prague's assassinated Spring—the Soviet Union will ask the United States to ratify the borders established after the end of World War II, and it is possible that Washington will then demand some type of compensation in the southern flank of its national territory. That would contribute to the poisoning of relations between Havana and Moscow. Because Havana, as occurred during the missile crisis, is incapable of understanding that the big powers answer to different interests than Cuba's.

These hypothetical examples could be multiplied a thousandfold. There will always be reasons for friction. Firm also was the eternal love that Albania and China swore to each other hardly a few years ago, and today relations between Peking and that remote European satellite are about to freeze. Enver Hoxha, a national hero (like Castro), a David (like Castro) battling a Goliath of a hostile power a few miles away—this fervent believer in Maoism's planetary triumph, in the face of uncontrolled events (Mao's death and his successors' deradicalization)—Albania's Hoxha today holds beliefs different from the ones he held a few years ago, and consequently he tries out other solutions. Who can be sure that the rise of Gorbachev has not affected the Soviet Union's relations with its satellites? Cuba is situated thousands of kilometers from the Soviet Union, and falls, due to geographic fatality, within the American sphere of influence. Cuban Communism is not the product of the death of 20 million Russians who immolated themselves during World War II. It has cost the Soviet Union billions of irrecuperable dollars to support Cuban Communism. That pertinacious bleeding will continue through costly subsidies. That remote island is not defensible in case of an armed confrontation, and its conversion into an offensive military base is explicitly prohibited by the secret pacts which followed the missile crisis.

Why believe that the allegiance between Moscow and Cuba will be eternal? In that relationship the balance is not favorable to the Soviets, but neither is it to the Cubans. Cuba is very expensive to the Soviet Union—until now some

$30 billion—but that help has not been able to develop the island, only keep it breathing. Throughout the years there have been eloquent symptoms of fatigue. The Escalante affair, the microfaction, or the "Marquitos" affair are not episodes that have been completely forgotten.

New Beliefs Also Crumble

In a few years, and who knows whether it will be at the end of other imperialistic adventures, Havana will discover that Africa's battles do not necessarily lead to the eradication of capitalism, and will thus learn that it is very difficult to justify from an ethical point of view—even Marxist ethics— the support given to the bloody assemblage of procommunist dictators of the Macías, Amin, or Mengistu type. Moscow and Havana, in spite of any cynical considerations of realpolitik, will someday have to explain to their citizens the support offered to certain despicable dictatorships. Or at least they should, in some autocritical gathering, reevaluate the sacrifices and allegiances made taking into account the real and objective course of events and the validity of the reasonings which originated the Cuban acts. The contradictions, in the end, should have a limit. One of the tasks of the counterguerrilla intervention of Castro in Angola is to guard the oil installations of the capitalist countries. Half of the army kills Maoists, and the other half protects Gulf Oil. Of course, Havana and Luanda consider the paradoxical situation as an unavoidable phenomenon in the transition toward socialism, but when that concrete phenomenon disappears, another twenty contradictions will crop up to undermine the logical base of the belief of Castro and his group, no matter how obstinate and dogmatic they might try to be. When the Soviet Union, the world's second military power, ends up by yielding to Fiat, Pepsi Cola, or making concessions to Japanese companies (the operation of obtaining Siberian gas), what contradictions cannot occur in Africa, whether it be governed by the right, left, or simple military autocrats?

In the next few years conditions for the de-Sovietization of Cuba will exist. I am not talking about decommunization—that might or might not happen in the future—but about Cuba's distancing from the Soviet orbit. Castro and his generation, overwhelmed by contradictions, exhausted by the tense revolutionary effort, defeated by old age, will lose faith in the inevitability of world socialism, and may even become disenchanted with a system as ineffective as Communist collectivism. If in 1959 someone had said that Castro and his entourage would lose faith in the possibilities of developing Cuba, we all would have made fun of the prediction. If in the Sino-Guevara stage of the revolution—that fateful decade of the sixties—someone had repudiated the utopian fabrication of the new man, he would have been dismissed as a fool.

That impetuous young man and those raving guerrilla fighters appeared to be cockeyed optimists. That disillusionment might take place. It may even be the natural outcome of this renewed euphoric excess.

The Strategy of Washington and the Democrats

But perhaps—and here we arrive at the sensitive part of these reflections—perhaps it would be opportune to foster this attitude among the Cuban leaders. At this point, it would correspond with a strategy defined by the American Department of State and the most politically aware Cuban emigration.

Within a scenario of Cuban de-Sovietization, Washington might guarantee Havana total nonbelligerence, suspension of the economic blockade, and perhaps, in exchange for the elimination of Soviet economic aid, offer Cuba a subsidy which would permit its economic survival, at least at the level of present Soviet aid.

Unconditional elimination of the economic blockade, renovation of the sugar quota, or any type of loan or aid from the United States to Cuba is not presently advisable. Those and other friendly gestures are only prescribed if Cuba were to distance itself from the Soviet Union. That should be the reward if Cuba were to abandon its condition of Soviet satellite. It is politically correct to offer Castro an alternative, but it would be foolish to do it gratuitously. This rough plan, of course, cannot be stated publicly, as Castro has a very developed sense of propriety—a result more of his temperament than of ethical convictions—and is thus incapable of negotiating face to face on issues which he believes are fundamental. That negotiation would be secret, discreet, full of circumlocutions, and always respectful of Castro's image, allowing him to "save face," as the Soviet Union did with him after the 1970 meetings. Privately, without witnesses, Castro then accepted the humiliating satellization of Cuba. The offer which might be presented to him in the future will have to be surrounded by the utmost secrecy. We are in the presence of a heroic Latin American macho, with all the deplorable consequences this entails.

The primary objective of democratic-minded persons should be, for the time being, to disengage Cuba from the Soviet orbit. It would be advisable that Castro be "guaranteed" the survival of his Communist dictatorship were it to break away from Soviet economic and military protection. What would Cubans gain with that hypothetical de-Sovietization, if in the end the country remained submerged in a communist dictatorship? In that event, Cubans who do not believe in the dictatorship of or for the proletariat, in communism as a system of government or a theoretical formula, will have won an opening for the possibility of change when Castroism exhausts its vital cycle, when the

Moncada generation surrenders, due to old age or death. Then there would be a possibility for evolution in the system, which today is impeded by the Soviet presence.

It is true that until now Communism has not evolved anywhere toward democratic forms of government, but it is also true that no one could have predicted Hungary's future if the 1956 revolution had triumphed, or Czechoslovakia's if the Soviet Union had not interfered during that sad spring of 1968. There are clear symptoms of division and struggle among Communist parties. Those symptoms cannot sprout in the present Cuban situation, but they will be irrepressible as the Moncada generation grows old and deteriorates, and the Soviet dike ceases to exist. Neither communism, capitalism, nor any other government system can permanently avoid the evolution of contradictions in their core. Although there are great differences in its background and form, the Spanish case is eloquent: Franco, without resolving the problem, unwittingly established the basis for the liberal multiparty democracy which today is being tested in the Iberian peninsula.

Twenty years after Gottwald and the Czech Stalinists destroyed Benes's Republic, Dubcek, Otta Sik, Arthur London, and the hierarchy of the Czech Communist party tried to restore to the country the human face erased by the dictatorship. There are no eternal systems, nor can the luck of political theories be prejudged. The Third Reich was going to last a millennium. Mussolini planned no less than the resurgence of the Roman Empire. A few years later all the fascist fantasies had disappeared.

The recent history of Cuba is not definitive. Neither the geography, the history, economy, nor Cuba's sociopolitical tradition indicate that the Communist dictatorship is an irreversible fact. It might be a long-term phenomenon, as was the Franco dictatorship, but there are indications that permit us to believe in its potential disappearance. The present adventure began when a group of delirious dilettantes embarked on the precipitous and forced development of the country. Those wrathful young men are now old dogs, tired of utopias. The road is open to start a slow and cautious recovery.

Appendix

ABC. A broad-based Cuban political movement with supporters among many different social classes which, together with other organizations, led the struggle against the dictatorship of General Machado y Morales. It included the cream of the Cuban middle and working classes and its underground activity finally forced Machado and his collaborators to flee in 1933.

Corner of 12th and 23rd Streets. A traditional meeting-place at the intersection of 23rd and 12th Streets in the upper part of El Vedado. It is well known for the many open-air cafés, shops, and two movie houses.

Cuba Moves Away from the Soviet Union. Mikhail Gorbachev's *perestroika* and *glasnost* policies are viewed with suspicion by Castro who indirectly attacks them—as in his 8 October 1987 speech marking the twentieth anniversary of "Che" Guevara's death in Bolivia and the 1988 26 July's anniversary speech. But he makes sure the Cuban press does not carry information about such discrepancies.

Exploitation by Foreign Companies. It is an article of faith in most political circles that Cuba was exploited by companies like Shell and Esso or, in Camagüey, the United Fruit Co., and that this prevented it from accumulating enough capital to enable it to achieve economic takeoff. Time has shown that even though these factors have been eliminated the country has not become developed.

Imperialism's Weak Flanks. Castro does his best to make as much trouble as possible for U.S. "imperialism" by financing guerrilla movements and intervening in countries which, according to the theory of the Egyptian ideologue Samir Amin, are on the periphery of the industrial world.

Marquitos Affair. The trial and execution by firing squad of Marcos Rodríguez, a former PSP (communist) activist, caused splits between the directorate and veteran Communists. Rodríguez was accused of betraying members of the directorate to Batista's police because of sectarian squabbles within the PSP.

The Microfaction. A faction of the Cuban Communist party that, when relations were cool in 1968, pressed for closer links with the Soviet Union. It is formed mainly by former PSP militants led by Aníbal Escalante. It opposed some of Fidel Castro's more grandiose initiatives such as the "10-million-ton harvest" (this finally reached 8.5 million tons).

Petroleum. Little oil has been found in Cuba itself or in offshore areas despite exploration and the purchase of oil derricks from Rumania. The quantities discovered have been far too small to justify exploitation. Nonetheless, for years Cuba has been paying Rumania for the oil derricks with shipments of oranges.

Present Situation. It is hard to explain how Cuba, thirty years after having eliminated the "causes" of its underdevelopment, still has much the same per capita income as before and remains an underdeveloped Third World country.

Soviet Generosity—Strings Attached. It is taken for granted that such Soviet "aid" as is represented by the sugar quota is conditional on Cuba repaying the favor by sending money, providing troops, or by accepting Soviet domination. This belief has proved justified.

Sugar Rationing in the United States. The naive popular belief that if Cuba refused to sell sugar to the U.S., Washington would have to impose sugar rationing.

Support for Dictatorships. Not surprisingly, the Cuban regime has been supported by the Communist dictatorships of Eastern Europe. But it has also been supported by and has given support to the Argentine dictatorship of Videla, Viola, and Galtieri, and it always enjoyed excellent relations with Francisco Franco's Spain.

14

Castro's Cuba in Gorbachev's Era: Factors That Weaken/Consolidate Castroism— Possible Outcomes

All the symptoms suggest that Castroism today is passing through a period of change. Such expressions as "this has to change," "something has got to happen," or "things can't go on like this" can be heard from many different quarters. I am not referring to isolated comments coming from people who are opposed to the regime but to expressions of discouragement made by individuals connected to the power structure; in other words, people who are close to Castro but who are aware that the decline of Cuban society in almost all its aspects has become intolerable. In this respect, the most concerned— and revealing—voice is probably that of the former deputy economy minister Manuel Sánchez Pérez who defected in Madrid in December 1985.

Among other things, Sánchez Pérez says that not a single one of the fifty ministers and 250 deputy ministers in the Cuban cabinet takes an optimistic view of the ability of the *system* to overcome the serious problems affecting Cuban society.

In any event, this desire for change is a factor weakening Castroism, especially as Castro, who is himself aware that the country wants, indeed, *needs* a change, can offer nothing better than an attempt to save the revolution by restoring the collectivist spirit in accordance with the hoariest Marxist orthodoxy. For Castro, the only way out of the mess is to revive the revolutionary momentum and faith of 1959 and 1960 and, to this end, he started in 1986 to criticize publicly officials and administrators responsible for the most flagrant mistakes in the management of the economy. The trouble is, the punishment proposed by Castro for his most incompetent subordinates is not enough to appease Cubans, because after almost thirty years of dictatorship very few of them believe the revolution is a disaster merely because ten, 100, or 1000 individuals are dishonest or inept. The consensus is that the problem is the *system*, not certain people.

Let us look at another serious factor that tends to weaken Castroism: the economic crisis. To simplify matters, it is enough to say that the Castro regime is going through an extremely serious economic crisis for which it has no answers: with the West it has an unpayable debt of almost $5 billion; it owes the Soviet Union more than $20 billion. What is more, what is virtually its only export, sugar, fetches on the international market only half of what it costs to produce, so there is no way Cuba can meet its obligations, let alone pay its bills to the West. The country lives purely and simply off Soviet handouts and it can do this only as long as the Soviet Union is prepared to continue subsidizing its remote Caribbean satellite.

The third factor undermining Castroism is the aging of its leadership. It is possible, even though it does not happen very often, for a people to love and support its leaders for a very long time as in the case of Adenauer in Germany and Urho Kekkonen in Finland, President Lee in Singapore and Muñoz in Puerto Rico, but for this to happen members of the government and the ruling class as a whole must demonstrate their efficiency and deliver on their promises. Adenauer, Kekkonen, Lee—who has ruled Singapore since 1962—and Muñoz Marín, who led Puerto Rico for twenty years, all succeeded in developing their countries, in making the economy prosper so that in a single generation the societies they governed experienced a tremendous leap forward toward prosperity. There was no doubt about the relationship between their original promises and the results.

Fidel Castro, however, promised one thing and has achieved something quite different. Cuba has become a society characterized by misery, sacrifices, and social tensions. It is therefore legitimate to assume that disillusionment with Castroism is practically absolute. (If this were not the case, we would have to conclude that Cubans are completely unlike the other peoples on this planet. In fact, the people ruling Cuba today after taking power thirty years ago are perceived as elderly failures.)

The fourth factor contributing to weaken the Castro regime has to do with the wars in Africa. Cuban troops landed in Angola thirteen years ago, making this the longest war in which any American army has ever participated. Moreover, the contingent fighting in Angola alone—leaving aside the units in Ethiopia—is bigger than all the armed forces of Batista combined. Castro has had his Afrika Korps in Angola for twelve years and, according to general Rafael del Pino who recently left Cuba, this has cost Cuba's youth no fewer than 10,000 casualties and, in Cuba itself, there are over 50,000 desertors. Can there be any doubt that for Cuban families this bloody adventure by Castro is a permanent source of irritation and tension?

The fifth factor weakening the Castro regime is the appearance on the stage of the reformist Gorbachev. This is not because the new Soviet prime minister and president proposes to make Castro imitate the Soviet model with its *perestroika* and *glasnost* but because Gorbachev himself has become an element spreading demoralization within Cuba.

His is the voice that cannot be silenced—even though interviews with and statements by him are censored—a voice that has, in indirect fashion, joined in the chorus of those in Cuba, including Marxists, who are demanding liberal reforms to save the system from a complete catastrophe. I am here referring to officials such as Humberto Pérez and also the exhausted "superminister" Osmani Cienfuegos, an individual who would like to play at Gorbachevism were Castro to let him.

But nobody should cherish any illusions about an ideological clash between Moscow and Havana. Gorbachev (like the Soviet rulers of the Brezhnev era), does not seem to be overinterested in the way the satellites handle their economies as long as there are no doubts about their loyalty to the Soviet Union and their agreement on international strategy. Be this as it may, even without intending to, Gorbachev has become the guardian angel of the fairly large faction convinced that Castro has led the country into a blind alley.

A sixth factor weakening Castroism, which deserves a mention, is the absence of a true Communist party enjoying real hegemony that would buttress the system and underpin its authority at a time of crisis. Castroism is paying the price for its *petit bourgeois* origins and the fact that the inner circle of power, the ring surrounding Castro, was formed not by people drawn to the revolution for ideological reasons but by those who have attached themselves to the leader in ways that may be described in manuals of anthropology or sociology, but which are not mentioned in Marxist treatises. Castro has prevented the formation of a hegemonic Communist party. A skeleton of one exists, but it has no more life than whatever Castro chooses to grant it. In communist societies it is often said that men pass on but the party is immortal. In Cuba it seems the reverse is the case.

The seventh factor undermining Castroism is the welcome existence of radio stations such as The Voice of the CID and Radio Martí that reach the island with commentaries and reliable news reports. The current crisis would not be so serious were Castro able to concoct some alibi explaining it away. But these radio stations have made this impossible. Thanks to them, the Castro regime has been left without any answers. They have snatched away his chances of producing some rhetorical rationalization of the crisis.

A stage has now been reached in which Castro cannot explain anything. He cannot blame anyone for the setbacks. He cannot defend himself with sophistries because the very next day the exiles' radio station pulls his arguments to pieces. This is very serious for Castro because every system, even one with a million policemen ready to kill on its behalf, also needs a political discourse. It needs an ethical framework to justify its behavior. But Castro has lost this, hence his fury against these radio stations and his effort to get them closed down.

I could list a dozen more factors that help to weaken the Castro regime but—for the time being—I shall confine myself to mentioning in question form, an eighth one that is dictated by common sense: What would have happened in Hungary in 1956, in Czechoslovakia in 1968, or in the Poland of the seventies if the Soviet Union, instead of being on the frontier, had been 5,000 miles away with a wide ocean in between?

I do not think it is at all hard to work out the answer: These countries would have stopped being satellites. In other words, the geographic distance between Cuba and the Soviet Union is and will continue to be a factor tending to weaken the Castro regime. The defenders of Cuban Communism or, for that matter, its opponents, cannot take for granted the inevitable presence of the Soviet Union simply because the Soviet Union is not in the neighborhood and could do nothing to prevent certain things taking place in the country even though it would undoubtedly try to control them. But this geographical fact is very important. It is the sword of Damocles which always hangs over the Cuban-Soviet alliance.

Thus far we have been looking at some of the factors that serve to weaken the regime. Now we are going to look at others that tend to consolidate it because there can be no doubt that these too can be found in the Cuban panorama.

The first and most decisive factor conducive to the consolidation of the Castro regime is the determined support of the Soviet Union. Moscow's aid to Cuba has been estimated at $5 billion a year, a fantastic sum if regarded as "conventional foreign aid" but a pittance when you take into account the military advantages stemming from having an aircraft carrier measuring over 42,000 square miles just sixty miles off the U.S. coast.

What is more, it is highly unlikely that anyone in the Kremlin would do anything to jeopardize the alliance with Cuba because for thirty years the Soviet propaganda machine has devoted itself, within the Soviet Union, to singing the praises of the Cuban revolution and to exalting the virtues of the "younger brother" who in the Caribbean repeated Lenin's "feat" of 1917.

It would in consequence be very hard for Moscow to leave Cuba suddenly in the lurch. This would have a serious effect on Soviet public opinion, especially now that Mr. Gorbachev is going ahead with his halfhearted experiments in letting the people know what is happening and is, moreover, trying to strengthen his own personal hegemony.

The second factor consolidating Castroism derives from reasoning by analogy: No society controlled by communists has ever been able to escape its fate. There can be no doubt that this fact serves to discourage dissidents.

The third factor favoring the consolidation of Castroism is perhaps the efficiency of the repressive apparatus. Nothing works well in Cuba except the legion of informers, spies, and enforcers linked to the Interior Ministry, State Security, an organization spawned by the Soviet KGB. Minint and Security are without doubt formidable organizations and quite capable of drowning any conspiracy in blood. At any rate, this is what history has taught us so far even though the recent defection of intelligence colonel Azpillaga shows that these organizations are less monolithic than was once thought.

The fourth element helping to consolidate the Castro regime comes from outside. The international community, including the United States, sees communist Cuba as a fact of political life that may be unpleasant but which cannot be changed. The United States, all of Latin America and the rest of the West, simply accept that the Castro regime is here to stay and this resigned attitude strengthens the system.

Another factor that helps consolidate the Castro regime is the absence among the opposition of a credible alternative. As is natural when such lengthy historical processes are involved, time, quarrels, the genuine impossibility of doing anything in the short term—and this is an indispensable requisite for political activity—have prevented the vast forces opposed to the Castro regime from presenting a solid resistance front that could be recognized everywhere as representing a valid alternative to Castro's government. This does not mean that there have been no efforts in this direction, merely—unfortunately—that around the world the public image of the exile is not very helpful.

It would be possible to list another dozen factors contributing either to the weakening or to the strengthening of the Castro regime, but those mentioned already are significant enough to let us proceed to consider a series of possible outcomes resulting from the present situation.

Let us look at the first scenario, based on an analysis of Castro's own proposals. In other words, let us assume that the government rectifies its mistakes, Cuban society recovers its faith in the revolutionary process, and there is a gradual reconciliation between the people and Castroism that ends by consolidating the system and guaranteeing the handing on of power without any traumas when Castro leaves the scene.

In theory, this is not impossible. In 1956, Janos Kadar was the most hated man in Hungary, but in 1987, thirty-one years later, he seems to have recovered some of his prestige and managed to create under communism a society somewhat less dissatisfied with the system. In other words, such miracles can happen.

But in the Cuban case there is a serious drawback: If Janos Kadar succeeded in restoring some of his prestige, it was because he was able progressively to diverge from the Stalinist norms of behaviour that had brought so much misfortune on the Hungarian people. Castro, however, has taken the opposite course, choosing to crack down harder on discontent and press ahead with collectivization.

It can therefore be predicted that the Castroite road toward the restoration of revolutionary prestige will prove counterproductive for the regime, that there will be an increase in tensions, worse economic failure and further demoralization in the power apparatus. In all frankness, this is what I think will happen in this neo-Stalinist period.

Let us consider a second scenario. As expected, mass discontent increases and work habits get even more undisciplined so the economy deteriorates still further. There can be no doubt that this would mean greater tensions in the power structure because it is there that the steps to deal with the crisis must be taken. It is there, in Juceplán, in the economic ministries, and in the bureaucratic structure as a whole where it must be decided just how to further tighten the country's belt, just where to cut back, and where to take away because economic crises mean less bread, less water, fewer schools, fewer medicines, and so on and so forth item by item right across the country's life. What is more, we cannot assume that communist regimes are immune to the effects of economic crises. The Polish government that preceded Jaruzelsky's was a victim not merely of the Solidarity union but also of the high cost of living and shortages.

Much the same will take place in Cuba and it is not inconceivable that there will be a new clash between Castro and the regime's reformist wing, which is getting steadily bigger and is concentrated in the administrative sector.

This is one of the hairline cracks in the Castro regime. On one side are those who know that the regime can increase its lifespan only if it introduces liberalizing measures in the economy and in public life as a whole. On the other side are those who think that liberalization would mean the beginning of the end of Cuban communism because once this process has got under way the capitalist germs would eventually devour the Castro Communist system in its entirety.

There is no contradiction between these two postures. Economic and political liberalization might enable the Castroite oligarchy to stay in power a bit longer, but in the long term an evolution toward a market economy and more democratic freedom would lead to the demise of the Cuban Marxist regime. On the other hand, however, were the Castro regime to retreat into a sort of bunker and dig in so as to fight against the inevitable, it might preserve its essential character but it would find itself up against the growing hatred of the Cuban people and increasingly out of touch with the country's real problems and with nothing to look forward to but the definitive crisis. This could well arise after Castro's departure.

This scenario cannot be written off: A military conspiracy is possible because Castro is leaving his own government clique with no alternatives. All the generals, everyone in a position of power in Cuba, know that were Castro to retreat into a bunker and cling to neo-Stalinism whatever the cost, this would be equivalent to a death sentence for the system, because even should Castro manage to keep power until the day he dies, the longer he lives the weaker will be his regime and the more vulnerable his heirs. My hypothesis is this: If Castro insists on tightening the screws instead of loosening them there is a genuine possibility of a palace plot. Cuba is full of generals like Del Pino and colonels like Azpillaga. These are people close to the powder kegs and who are fed up with Castro's mad impulses.

We shall now take a look at another scenario. Let us suppose that the economic and social situation in the country gets even worse and that a group close to Castro, led perhaps by Raúl, who is his very worried heir apparent, faces Castro with the need to change course: to liberalize the economy and relax the political pressure because otherwise the revolution will suffer irreparable damage and the fate of Cuban communism will be endangered.

In this case, Fidel Castro, the failure of his neocollectivist campaign having been demonstrated, would probably be forced to accept his subordinates' line, but with an obvious twist: As he himself would not be in a position to propose the new revolutionary course he would have to change roles, perhaps adopting that of a kind of living mummy uninvolved in the day-to-day problems of the revolution. In this scenario, Fidel Castro would reign, but he would not rule.

Appendix
State of the Cuban Economy before Castro

If in 1959 the economic scene in Cuba had been that of Bangladesh or Haiti, much of the reasoning in this book would not be valid. In a country where people die of hunger in the middle of the streets, almost any measure to alleviate such a situation would be acceptable. Such was not the case in Cuba. To prove this, I am summarizing the work of Leví Marrero (foremost geographer and historian of the Cuban economy), which appeared in the third edition of his *Geography of Cuba*, published by Editorial Minerva in 1966, and which has been translated in the Soviet Union. Lacoste has selected fifteen characteristics of underdevelopment as a guide for the social scientist to draw his own conclusions from the data available. The following is a review of such characteristics in Cuban society in the 1950s.

1. Nourishment
2. Agriculture
3. National income per capita and standard of living
4. Industrialization
5. Energy consumption
6. Economic dependency
7. Commercial sector
8. Social structure
9. Importance of the middle class
10. National integration
11. Unemployment and underemployment
12. Education
13. Demographic growth
14. Health
15. Political consciousness

1. Nourishment

Cuba was in twenty-sixth place with 2,730 calories per day in the chart regarding the caloric intake of 93 countries computed on a world scale by Ginsburg (according to FAO, it had 2,870 calories). The minimum adequate requirement is 2,500 calories per day. In America, only Argentina (3,360), the United States (3,100), Canada (3,070), and Uruguay (2,945) were ahead of Cuba. Regarding sources of animal protein, Cuba was one of the most proportionately supplied with 6 million head of cattle, equivalent to one head per inhabitant. The slaughter of cattle and hogs in 1957 yielded an annual per capita of 34 kilograms of meat, not including poultry and fish. Milk production in 1958 reached 800,000 tons and 315 million eggs were produced.

2. Agriculture

There is an evident relationship between the proportion of the population working in agriculture and level of development. In 1955, southern Europe employed 58 percent of its population in agriculture; North Africa, 73 percent; Black Africa, 76 percent; Southeast Asia, 70 percent; meridional North Asia, 74 percent; Western Asia, 71 percent; the United States and Canada, 13 percent. Cuba employed 30.5 percent and was placed thirtieth among 97 countries researched by Ginsburg. Nevertheless Cuba placed second among Latin American countries regarding the proportional use of agricultural soil. In the chart regarding the use of kilograms of fertilizers per hectare, Cuba placed thirty-fifth, together with Spain, among the 102 countries analyzed, with an average of 26 kilograms (the world figure was 22 kilograms per hectare).

3. National Income per Capita and Standard of Living

According to H.T. Oshima of Stanford University, California, the per capita income of the Cuban people (1953) was the same as that fixed for Italy and the Soviet Union by Gilbert and Kravis in their *International Comparison of National Products and Purchasing Capacity of Currencies,* and by Bornstein in *Comparison of the Economies of the United States and the Soviet Union.* In the 1950s, several socialist countries had less per capita income than Cuba: Rumania, $320; Yugoslavia, $297; Bulgaria, $285; China, $56; Cuba, $520 (J.M. Illán).

Automobiles

One per every 40 inhabitants. Third place in Latin America after Venezuela and Puerto Rico. Third place in the world regarding kilometers of roads per thousands of vehicles.

Telephones

One per every 38 inhabitants. Fourth place in Latin America, after Puerto Rico, Argentina, and Uruguay (Brazil: one per 68 inhabitants; Mexico: one per 72 inhabitants).

Radio

One per every 6.5 inhabitants. Third place in Latin America. There were 270 transmitting stations.

Television

One per every 25 inhabitants. First place in Latin America, 5 television stations, one of them in color (1958).

4. Industrialization

According to Lacoste, in 1959 the world labor population reached the following percentages: Africa, 11 percent; Asia, 10 percent; Latin America, 17 percent; United States and Canada, 37 percent; Western Europe, 42 percent. In Cuba, 24 percent of the labor force in 1953 was employed in the industrial sector. Nonsugar industrial production was at that time greater than sugar production. Cuba was producing 10,000 different products. Regarding the consumption of steel per inhabitant, Cuba was in thirty-ninth place among 108 countries, ahead of Mexico and Brazil.

5. Energy Consumption

Among the 124 countries analyzed by Ginsburg, Cuba was in twenty-fifth place with 11.8 megawatt hours per annum per capita. It was the first country in Latin America, followed by Venezuela. The Soviet Union was in twenty-second place with 16 megawatt hours. Mexico was in forty-second place with only 6.4 megawatt hours.

6. Economic Dependency

In 1929—the highest point in the curve—the economic penetration of the United States in Cuba reached $1,525 million, of which $800 million were in the sugar industry. From 1935 on, this situation started to change. In that year, of the 161 sugar mills, only 50 of small capacity were Cuban-owned and produced hardly 13 percent of the total sugar production. In 1958, 121 of the 161 mills were Cuban-owned and made up 62 percent of the total. There was also an acknowledged Cuban participation in corporations, which owned the remaining sugar mills.

U.S. investments in 1958 reached $861 million. At the same time, the capitalization of Cuba in the industrial, commercial, and agricultural sectors was estimated to be over $6,000 million, which reduced the percentage of U.S. capital investment to less than 14 percent (Illán). Cuban urban properties not included in the previous estimates represented another 6 billion. British investments, mainly in railroads, which were estimated at $150 million thirty years before, were then only $400,000. Internal autonomy was shown in another fact: In 1939 Cuban banks had 23.3 percent of private deposits. In 1951, when the National Bank was founded, it had 53.2 percent and reached 61.1 in 1958.

7. Commercial Sector

Cuba, with a society totally within the monetary economy, had a very highly populated commercial sector. Illán has given the following figures for 1958: 65,000 commercial firms, that is, 1 per 1,000 inhabitants, which employed 254,000 persons and produced an average sales per year of 2,500 million dollars.

8. Social Structure

Noyola, the Mexican Marxist economist, in a series of speeches given at the National Bank of Cuba by invitation of the government, stated: "The regional and cultural differences among the different sectors of the population are much less distinct in Cuba than in other countries. The reasons for such a social flow are due in part to a great social and cultural homogeneity and because since colonial times the feudal institutions or working relationships were either nonexistent or did not develop or disappeared in Cuba. Fast economic development and the tendency to high salary scales were also factors that allowed a greater social flow." He added that contrasts between poverty and wealth are much less noticeable in Cuba. Perhaps with the exception of Costa Rica and Uruguay, Cuban income is the least badly distributed in all of Latin America.

9. Importance of the Middle Class

Gino Germani in a study made for UNESCO in 1963 calculated that the middle class constituted 22 percent of the total population, which was equivalent to that of Chile and Colombia, slightly less than Argentina (26 percent), and greater than that of Peru (18 percent) and Brazil (15 percent). A. Díaz, an Ecuadorian, in a study published in *Política* (Caracas, 1961), estimated the Cuban middle class as 33 percent of the population; Goldenberg, quoting professors MacGaffey and Barnet (1962), reiterated that "there is no doubt that the income in Cuba was the greatest of Latin America. This could be confirmed by anyone who would walk with his eyes open through the best areas and would see the new middle-class suburbs which were sprouting like mushrooms." American historian T. Draper stated, "A social interpretation of the Cuban revolution should start by looking at the Cuban society as much more urban, less agrarian, more middle class, and much less backward than what Castroism has made it appear."

10. National Integration

In Ginsburg's atlas one repeatedly notices the prominent world rank reached by Cuba regarding means of communication and transportation.

Table A.1

Cuba		World Rank
Density of railroad tracks (Km or tracks per Km²)	8.27	13
Km of railroad tracks per 100,000 inhabitants	16.0	9
Millions of cargo ton/Km per 100,000 inhabitants	16.3	42
Density of roads (Km of roads per 100 Km²)	4.0	75
Density of motor vehicles	29.7	28

(Soviet Union: 12.5 vehicles per 1,000
inhabitants in 1957; world rank: 46)

Goldenberg has stated, "The great majority of the population formed a nation which was lacking the taboos and traditions which in many underdeveloped countries interfere in the road towards development and modernization."

11. Unemployment and Underemployment

Lack of national economic planning contributed to the perpetuation of high unemployment and underemployment rates, in spite of the relative bonanza periods of sugar prices which since the end of World War II favored the Cuban economy. The encouragement of highly technologized commercial agriculture, as the rice crop, and the development of new industries, absorbed a minimal proportion of the large unemployed and underemployed masses in the cities and countryside. The National Economic Council admitted in 1957, as a result of its *Survey on Employment, Unemployment, and Underemployment in Cuba,* that of a work force of 2.2 million, equivalent to 53 percent of the population over 14 years of age, there were 16.4 percent chronically unemployed and 7 percent working within the family circle without remuneration.

12. Education

Since 1940, all Cuban teachers, whether at the elementary or secondary level, held degrees from teachers' colleges or universities. Cuba was the only Latin American country to achieve such a standard. There were more than 30,000 elementary classrooms with more than 34,000 teachers. Enrollment had reached 1,300,000. Private education, represented by more than 1,000 schools, had an enrollment of more than 200,000 students, all under the official supervision of the Department of Education. The quality of textbooks was usually high. In 1959 Cuba exported textbooks valued at $10 million.

Literacy

According to Ginsburg, Cuba, thirty-fifth among 136 countries studied, had a literacy rate of 80 percent, placing it in the same category as Chile and Costa Rica, and thus exceeded in Latin America only by Argentina (which held 85–90 percent literacy) and Uruguay (80–85 percent). These figures are impressive if we realize that at the end of the Spanish colonial regime, only 28 percent of Cubans were literate.

The Press

Among the 112 countries studied, Cuba ranked thirty-third, with a daily circulation of 101 newspaper copies per 1,000 inhabitants. In Latin America, only Uruguay (233/1,000), Argentina (154/1,000), and Panama (111/1,000) excelled Cuba.

University Students

According to the 1959 *Statistical Annual of the United Nations,* Cuba, together with Argentina, Uruguay, and Mexico, held the leading positions in Latin America with 3.8 university students per 1,000 inhabitants.

13. Demographic Growth

At the end of the 1950s, Cuba had an annual rate of 25.1 births per 1,000 inhabitants, comparable to that of the United States (22.4) and Canada (25.5), and was third in Latin America, after Uruguay (21.3) and Argentina (22.4), while in the rest of the region figures reached among the highest levels in the world: Costa Rica (50.5); Guatemala (49.9); Mexico (44.9); El Salvador (45.3); and Venezuela (44.4).

The mortality rate in Cuba was among the lowest in the world: 5.8 annual deaths per 1,000 inhabitants. The United States had 9.5; Canada 7.6; Chile 20.6; and Mexico and Peru 10.6. Toward 1955 the Cuban population was growing at a yearly rate of 2.4 per 100 inhabitants. This was high with respect to the median world populations, which was 1.6 per 100, but low in terms of Latin America, which had 13 countries with higher rates than Cuba's.

14. Health

According to Ginsburg, in a chart describing the health of 122 countries, Cuba ranked twenty-second with 128.6 medical doctors and dentists per 100,000 inhabitants. The only two Latin American countries with a larger percentage of professionals were Argentina and Uruguay. Far behind Cuba were socialist countries such as Poland, Yugoslavia, Hungary, Bulgaria, and China. In 1953, even countries such as Holland, France, the United Kingdom, and Finland had proportionately fewer medical doctors and dentists than Cuba. As to hospital capacity, according to a study conducted from 1952 to 1953 by the Center for Latin American Studies of the University of California, Cuba had 1 bed per 300 inhabitants. Only Costa Rica (1/135), Argentina (1/160), Uruguay (1/175), and Chile (1/185) exceeded Cuba in Latin America.

15. Political Consciousness

Awareness of underdevelopment, which according to Lacoste is the first step toward development itself, took place in Cuba early in the thirties, when the island's economic crisis, originated by the world depression, coincided with the struggle against the last caudillo-type dictatorship, which was a product of the traditional society.

How Far Had Cuba Advanced on the Road to Development?

A quantitative analysis of the capacity reached by the Cuban economy to generate savings and self-finance its development has brought such distinguished economists as José Alvarez Díaz and José M. Illán to place Cuba at the end of the 1950s in the exact instant that W. W. Rostow graphically calls the takeoff stage toward the economic maturity of developed countries. In order to support this, it is pointed out that the internal capital net formation reached in Cuba in 1957 was 15.5 percent of the national income, and in 1958, 13.5 percent. Both figures amply exceeded the minimum 10 percent pointed out by Rostow as sufficient to feed the autonomous development process of a national economy.

Selected Bibliography

General Introductory Works

Chapman, Charles E. *A History of the Cuban Republic*. New York: Mac-Millan, 1927.

Guerra, Ramiro. *Manual de historia de Cuba* [from the Discovery until 1868]. Madrid: Ediciones R, 1975.

_____. *Historia de la nación cubana*. 10 volumes. Havana: Editora Nacional de Cuba, 1958.

Marrero, Leví. *Cuba: economía y sociedad*. Madrid: Editorial Playor. [13 volumes were published between 1977 and 1987; when completed the work will consist of 15 volumes.]

Masó, Calixto. *Historia de Cuba*. Miami: Ediciones Universal, 1976.

Portell Vilá, Herminio. *Historia de Cuba en sus relaciones con los Estados Unidos y España*. Miami: Mnemosyne, 1969.

Portuondo, Fernando. *Historia de Cuba*. Havana: Editora Nacional de Cuba, 1965.

Santovenia, Emeterio, and Shelton, Raúl M. *Cuba y su historia*. Miami: Cuba Corporation, 1966.

Suchlicki, Jaime. *Cuba: From Columbus to Castro*. New York: Pergamon, 1986.

Thomas, Hugh. *Cuba: The Pursuit of Freedom, 1762–1969*. New York: Harper & Row, 1971.

Books on the Cuban Revolution

Aguila, Juan del. *Cuba: Dilemmas of a Revolution*. Boulder, Colo.: Westview, 1984.
A brief but exhaustive analysis of Cuba's history and the effects of the revolution.

Aguilar, Luis E. *Cuba, 1933: Prologue to Revolution*. Ithaca, N.Y.: Cornell University Press, 1972.
The author makes a comparative study of the revolution of 1933 and the one led by Castro.

Alvarez Díaz, José, et al. *Estudios sobre Cuba*. Miami, 1963.
The first scholarly treatment of Castroism by Cuban exiles.

Barkín, Ramón M. *Las luchas guerrilleras en Cuba.* 2 volumes. Madrid: Editorial Playor, 1972.
A detailed description of the fighting against Batista and the number of casualties. The study shows that the conflict was far from ferocious.

Batista, Fulgencio. *The Growth and Decline of the Cuban Republic.* New York: Devin-Adair, 1964.
The former Cuban dictator stresses his own role in Cuban history.

Bonachea, Rolando, and Valdés, Nelson (editors). *Che: Selected Works of Ernesto Che Guevara.* Cambridge, Mass.: MIT, 1969.
A selection of speeches and writings of the famous (Argentine) Cuban guerrilla leader.

————. *Revolutionary Struggle: The Selected Works of Fidel Castro.* Cambridge, Mass.: MIT, 1971.
Speeches and writings by Castro, carefully selected.

Bonsal, Philip W. *Cuba, Castro, and the United States.* Pittsburgh: University of Pittsburgh Press, 1971.
Former ambassador Bonsal describes his experiences and his efforts to improve relations between Cuba and the United States during his tour of duty.

Burks, David D. *Cuba under Castro.* New York: Foreign Policy Association, 1964.
An interesting monograph detailing Castro's relations with the Soviet Union and his discrepancies with the United States.

Castro Ruz, Fidel. *El pensamiento de Fidel Castro.* Volume 1, books 1, 2. Havana: Editora Política, 1983.
A good selection of Castro's key speeches.

Casuso, Teresa. *Cuba and Castro.* New York: Random House, 1961.
A former aide of Castro describes the future leader's activities in Mexico in his prerevolutionary days.

Conte Agüero, Luis. *Cartas de Presidio.* Havana: Editorial Lex, 1959.
A collection of personal letters written by Castro. Provides useful information about the political atmosphere in the circles in which Castro moved before he embraced communism.

Crassweller, Robert D. *Cuba and the U.S.: The Tangled Relationship.* New York: Foreign Policy Association, 1971.
An analysis of Castro's role in the development of the revolution and of the factors that brought about his anti-American posture.

Debray, Régis. *Revolution in the Revolution.* New York: Monthly Review Press, 1967.
The theoretical defense of *foquismo,* the Castroite contribution to strategies for seizing power in the Third World. The book is of interest for the light it throws on the differences regarding revolutionary methods between Castroism and traditional Leninism.

Dewart, Leslie. *Christianity and Revolution: The Lesson of Cuba.* New York: Herder & Herder, 1963.
A study of some of the points of conflict between the Roman Catholic Church in Cuba and Castro.

Domínguez, Jorge I. *Cuba: Order and Revolution.* Cambridge, Mass.: Harvard University Press, 1978.
A conscientious analysis of Cuban politics in the twentieth century, with special attention paid to the revolution.
Dorschner, John, and Fabricio, Roberto. *The Winds of December.* New York: Coward, McCann, & Geoghegan, 1980.
A well-written and incisive account of how and why Batista fell. An excellent book "Cubanologists" have ignored because of its journalistic style.
Draper, Theodore. *Castroism: Theory and Practice.* New York: Praeger, 1965.
A well-documented study of Castroism in Cuba.
————. *Castro's Revolution: Myths and Realities.* New York: Praeger, 1962.
An exhaustive analysis that makes it easier to understand Castroism.
Dubois, Jules. *Fidel Castro: Rebel, Liberator, or Dictator?* Indianapolis, Ind.: Bobbs-Merrill, 1959.
Includes valuable details about the struggle against Batista.
Dumont, René. *Socialism and Development.* New York: Grove, 1970.
A critical approach to the economic and social errors committed by Castro from the viewpoint of the author, who, as well as being at one time an advisor to the Castroite government, is also a recognized Marxist agronomist.
————. *Cuba est-il socialiste?* Paris: Seuil, 1970.
A severe criticism of the erratic behavior and clumsiness of the Castroite bureaucracy.
Fagen, Richard R. *The Transformation of Political Culture in Cuba.* Stanford, Calif.: Stanford University Press, 1969.
An objective analysis of the cultural and political changes that have taken place in Cuba under Castro's government.
Fagen, Richard R., et al. *Cubans in Exile: Disaffection and the Revolution.* Stanford, Calif.: Stanford University Press, 1968.
The political currents at work in the Cuban exile community and its social groups are analyzed in this interesting work.
Fernández, Manuel. *Religión y revolución en Cuba.* Miami: Saeta Ediciones, 1984.
The best analysis of the conflictive and changing relations between the Roman Catholic Church and the Castro government.
Franqui, Carlos. *Family Portrait with Fidel.* New York: Random House, 1984.
Franqui, who was one of Castro's closest collaborators and also editor of the daily newspaper *Revolución,* writes his memoirs.
————. *Diary of the Cuban Revolution.* New York: Viking, 1980.
This book contains a selection of documents without which it is hard to understand the anti-Batista insurrection. Among them are letters from Castro to his mistress in which he reveals, from 1958 onward, his intention of making himself the apostle of anti-Americanism.
Goldenberg, Boris. *The Cuban Revolution and Latin America.* New York: Praeger, 1965.

Goldenberg lived in Cuba for many years and provides incisive comparative analysis on the Revolution's impact on the rest of Latin America.

González, Edward. *Cuba under Castro: The Limits of Charisma.* Boston: Houghton Mifflin, 1974.
An excellent work on revolutionary politics and Castro's role in them.

————. *Partners in Deadlock: The United States and Castro, 1959–1972.* Calif.: The Southern California Arms Control and Foreign Policy Seminar, 1972.
A brief study of the relations between Cuba and the United States, indicating possible alternatives that could lead to a rapprochement.

Grupo Cubano de Investigaciones Económicas. *A Study on Cuba.* Coral Cables, Fla.: University of Miami Press, 1965.
This book contains first-rate information on Cuban economic history from exiled Cuban economists.

Halperin, Ernst. *Castro and Latin American Communism.* Cambridge, Mass.: Center for International Studies, Massachusetts Institute of Technology, 1963.

————. *The Ideology of Castroism and Its Impact on the Communist Parties of Latin America.* Cambridge, Mass.: Center for International Studies, Massachusetts Institute of Technology, 1961.
Two studies of Castro and Latin America by an acute observer of Communism.

Horowitz, Irving Louis (editor). *Cuban Communism.* 6th edition. New Brunswick, N.J.: Transaction, 1987.
Essays on most aspects of the Cuban Revolution.

James, Daniel. *Che Guevara: A Biography.* New York: Stein & Day, 1969.
An important biography of the noted guerrilla leader emphasizing his death in Bolivia.

Johnson, Haynes. *The Bay of Pigs.* New York: W. W. Norton, 1964.
An unbiased account of what happened. The author had access to the personal testimony of the principal leaders of Brigade 2506.

Karol, K. S. *Guerrillas in Power.* New York: Hill & Wang, 1970.
The author, who is strongly sympathetic toward Chinese communism, argues that most of the problems afflicting the Cuban Revolution are due to the dependence on the Soviet Union Castro has encouraged.

Lazo, Mario. *Dagger in the Heart: American Policy Failure in Cuba.* New York: Funk & Wagnalls, 1968.
A critical approach to the clumsiness shown by the U.S. government in the Cuban case.

La Vesque, Jacques. *The U.S.S.R. and the Cuban Revolution: Soviet Ideological and Strategic Perspectives.* New York: Praeger, 1978.
The influence of the Cuban Revolution on Soviet perceptions of the world.

Levine, Barry B. *The New Cuban Presence in the Caribbean.* Boulder, Colo.: Westview, 1983.

A series of essays by experts on Caribbean affairs analyzing not just Cuba's influence in the area itself but also in Mexico and Central America.

Le Riverend Brusone, Julio. *Economic History of Cuba.* Havana: Havana Book Institute, 1967.

A well-known Cuban economist analyzes, from a Marxist perspective, the Cuban economy over the centuries.

Llerena, Mario. *The Unsuspected Revolution: The Birth and Rise of Castroism.* Ithaca, N.Y.: Cornell University Press, 1978.

An intelligent account of the Cuban Revolution by a former collaborator of Castro.

López-Fresquet, Rufo. *My Fourteen Months with Castro.* New York: World, 1966.

The author, once treasury minister in Castro's government, describes the beginnings of the revolutionary order.

Mallin, Jay (editor). *Che Guevara on Revolution.* Coral Gables, Fla.: University of Miami Press, 1969.

The most important speeches and writings of the famous guerrilla leader, together with biographical information and commentary on Guevara's different activities in the area of the economy and in the guerrilla struggle.

Mesa-Lago, Carmelo (editor). *Revolutionary Change in Cuba.* Pittsburgh: University of Pittsburgh Press, 1971.

An authoritative series of essays covering different aspects of Castro's Cuba.

_____. *The Economy of Socialist Cuba.* Albuquerque: University of New Mexico Press, 1981.

An analysis, with abundant economic data, of the Cuban economy under Castro's government.

Montaner, Carlos Alberto. *Informe secreto sobre la revolución cubana.* Madrid: Editorial Sedmay, 1976.

A critical view of the revolution written in a series of brief essays on such different aspects as Castro, racial problems, power, etc.

Morán Arce, Lucas. *La revolución cubana: una versión rebelde.* Ponce, P. R., 1980.

A first-rate history of the struggle against Batista narrated by one of its leading protagonists. It includes a very interesting analysis of "revolutionary justice" as it was applied in the Sierra Maestra and of the discrepancies between the anti-Communist members of the July 26 organization on the one hand and Che Guevara and Raúl Castro on the other.

Nelson, Lowry. *Cuba: The Measure of a Revolution.* Minneapolis: University of Minnesota Press, 1972.

An excellent summary of the influence of the Cuban Revolution in the political socioeconomic fields, emphasizing the grim reality of the effect of Castro's regime on Cuba and its inhabitants.

Núñez Jiménez, Antonio. *En marcha con Fidel.* Havana: Letras Cubanas, 1982.
This work is useful because it shows how Castro's closest collaborators see their leader.

Padilla, Heberto. *Fuera de Juego.* Río Piedras, P. R., 1971.
The trial of Padilla—and the subsequent rupture between Castroism and the Latin American *intelligentsia*—began with the appearance in Havana of this book of poems.

Pérez, Louis A. *Army Politics in Cuba, 1898–1958.* Pittsburgh: University of Pittsburgh Press, 1976.
An exhaustive analysis of militarism in Cuban political development.

Roca, Sergio. *Cuban Economic Policy and Ideology.* Beverly Hills: Sage, 1976.
A detailed analysis of economic problems and development in the context of the Cuban revolutionary process.

Ruiz, Ramón Eduardo. *Cuba: The Makings of a Revolution.* Amherst, Mass.: University of Massachusetts Press, 1968.
The influence of nationalism and anti-Americanism on the leaders of the Cuban Revolution and their effects on its subsequent orientation.

Sanford, Gregory, and Vililante, R. *Grenada: The Untold Story.* Lanham, Md.: Madison, 1984.
This book describes the documents discovered in Grenada. These demonstrate the real extent of Cuban penetration of Bishop's government.

Smith, Earl E.T. *The Fourth Floor.* New York: Random House, 1962.
The last U.S. ambassador to Cuba before the rise of Castro describes the reasons for his failure and blames other officials of the U.S. government for the course of events.

Suárez, Andrés. *Cuba: Castroism and Communism, 1959–1966.* Cambridge, Mass.: MIT Press, 1967.
This book is of great help toward understanding the Cuban revolutionary process. It is a painstaking analysis of relations between Castro and the Soviet Union and with the Cuban Communist Party.

Suárez Núñez, José. *El gran culpable.* Caracas, 1963.
An extremely harsh criticism of Batista and his behavior while in power. The author was the dictator's private secretary and the leader of his party's youth wing.

Suchlicki, Jaime. *University Students and Revolution in Cuba.* Coral Gables, Fla.: University of Miami Press, 1972.
In this collection of essays a group of prestigious specialists analyze the Cuban Revolution.

Szulc, Tad. *Fidel: A Critical Portrait.* New York: William Morrow, 1986.
Even though this biography is virtually a defense of Castro, the author's research has some interesting features, especially with regard to the first year of the revolution.